Toni Morrison's

Beloved

A CASEBOOK

CASEBOOKS IN CONTEMPORARY FICTION

General Editor, William L. Andrews

With the continued expansion of the literary canon, multicultural works of modern literary fiction have assumed an increasing importance for students and scholars of American literature. Casebooks in Contemporary Fiction assembles key documents and criticism concerning these works that have so recently become central components of the American literature curriculum. The majority of the casebooks treat fictional works; however, because the line between autobiography and fiction is often blurred in contemporary literature, a small number of casebooks will specialize in autobiographical fiction or even straight autobiography. Each casebook will reprint documents relating to the work's historical context and reception, representative critical essays, an interview with the author, and a selected bibliography. The series will provide, for the first time, an accessible forum in which readers can come to a fuller understanding of these contemporary masterpieces and the unique aspects of the American ethnic, racial, or cultural experiences that they so ably portray.

Toni Morrison's
Beloved: A Casebook
edited by William L. Andrews
and Nellie Y. McKay

Maxine Hong Kingston's
The Woman Warrior: A Casebook
edited by Sau-ling C. Wong

Maya Angelou's
I Know Why the Caged Bird Sings: A Casebook
edited by Joanne M. Braxton

Forthcoming:

Louise Erdrich's
Love Medicine: A Casebook
edited by Hertha D. Sweet Wong

TONI MORRISON'S
Beloved

◆ ◆ ◆

A CASEBOOK

Edited by
William L. Andrews
Nellie Y. McKay

New York   Oxford

Oxford University Press

1999

Oxford University Press

Oxford New York
Athens Auckland Bangkok Bogotá Buenos Aires Calcutta
Cape Town Chennai Dar es Salaam Dehli Florence Hong Kong Istanbul
Karachi Kuala Lumpur Madrid Melbourne Mexico City Mumbai
Nairobi Paris São Paulo Singapore Taipei Tokyo Toronto Warsaw

and associated companies in
Berlin Ibadan

Published by Oxford University Press, Inc.
198 Madison Avenue, New York, New york 10016

Oxford is a registered trademark of Oxford University Press

Library of Congress Cataloging-in-Publication Data
Toni Morrison's Beloved : a casebook / edited by William L. Andrews
and Nellie Y. McKay.
p. cm. — (Casebooks in contemporary fiction)
Includes bibliographical references.
ISBN 0-19-510796-9 (cloth); ISBN 0-19-510797-7 (pbk.)
1. Morrison, Toni. *Beloved* 2. Historical fiction, American—
History and criticism. 3. Afro-American women in literature.
4. Infanticide in literature. 5. Slaves in literature. 6. Ohio—In
literature. I. Andrews, William L. 1946– . II. McKay, Nellie Y.
III. Series.
PS3563.08749B43 1998
813'.54—dc21   98-10126

3 5 7 9 8 6 4 2

Printed in the United States of America
on acid-free paper

Credits

Lori Askeland, "Remodeling the Model Home in *Uncle Tom's Cabin* and *Beloved*," *American Literature* 64:4 (Janurary 1992), pp. 785–805. Copyright Duke University Press, 1992. Reprinted with permission.

Barbara Christian, Deborah McDowell, and Nellie Y. McKay. "A Conversation on Toni Morrison's *Beloved*," previously unpublished. Printed with permission of Barbara Christian, Deborah McDowell, and Nellie Y. McKay.

Trudier Harris, "*Beloved*: Woman Thy Name Is Demon" in *Fiction and Folklore: The Novels of Toni Morrison* (University of Tennesee Press, 1991), pp. 151–183, 209–211. Reprinted with permission of the author.

Mae G. Henderson, "Toni Morrison's *Beloved*: Re-membering the Body as Historical Text." Hortense J. Spillers, ed., *Comparative American Identities: Race, Sex, and Nationality in the Modern Text* (New York: Routledge, 1991), pp. 62–86. Reprinted with permission.

Karla F. C. Holloway, "*Beloved*: A Spiritual." *Callaloo*, vol. 13 (Summer 1990): pp. 516–525. Reprinted by permission of the Johns Hopkins University Press.

Linda Krumholz, "The Ghosts of Slavery: Historical Recovery in Toni Morrison's *Beloved*," *African American Review*, 26 (Fall 1992), pp. 395–408. Reprinted with permission.

Rafael Pérez-Torres, "Betwen Presence and Absence: *Beloved*, Postmodernism, and Blackness," previously unpublished. Printed with permission of the author.

Ashraf H. A. Rushdy, "Daughters Signifyin(g) History: The Example of Toni Morrison's *Beloved*," *American Literature*, 64:3 (September 1992): pp. 567–597. Copyright Duke University Press, 1992. Reprinted with permission.

Contents

Toni Morrison's

Beloved

A CASEBOOK

Introduction

* * *

> There is no place you or I can go, to think about or
> not think about, to summon the presences of, or
> recollect the absences of slaves; nothing that re-
> minds us of the ones who made the journey and of
> those who did not make it. There is no suitable
> memorial or plaque or wreath or wall or park or
> skyscraper lobby. There's no 300 foot tower. There's
> no small bench by the road. There is not even a tree
> scored, an initial that I can visit or you can visit in
> Charleston or Savannah or New York or Provi-
> dence or, better still, on the banks of the Missis-
> sippi. And because such a place does not exist (that
> I know of), the book had to.
>
> —Toni Morrison,
> "A Bench by the Road"

Beloved, TONI MORRISON'S fifth novel, is "the book [that] had
to" exist. The author's eloquent and serious justification befits its *raison
d'être*. For Morrison, this publication was a conscious act toward healing a
painful wound: a studied memorial to the great social wrong of the enslavement of Africans. Her powerful words, on behalf of millions, give
voice to a profound lament: the absence of a historical marker to remind
us never to let this atrocity happen again. For its absence has neither erased
nor diminished its pain; rather, it reminds us only of itself: of what is missing. "I think I was pleading for that wall or that bench or that tower or
that tree when I wrote the final words," Morrison told *The World* (Morrison
and Richardson 4). It is also significant though not surprising that Toni
Morrison accepted the responsibility for action to rectify the neglect. She
often speaks of the role of the black novelist in the world as one to address
and explore issues meaningful to the welfare of the whole world community. As if responding in kind to her expression of grief, and accepting her

offering, readers almost unanimously acknowledge the book as a major literary achievement of great purpose. The momentum it generated on its appearance has not abated a decade later. In the attention that they give to it, scholars, general readers, students, and critics alike continue to assess *Beloved* as one of the great books of this century.

By the time Morrison published *Beloved*, she had four previous successful novels to her credit and enjoyed wide national and international fame. By then, for years most readers had considered her one of the most significant contemporary American novelists and literary/cultural critics in this century. This, in spite of the fact that only one of her earlier works, *Song of Solomon* (1977), rivaled *Beloved* in the immediacy of the glowing public response it received. *Beloved* made its way onto the *New York Times* Bestseller List in the week of its official publication date, and within a month, after an initial run of 100,000 copies, it was in its third printing. There is little question at this time that of all her novels, this is the one most often taught and the one most written about across the world. A work recognized for outstanding literary worth, *Beloved* represents a signal achievement in African-American and American letters.

A native of Lorain, Ohio, Nobel laureate Toni Morrison is the daughter of Southerners (from Alabama and Georgia) who migrated to the North in the early part of this century. Born Chloe Anthony Wofford in 1931, she learned to read (still a devouring passion easily recognized in her own writing) before she entered the first grade. In the close-knit three-generational family in which she grew up, storytelling of all kinds, including ghost stories, animal tales, and yarns of magical happenings were an important facet of her home-life education. An honors student at Lorain High School, there she became acquainted with and developed great admiration for the craft of such writers as Jane Austen, Tolstoy, and Dostoyevsky. After graduation she went to Howard University, the first woman in her family to attend college. She was a member of the campus theater company and saw the South for the first time while on tour with a student-faculty group. Her family's roots in the region made that trip very important to her. In those years she also changed her first name, because, she said, most people did not pronounce it correctly. She followed up her 1953 B.A. as an English major and classics minor with an M.A. in English from Cornell University in 1955. Her thesis explored the theme of death in the writings of Virginia Woolf and William Faulkner.

Morrison held a teaching appointment at Texas Southern University in Houston from 1955 to 1957, then one at Howard from 1957 to 1964. When her 1958 marriage ended in 1964, she joined a writers' group in Washington and began to pay attention to that aspect of her creativity. Even so, she had no idea of making a career of writing. However, she resigned from Howard and, with her two young sons in tow, took a position in Syracuse, New York, as a textbook editor for a subsidiary of Random House. In Syracuse, she turned feelings of isolation from the loss of more familiar communities to the profitable end of writing much of the narrative that led to her first novel, *The Bluest Eye* (1970).

In 1968, Morrison left Syracuse for New York City and a position as a trade book editor at Random House. Over time she rose to the rank of senior editor with that publisher, one of only a very few blacks and the only black woman until then to hold such high standing in that profession. Under her editorship, Random House published the work of many up-and-coming new black writers including Toni Cade Bambara, Claude Brown, Leon Forrest, Angela Davis, and Gayle Jones. She used her position to make it possible for a group, until then denied representative access to the mainstream publishing industry, to break through that barrier.

Nor did Morrison neglect her own budding writing career as she promoted those of others. In 1970, Holt, Rinehart, and Winston brought out her first book, *The Bluest Eye,* a success that, though long in coming (the manuscript was rejected many times before it was accepted), was quickly followed by Knopf's publication of *Sula* in 1973. *The Bluest Eye* explores issues of black identity, self-love, and self-hatred in a world in which the violence of race, gender, and class makes it extremely difficult for large numbers of people to find dignity in their lives. At the center of the action, a young black girl believes that what is most beautiful has the power to restore order and balance to the chaos she experiences in her world, but in a futile search for that beauty, the bluest eye, she eventually goes insane. At the time of its publication, most reviewers of this novel were white critics who approached its unsettling plot with caution but heaped praise on Morrison's fine evocative lyrical prose. However, black women critics like Ruby Dee engaged it both for its artistic qualities and for the ways in which the new writer captured the pain of young black female experience against a background of material and psychological conditions that diminished her personhood.

Sula generated more negative and positive critical responses than *The Bluest Eye*. In this story, the focus is on the inversion of conventional systems of thought and values through oppositions between self and other, good and evil, social approbation and community rejection. The novel posits a binary structure centered in the relationship between two black female friends with opposite upbringings and behavior patterns, Sula and

Nel, and follows them from childhood through their adult years. As an alternate selection of the Book-of-the-Month Club, *Sula* brought Morrison to larger public attention. As with *The Bluest Eye*, critics unanimously approved her literary skills, but some expressed impatience with her insistence (as they read it) on working on the small canvas of the lives of black girls and women instead of on larger subjects in American life.

Although there is no evidence in the text to indicate it, in 1974 Morrison took on one of the most important projects of her career: editorship of *The Black Book* (published under the names of Harris, Levitt, Furman, and Smith). A collection of nineteenth- and twentieth-century black memorabilia woven into a complex documentation of the African-American experience in America, *The Black Book*, as Morrison perceived it, was a corrective to much of the rhetoric of the radical wing of the Civil Rights Movement, which she feared was disrespectful of the lived experiences of many who survived slavery and/or the oppressions that came in its aftermath. Over time she had heard fragments of stories of slave mothers who killed their children, but it was while researching *The Black Book* that she discovered a newspaper item that documented an actual incident. In the 1850s, Margaret Garner, a fugitive slave woman from Kentucky, was tracked to Ohio and caught by proslavery authorities in a small settlement outside of Cincinnati. Resisting the family's return to slavery, Garner killed one of her three children and would have killed all three had she not been stopped. Morrison was struck by the enormity of the mother's deed and filed the information away for almost a decade before acting on it. That news item was the kernel from which *Beloved* emerged in the late 1980s.

Meanwhile, in 1977 Morrison published her third novel, *Song of Solomon*, which immediately brought her into great acclaim. Unlike the two early novels, each set in a small Midwestern black community, *Song of Solomon* is panoramic in its geographical movement from North to South, the prominence of its African heritage, its complex cross-generational conflicts, and its cross-cultural mythological framework. Milkman Dead, the central character, is Morrison's first male hero. However, in spite of its differences from the earlier novels, *Song of Solomon*, much like them, also focuses on identity, fragmentation, alienation, and the merits and demerits of Western values. When Milkman, after many personal trials, finally recognizes and accepts his familial history, he comes to understand himself within a communal structure and claims his complicated collective identity. *Song of Solomon* was a Book-of-the-Month Club selection, the first by an African-American since Richard Wright's *Native Son* in 1940. It also received the National Book Critics Circle Award in 1977. In 1978 the

American Academy of Arts and Letters named Morrison Distinguished Writer of the Year, and in 1979 President Jimmy Carter appointed her to the National Council on the Arts. At this time, Morrison's fiction began to be compared to that of writers such as Thomas Hardy and William Faulkner.

In 1981, when *Tar Baby* appeared, *Newsweek* featured Morrison on its cover, the first black woman to receive such notice since 1943 when Zora Neale Hurston (the first ever) did. In *Tar Baby,* Morrison further expands her geographical and racial reach by setting her plot in the Caribbean and including white characters who are central to the story. Divided and/or dysfunctional identities, fragmentation, displacement, materialism, and white hegemony are but some of the elements that Morrison explores in her fourth novel. Issues of class and cross-gendered conflicts are also at the core of the separation between the characters, not only in the division between the racial groups but also between Jadine, the beautiful African-American Sorbonne-educated pin-up girl heroine and Son, the uneducated, provincial, uncouth young black man who rejects the social ethic of the upwardly mobile black middle class.

Additional awards and important changes in Morrison's life occurred after the publication of *Tar Baby*. In 1981 she was elected to the American Academy and Institute of Arts and Letters, the Writer's Guild, and the Author's League, and in 1984 she decided to leave publishing for the Albert Schweitzer Professorship of the Humanities at the State University of New York at Albany. In 1986, her play, *Dreaming Emmett,* commissioned by the New York State Writers Institute at SUNY-Albany, was performed and won the New York State Governor's Art Award. The play, which uses a dream motif and elaborate masks, is based on the murder of Emmett Till, the fourteen-year-old Chicago boy lynched in Mississippi in 1955 for allegedly whistling at a white woman. This is Morrison's only venture into drama. The script has never been published.

Beloved appeared in 1987, almost two decades after Morrison discovered the record of Margaret Garner's story and began considering its adoption for a book. She wanted to explore the nature of slavery, not from an intellectual or slave narrative perspective, but from within the day-to-day lived experiences of the slaves themselves. Margaret Garner wanted to save her children from a fate she considered worse than death, to remove them from the clutches of slavery. On one hand, Morrison saw no moral justification for Garner's crime, even in the face of the brutality of the institution in question. On the other, she wondered if it were a worse thing for a mother to do to turn her children over to a living death. Therein was her dilemma. The Garner incident was well known when it occurred and was taken up as a cause célèbre by abolitionists such as Frederick Douglass and by abolitionist newspapers. Was Garner the only slave mother who responded as drastically to slavery? No one knows how many women engaged in similar deeds or how many undetected or undetectable means such women surreptitiously employed to save their young from servitude. Infanticide (although not abortion) has always carried the marks of a taboo in our culture, and the real and imagined virtues and values of African mother-women, under all circumstances, have served as muse for many inspired bursts of creativity in diverse black cultures.

Set in 1873, roughly a decade after the Emancipation Proclamation ended slavery, *Beloved* is the story of a former slave, Sethe, who eighteen years earlier had escaped from Kentucky to Ohio. Ahead of her she sent her three babies, one yet-unnamed girl and two little boys. On the way she gave birth to another daughter, Denver. Tracked to her new home by her slave owner, Sethe reacted by cutting the throat of her "crawling-already" older daughter and would have done the same with the other children had she not been stopped. For destruction of property (the child as slave), she served a jail sentence. By the time she is released, the ghost of the dead baby, Beloved (the name Sethe has inscribed on the headstone of her grave), has come to haunt the house the family occupies. Unresigned to the mischievous spirit and out of fear of their mother, the two boys leave home as soon as they feel they can take care of themselves, but Sethe and Denver accept the baby ghost and the disruptions she causes as part of their lives. This situation changes when Paul D, another former slave from Sweet Home, the plantation on which Sethe previously lived, arrives. First, with brute force, he rids the house of the ghost and he and Sethe become lovers. Soon after, an unknown young woman, who behaves strangely and appears to be the age that the dead baby would have been had she lived, arrives. She calls herself Beloved. Although she seems to know almost nothing else about herself that would usefully identify her, Beloved soon becomes a powerful force in the house. Against his will, she forces Paul D out, first from the house and then from Sethe's life. Meanwhile, Sethe, the target of Beloved's attention and the person from whom she seeks retribution, cannot keep from becoming completely enthralled by the intruder, for Sethe believes that Beloved is the reincarnation of the child she murdered. As a result, Sethe suffers physical and psychological deterioration until Denver, anxious for her mother's life, seeks help from the black women in the community. Under the gaze of the collective force of the women who respond to the call, Beloved disappears, and for the first time in her life Denver finds the courage to make life plans that promise positive changes for the entire community. The story concludes with Paul D's return to a recovering Sethe, to whom he offers himself in a partnership for a life they might build together.

Morrison was not concerned with the social consequences Garner suffered as a result of her act. She admits to doing research to secure information to make her plot narrow and deep; for instance, she learned exactly what the bit, an instrument of slave torture, looked like, how it was obtained, and how it was used. But Morrison did not delve into Garner's life story, opting instead for the freedom to invent the lives of her characters. She wanted to be fully accessible to those characters and to choose her own place in the political, philosophical, and moral discourse surrounding her story. So she turned to her imaginative powers and wove together fragments from the Garner episode into a new creation that explores the complexities of the situations of the former slave mother and those around her and the return of her murdered "already-crawling baby." In plotting the action, Morrison has said that she came to a point where, after asking herself who had the right to judge Sethe's action, she knew that she did not, nor did anyone else except the child Sethe killed. Then Beloved inserted herself into the narrative.

Morrison claims she had many more difficulties in writing *Beloved* than with any of her previous books. For one thing, there was the problem of making the ghost-child believable. But, she noted, "everybody believes in [ghosts], even those of us who don't believe in them" (Morrison and Richardson, 36). Also, this book seemed to her very different from the others. She explains:

> For *Beloved*, . . . I could take nothing that I knew that I seemed sure of, nothing I could really use. All of my books have been different for me, but *Beloved* was like I'd never written a book before. . . . I knew that I was in the company of people whom I absolutely adored, in a situation which I absolutely abhorred. To stay in their company, to listen, to imagine, to invent—and not to write—was exhausting. (Morrison and Richardson, 40)

Fortunately, she stayed, listened, imagined, invented, and wrote to release that exhaustion.

Another difference for Morrison between *Beloved* and the previous novels was the sense of melancholy she felt over the story. For instance, in writing the scene in which the child is killed, she recalls getting up periodically to take long walks and returning to rewrite, "over and over again," the sentence written just prior to each walk. While she wanted the fact of infanticide to surface early in the narrative so that the information would

be known, the horror of the act was as difficult for her as it is for her readers. She was forced to struggle to find language in which the violence
would not "engorge" her or her readers, or compete with the language itself. She struggled against producing either obscenity or pornography
(Schappell and Lacour 110–11).

Again, more than with any of her other novels, the demands of *Beloved*
made Morrison less confident that she could execute the book successfully. Still, she wanted to do it. Never having read a book that did what she
wanted this one to do, she persevered. She felt only the highest regard for
the lives of those who endured slavery, both its victims and its survivors,
and the idea that the enormity of the institution of African slavery might
be beyond the scope of art depressed her. Nevertheless, she kept going.

Much of *Beloved* is given over to the tortured internal lives of the former
slaves: Sethe, Paul D, Baby Suggs (Sethe's mother-in-law, whose son Halle,
Sethe's husband, worked years of Sundays to buy his mother's freedom but
did not himself survive slavery), and Stamp Paid, a former slave and Underground Railroad conductor who ferried escaping slaves across the Ohio.
So grotesque were many of their experiences, and so vulnerable did they
feel, that for them the act of remembering was risky, shameful, and dangerous. In addition to the wrongs she suffered, Sethe was haunted by the
memory of killing her child. She observed that much of her life was a
struggle to "keep the past at bay." Always as concerned with process as
product, Morrison focuses in *Beloved* on the healing process that returns
dignity to a people from whom it had been unceremoniously stripped. But
only in remembering, recounting, listening to, and accepting their individual and collective pasts does healing take place. In reclaiming and recreating the lives of those who lived through slavery Morrison writes a
new history that enables her characters and readers to reconsider the
wounds of a shameful past in a manner that exorcizes the ghost of
Beloved.

Beloved is a *big* book, not in its 273 pages (which disqualifies it for that sort
of bigness) but in the depth of the feelings it invokes by way of what critic
Ann Snitow calls "the terror of its material" as well as its spiritual richness;
in the complexities of its layers of meaning embedded in meticulously
crafted yet passionate prose; in the author's powers of imagination and
mastery of language; and in its impact on readers. It is also a text that is
part of a larger project: the first volume in Toni Morrison's trilogy of black
life in America. In this novel, Morrison takes large steps beyond the genre
of the slave narrative tradition to excavate, then to reclaim and re-create,
the hitherto hidden lives of those who survived the ravages of the inhu-

man institution. Her goal, she said, was to translate the historical into the personal. She wanted her characters to move from the page into the imagination of the reader. "I don't want to write books that you can close . . . and walk off and read another one right away—like a television show, you know, where you flick the channel." She writes intending to be as understated as possible, as quiet, clean, and lean as possible to elicit a complex response from her readers (Darling 253).

As *Beloved* garnered many accolades, Morrison's reputation soared. Among others, critic John Leonard agreed with her that it fulfilled her intended purpose: "Where *was* this book that we've always needed? Without *Beloved,* our imagination of America has a heart-sized hole in it big enough to die from" (Leonard 46). In the year of the novel's publication, Morrison was named a member of the Helsinki Watch Committee and the Board of Trustees of the New York Public Library. She also became chairperson of the New York State Education Department's Committee on Adult Literacy and a regent's lecturer at the University of California, Berkeley. She received the Pulitzer Prize for Fiction, the Robert Kennedy Book Award, and the Melcher Book Award from the Unitarian Universalist Association in 1988. The following year Morrison left Syracuse for the Robert Goheen Professorship in the Humanities Council at Princeton University, where she holds a joint appointment in African-American studies and creative writing. She also received the Modern Language Association's Commonwealth Award in Literature in 1989 and the Chianti Ruffino Antico Fattore International Award in Literature in 1990.

Jazz, which Morrison published in 1992, is her sixth novel and the second volume in her trilogy. Its characters are the children and grandchildren of Sethe's and Paul D's generation who left the rural areas and life on the land with dreams of success in the urban centers. In 1906, Joe Trace and his wife Violet, like many others of their group from across the South, rode the train north to Harlem and elsewhere. Seeking escape from poverty and white violence, they danced into the City (capitalized C), with high expectations. The action in the novel begins in 1926, in the jazz age. Ironically, by then, the dreams of the ordinary migrants no longer sparkled with hope, and Joe, now a fifty-year-old door-to-door beauty products salesman, traces his eighteen-year-old girlfriend, Dorcas, to a party in Brooklyn and shoots her. She dies without revealing the identity of her assailant. Then Violet, who already acts strangely and is angered by Joe's infidelity, disrupts the girl's funeral by attempting to mutilate the face of the corpse.

Just as *Beloved* interested Morrison as a result of her reading of the Margaret Garner story, so the plot of *Jazz,* as an extension of *Beloved,* suggested itself to her from the photograph of a dead girl in her coffin in James Van Der Zee's *The Harlem Book of the Dead*. The story behind the picture reveals that Dorcas did exactly as this girl, who also refused to name her killer. Like Sethe, who considered her children her "best parts," Dorcas loved someone else so much more than herself that she was willing to bleed to death rather than reveal her lover's name. This willingness to replace the self with a love object outside of the self is, Morrison says, a way in which women sabotage themselves. The idea intrigued her. How Joe and Violet came to the place in which they find themselves at the time of Dorcas's death and where they will go from there is the burden of the narrative, which takes readers on a journey into black history and returns to many of the themes Morrison used in her previous novels. As always, the struggles with alienation, fragmentation, self, and identity are all present. This time Morrison explores them in light of the unfulfilled promises of the black migrant urban experience.

Toni Morrison received the Nobel Prize for Literature in 1993. In the great hall of the Swedish Academy in Stockholm, in her acceptance speech she focused on language. She explained that having had a childhood full of stories, she had never thought of narrative as just a source of entertainment but rather as a conduit for the flow of knowledge. She spoke to the distinguished audience on the responsibility that writers, readers, thinkers, and speakers have to keep language alive and regenerative. For, she reminded them, a living language is vital, continually renewing itself in the imaginations of those who use it in any of its many ways. Without that continual regeneration, language dies.

Morrison's vast cultural knowledge is the source of the richness in her novels. She is also a gifted writer with a keen grasp of detail and the skills to invent compelling narrative. Nowhere are her talents more evident than in *Beloved*. In the many voices and memories in this text, Morrison explores and dramatizes the past and present of African-American history through the myth and folklore of many nations and peoples. Her themes revolve around the wish to forget and the necessity to remember, to reject and to reclaim; and to elide the boundaries between past and present. She imagines and fills in what was not written into the slave narratives. Who else writes a ghost story to re-create history and raise a monument? Where else do we find

[g]host story, history lesson, mother-epic, incantation, folk and fairy tale . . . lost children and men on horseback; a handsaw, an icepick and a wishing well; Denver's "emerald light" and Amy's velvet; spiders and roost-

ers and the madness of hummingbirds with needle beaks[;] . . . a devouring past of everything that is unforgiven and denied; a hunger to eat all of the love in the world[?]—*Beloved* belongs on the highest shelf of our literature. (Leonard 45)

The task of choosing seven essays for this *Casebook* was not easy. The large number of excellent essays already published on the novel presented a formidable challenge to the process. We could easily have assembled an anthology three times as large as the one we have created and not have exhausted the base of our resources. Readers are well advised to continue their explorations of *Beloved* by taking advantage of reading well beyond the titles of the suggestions we offer. Nevertheless, our goal here is to present teachers and scholars with a small group of essays that not only are worthy of inclusion but that also address some of the issues that readers often raise about the book. We believe they will be valuable to those who teach or write about the novel. Some degree of repetition of viewpoint within the group was unavoidable, but we tried to choose with an eye to the breadth of perspective among the individual pieces to lend as much variety as possible to the collection.

The seven essays are framed on one side by two prefatory items—a poem written by Frances Ellen Watkins Harper in the immediate aftermath of the Margaret Garner incident and a contemporary review of that incident by a white antislavery activist—and on the other side by a conversation on *Beloved* among Barbara Christian, Deborah McDowell, and Nellie Y. McKay. We hope that this unstructured exchange will contribute to the value of the whole by helping to keep open the larger ongoing conversation in which teachers in classrooms and scholars have engaged since the publication of the book in 1987. *Beloved* is truly one of the great novels of our time.

Frances Ellen Watkins Harper's poem, "The Slave Mother (A Tale of Ohio)," one of her best-known works, was written in reaction to Margaret Garner's murder of her child in 1856. Harper (1825–1911), a free black woman, was a successful novelist, poet, journalist, and essayist and was an outspoken abolitionist, women's rights activist, and temperance advocate for almost all of her life. "The Slave Mother" makes the point that the murder of the child manifests the great love this mother has for her children, who, she believes, will be worse off enslaved than dead. Harper concludes the poem with a call to her (white) countrymen and women to join the crusade for black freedom and end the dishonor of slavery.

A lengthy review of the Garner case in *The Fugitive Slave Law and Its Victims*

(1856), by the white abolitionist Samuel May, follows the poem. May was deeply concerned about the injustice of the Fugitive Slave Act (1850), which enabled the apprehension of escaped slaves like Margaret Garner and her family, even when they were discovered in free states. May, who wrote his account from local newspaper articles and included an excerpt from an antislavery sermon delivered in Cleveland, Ohio, by the Reverend H. Bushnell, concluded the tract with a plea for the abolition of slavery, asking especially that special thought be given to the thousands of fugitives living in free states in great fear of becoming the next victims of the Act.

In the first essay in this collection, "Daughters Signifyin(g) History: The Example of Toni Morrison's *Beloved*," Ashraf H. A. Rushdy studies *Beloved* from the perspective of its contribution to the African-American literary tradition based on the idea of the interdependence between the black past and present. Rushdy situates Morrison within revisionist historiography and contemporary fiction, creating daughters signifyin(g) history. The essay addresses five aspects of the way in which Morrison achieves her goal. "Raising *Beloved*: A Requiem That Is a Resurrection" posits *Beloved* as the story of an anonymous people who were slaves. As a character in the story and the embodiment of the past, Beloved must be remembered to be forgotten, reincarnated to be given proper burial. "Toward *Beloved*: Margaret Garner" briefly traces the history of the influence of Margaret Garner's murder of her child through nineteenth-century abolitionist agitations to Morrison's fiction. Also brief, "Signifyin(g) on History" reinforces Rushdy's argument regarding the multiple perspectives of the book's project, and "Reading *Beloved*" looks closely at how Sethe's killing of her child affects her and the rest of her community. Here Rushdy explores the development of relationships of understanding between Sethe and the other characters in the book as they discover themselves within a communal framework. Sethe begins to heal only after she accepts her action and takes responsibility for it by recognizing why it happened and by understanding it in a framework larger than one of individual concern. "Hearing *Beloved*," the final section of the essay, addresses the relationship between the orality of the text and the "aural being" in the text represented by the signifyin(g) daughter. Classifying *Beloved* as a "speakerly" text with Denver as its ideal "listener," Rushdy concludes that she will tell and retell the story that she comes to understand through the course of the narrative. Denver is the site of hope, the daughter of history.

In "*Beloved*: A Spiritual," Karla F. C. Holloway argues for the significance of *Beloved* as one of the most effective documents in contemporary efforts to revise the historical and cultural texts of black women's experiences.

She bases her claim on the effectiveness of Morrison's revision of the strategic devices within the structure of the novel. For example, with myth as a dominant feature of *Beloved,* Morrison not only reclaims the Garner story from those who interviewed her after her child's death and expressed enormous surprise at her calm but also, as mythmaker, achieves a complete revision of the episode. The oral and written history that Morrison revises, consciously and unconsciously felt, considers many aspects of each life and reflects an alternative perspective on reality. Morrison's skillful manipulation of such elements as the interplay between the implicitly oral and explicitly literary structures of the novel; the novel's dominant contrapuntal structure, which mediates speech and narrative, visual and cognitive, and Morrison's manipulation of time and space; and signals of "telling" as a survival strategy are topics of discussion in this essay. In addition, Morrison, like many other African and African-American writers, often defies the boundaries separating past, present, and future time. This allows her to free *Beloved* from the dominance of a history that would deny the merits of slave stories. As Morrison's creation, Beloved is not only Sethe's dead child but the faces of all those lost in slavery, carrying in her the history of the "sixty million and more." Holloway sees *Beloved* as a novel of inner vision: the reclamation of black spiritual histories.

"Toni Morrison's *Beloved:* Re-Membering the Body as Historical Text," Mae G. Henderson's contribution to the collection, examines the novel in the context of contemporary historical theory on discourse and narrativity and offers a reading that links historiography and psychoanalysis. She believes that, insofar as Morrison's relationship to the slave narrators and the slave narratives is one in which her intent is to resurrect buried stories and express repressed ones, the comparisons between historian and informant, and analyst and analysand, are valid.

Morrison faces the challenge of transforming Sethe's "rememories" of a dreadful past into a discourse shaped by her own narrativity. For both, the question becomes: how does one, from a cluster of images (rememories), create history that represents the unspeakable and unspoken in narrative? At the center of the novel is Sethe's burden, a past dominated by an oppressive master text. With no discourse of her own, she needs to create her fragmented images into a sequential, meaningful narrative of her own. As a black woman, with no voice or text, she has no history. She must find a way to gain control of her story, her body, her progeny, and all that belongs to her by dismantling the authority of the master discourse and constructing her own. Henderson's essay addresses Morrison's achievement in resolving the dilemma by bringing together the personal and the social, the psychic and the historical in Sethe's experiences. This opens the way for the events of her life to be encoded in an alternative plot structure, a counternarrative to that of the shameful slave experience. In this new narrative, the story of oppression becomes the story of liberation as she subverts the master's code. Reconstituting the self is the act of storytelling that imposes sequence and meaning on images that shape and define the self.

"The Ghosts of Slavery: Historical Recovery in Toni Morrison's *Beloved,*" by Linda Krumholz, addresses Morrison's conceptualization of American history through the acts and consciousnesses of former African-American slaves. Krumholz believes that the goal of the novel is to subvert their shame of slavery in the collective African-American memory and convert it into a source of recovery or healing. Such a healing occurs on a psychological (personal) level as well as a national or historical (beyond the individual) level. As Krumholz sees it, Morrison promotes this process through specific rituals enacted by various characters in the novel. Krumholz delineates the nature of these rituals and their significance relative to the healing process. Central to the achievement of success in this undertaking is the combination of healing with knowledge, which Morrison sets in an African-American framework that challenges the basic premises of Western pedagogy and epistemology. *Beloved*, argues Krumholz, is the history that Morrison creates out of the African-American oral and literary tradition combined with the Euro-American novel tradition. *Beloved* also critiques the fact-based history that dominates Western intellectual traditions. Morrison reconstructs the national and personal history that, in addition to physical freedom, give freedom of the heart and the imagination to the formerly oppressed. Thus Krumholz argues that *Beloved* is a healing ritual, while Beloved is the forgotten spirit of the past that must be loved though unlovable and elusive.

The main issues of discussion in Trudier Harris's *"Beloved:* Woman, Thy Name Is Demon" include Morrison's portrayal of the female body as evil, demonic, satanic (a theme she uses in other novels as well); Morrison's art as a storyteller that allows her to wed successfully her novels to fiction, folklore, and oral history; the verbal art of preaching or calling people together to preach as manifest in Baby Suggs's preaching, a blend of the best of the sacred and secular in African-American traditions; and the creation of black myth and folktale such as Sweet Home. In this last instance, Harris points out that the reality of Sweet Home becomes blurred in their memories when the former slaves make contrasts between the Sweet Home they knew under Mr. Garner (a benevolent slave owner) and schoolteacher (a

Simon Legree character). Harris's exploration of these topics draws our attention to specific hallmarks of Morrison's fiction-making, especially the ways in which she shares the creative process with her characters and draws readers into the circle to fill in the gap; her consciousness of the transition from the oral to the written text; the ways in which her characters transcend the shame of their experiences to discover delight in small things like owning one's heart; and the creation of legend and myth out of pain and suffering survived.

In "Remodeling the Model Home in *Uncle Tom's Cabin* and *Beloved,*" Lori Askeland notes the similarities in geographical location, the authors' mutual opposition to slavery, and the remodeling of parts of slave history in Stowe's and Morrison's novels. Both authors produce narratives that remodel dominant ideologies within the nation's power structures. However, Askeland contends that Morrison's fiction revises Stowe's in that the former escapes the dominance of the white patriarchal structure while the latter remains within it. Stowe, an advocate for greater social recognition of the value of women's domestic activities, considered strengthening the traditional home a crucial part of her agenda. "Model homes" stressed more control for women. However, although the model in her novel is in a matriarchal Quaker community that provides shelter for slaves (vs. Simon Legree's "anti-home" in that novel), that community does not escape the domination of the patriarchal order. Morrison first explores the model house in the dwelling that Mr. Bodwin, an antislavery advocate, turns over to former slaves. When Baby Suggs lives there she transforms it into a communal center: a cheerful buzzing house, a station on the Underground Railroad, where everyone is welcome. But that community, situated within the white power structure, shatters after the assault by schoolteacher that prompts Sethe to kill her baby. Then Morrison configures another model that promises success. Although Beloved is the embodiment of slavery's legacy and her behavior pushes everyone to the edge of insanity, she is also the catalyst for change, first by forcing Sethe to face her suppressed memories. When she vanishes, Denver takes a job, and Paul D returns, their model home takes on the element of hopeful possibility. Morrison's revised model of the home rejects the patriarchal model by redefining manhood and goes on to suggest a more secure communal space where women and men share themselves through their stories.

The final essay in this collection, Rafael Pérez-Torres's "Between Presence and Absence: *Beloved,* Postmodernism, and Blackness," examines the conundrum implicit in African-American efforts to articulate black identity in a language in which blackness is a figure of absence and for a people whose impulse to speak was forced into silence. To overcome this dilemma, Pérez-Torres claims, black writers learned to construct a literary discourse that alters Western notions of blackness. In *Beloved,* Morrison transforms absence into a powerful presence by converting the shame her oppressed characters suffer from into self-awareness. She creates this aesthetic identity "by playing against and through the cultural minefield of postmodernism," challenging received notions of postmodernism and engaging some of the very complex issues that make up American cultural identity. Pérez-Torres carefully analyzes multiple discourses in the novel, which together, he argues, force a reconsideration of the relationship between the postmodern and the marginal. At the same time he claims that the novel's numerous forms of narrative and telling history evidence its resistant and critical postmodern qualities. Without special privilege going to any single form of storytelling and through an authenticity based on inclusiveness, the many voices within this text contribute to and give voice to those formerly excluded from history.

The "Conversation on *Beloved"* between Barbara Christian, Deborah McDowell, and Nellie McKay that concludes the essays in this text is an attempt on the part of the editors to add direct orality to the collection. As many critics, both in this *Casebook* and elsewhere, have observed, each of Morrison's novels contains strong components of orality. But perhaps more than in any other, that quality in her writing comes through in *Beloved.* The "Conversation," taped in the summer of 1997, took place as a spontaneous activity without notes or imposed directions on the topics we wished to discuss. The editors hope that along with the essays and the prefatory materials, the "Conversation" will be useful in prompting readers to continue to read, write, discuss, and teach this very profound novel.

Nellie Y. McKay

Works Cited

Darling, Marsha. "In the Realm of Responsibility: A Conversation with Toni Morrison." *Women's Review of Books* 5 (Mar. 1978): 5–6. Cited in *Conversations with Toni Morrison.* Ed. Danille Taylor-Guthrie. Jackson: University Press of Mississippi, 1992, 246–254.

Harris, Middleton A., et al., ed. *The Black Book.* New York: Random House, 1974.

Leonard, John. *"Jazz* (1992)." *The Nation,* May 25, 1992. Cited in *Toni Morrison, Critical Perspectives Past and Present.* Ed. Henry Louis Gates, Jr., and K. A. Appiah. New York: Amistad, 1993. 36–51.

Morrison, Toni, and Robert Richardson. "A Bench by the Road." *The World* 3, no. 1 (Jan/Feb 1989): 4, 5, 37–41.

Morrison, Toni. *Beloved.* New York: Knopf, 1987.

Schappell, Elissa, with Claudia Brodsky Lacour. Interview with Toni Morrison, "The Art of Fiction CXXXIV." *Paris Review* 35, no. 128 (Fall 1993): 82–125.

Snitow, Ann. "*Beloved* (1987)." *Village Voice Literary Supplement*, Sept. 1987. Cited in *Toni Morrison, Critical Perspectives Past and Present.* Ed. Henry Louis Gates, Jr., and K. A. Appiah. Amistad: New York, 1993. 26–32.

Van Der Zee, James. *The Harlem Book of the Dead.* Ed. Owen Dodson and Camille Billops. Foreword by Toni Morrison. Dobbs Ferry: Morgan and Morgan, 1978.

The Slave Mother

A Tale of the Ohio

FRANCES ELLEN WATKINS HARPER

◆   ◆   ◆

I have but four, the treasures of my soul,
   They lay like doves around my heart;
I tremble lest some cruel hand
   Should tear my household wreaths apart.

My baby girl, with childish glance,
   Looks curious in my anxious eye,
She little knows that for her sake
   Deep shadows round my spirit lie.

My playful boys could I forget,
   My home might seem a joyous spot,
But with their sunshine mirth I blend
   The darkness of their future lot.

And thou my babe, my darling one,
   My last, my loved, my precious child,
Oh! when I think upon thy doom
   My heart grows faint and then throbs wild.

Source: *Poems on Miscellaneous Subjects* (Philadelphia: Frances E. W. Harper, 1857).

The Ohio's bridged and spanned with ice,
　　The northern star is shining bright,
I'll take the nestlings of my heart
　　And search for freedom by its light.

* * *

Winter and night were on the earth,
　　And feebly moaned the shivering trees,
A sigh of winter seemed to run
　　Through every murmur of the breeze.

She fled, and with her children all,
　　She reached the stream and crossed it o'er,
Bright visions of deliverance came
　　Like dreams of plenty to the poor

Dreams! vain dreams, heroic mother,
　　Give all thy hopes and struggles o'er,
The pursuer is on thy track,
　　And the hunter at thy door.

Judea's refuge cities had power
　　To shelter, shield and save,
E'en Rome had altars: 'neath whose shade
　　Might crouch the wan and weary slave.

But Ohio had no sacred fane,
　　To human rights so consecrate,
Where thou may'st shield thy hapless ones
　　From their darkly gathering fate.

Then, said the mournful mother,
　　If Ohio cannot save,
I will do a deed for freedom,
　　She shall find each child a grave.

I will save my precious children
　　From their darkly threatened doom,
I will hew their path to freedom
　　Through the portals of the tomb.

A moment in the sunlight,
　　She held a glimmering knife,
The next moment she had bathed it
　　In the crimson fount of life.

They snatched away the fatal knife,
　　Her boys shrieked wild with dread;
The baby girl was pale and cold,
　　They raised it up, the child was dead.

Sends this deed of fearful daring
　　Through my country's heart no thrill,
Do the icy hands of slavery
　　Every pure emotion chill?

Oh! if there is any honor,
Truth or justice in the land,
Will ye not, as men and Christians,
　　On the side of freedom stand?

Margaret Garner *and seven others*

SAMUEL J. MAY

◆ ◆ ◆

MARGARET GARNER *and seven others,* at Cincinnati, Ohio, January, 1856. Of this recent and pecu-
liarly painful case we give a somewhat detailed account, mainly taken from the Cincinnati papers of
the day.

ABOUT TEN O'CLOCK ON Sunday, 27th January, 1856, a party of
eight slaves—two men, two women, and four children—belonging
to Archibald K. Gaines and John Marshall, of Richwood Station, Boone,
County, Kentucky, about sixteen miles from Covington, escaped from
their owners. Three of the party are father, mother, and son, whose names
are Simon, Mary, and Simon, Jr.; the others are Margaret, wife of Simon,
Jr., and her four children. The three first are the property of Marshall, and
the others of Gaines.

They took a sleigh and two horses belonging to Mr. Marshall, and
drove to the river bank, opposite Cincinnati, and crossed over to the city
on the ice. They were missed a few hours after their flight, and Mr. Gaines,
springing on a horse, followed in pursuit. On reaching the river shore, he
learned that a resident had found the horses standing in the road. He then
crossed over to the city, and after a few hours diligent inquiry, he learned
that his slaves were in a house about a quarter of a mile below the Mill
Creek Bridge, on the river road, occupied by a colored man named Kite.

He proceeded to the office of United States Commissioner John L. Pendery, and procuring the necessary warrants, with United States Deputy
Marshal Ellis, and a large body of assistants, went on Monday to the place
where his fugitives were concealed. Arriving at the premises, word was sent

Source: Samuel J. May, *The Fugitive Slave Law and Its Victims* (New York: American Anti-Slavery Society, 1856).

to the fugitives to surrender. A firm and decided negative was the response. The officers, backed by a large crowd, then made a descent. Breaking open the doors, they were assailed by the negroes with cudgels and pistols. Several shots were fired, but only one took effect, so far as we could ascertain. A bullet struck a man named John Patterson, one of the Marshal's deputies; tearing off a finger of his right hand, and dislocating several of his teeth. No other of the officers were injured, the negroes being rendered powerless before they could reload their weapons.

On looking around, horrible was the sight which met the officers' eyes. In one corner of the room was a nearly white child, bleeding to death. Her throat was cut from ear to ear, and the blood was spouting out profusely, showing that the deed was but recently committed. Scarcely was this fact noticed, when a scream issuing from an adjoining room drew their attention thither. A glance into the apartment revealed a negro woman holding in her hand a knife literally dripping with gore, over the heads of two little negro children, who were crouched to the floor, and uttering the cries whose agonized peals had first startled them. Quickly the knife was wrested from the hand of the excited woman, and a more close investigation instituted as to the condition of the infants. They were discovered to be cut across the head and shoulders, but not very seriously injured, although the blood trickled down their backs and upon their clothes.

The woman avowed herself the mother of the children, and said that she had killed one and would like to kill the three others, rather than see them again reduced to slavery! By this time the crowd about the premises had become prodigious, and it was with no inconsiderable difficulty that the negroes were secured in carriages, and brought to the United States District Court-rooms, on Fourth Street. The populace followed the vehicle closely, but evinced no active desire to effect a rescue. Rumors of the story soon circulated all over the city. Nor were they exaggerated, as is usually the case. For once, reality surpassed the wildest thought of fiction.

The slaves, on reaching the marshal's office, seated themselves around the stove with dejected countenances, and preserved a moody silence, answering all questions propounded to them in monosyllables, or refusing to answer at all. Simon is apparently about fifty-five years of age, and Mary about fifty. The son of Mr. Marshall, who is here, in order, if possible, to recover the property of his father, says that they have always been faithful servants, and have frequently been on this side of the river. Simon, Jr., is a young man, about twenty-two years old, of a very lithe and active form, and rather a mild and pleasant countenance. Margaret is a dark mulatto, twenty-three years of age; her countenance is far from being vicious, and her senses, yesterday, appeared partially stultified from the exciting trials she had endured. After remaining about two hours at the marshal's office, Commissioner Pendery announced that the slaves would be removed to the custody of the United States Marshal until nine o'clock Tuesday morning, when the case would come up for examination.

The slaves were then taken down stairs to the street-door, when a wild and exciting scene presented itself; the sidewalks and the middle of the street were thronged with people, and a couple of coaches were at the door in order to convey the captives to the station-house. The slaves were guarded by a strong posse of officers, and as they made their appearance on the street, it was evident that there was a strong sympathy in their favor. When they were led to the carriage-doors, there were loud cries of "Drive on!" "Don't take them!" The coachmen, either from alarm or from a sympathetic feeling, put the whip to their horses, and drove rapidly off, leaving the officers with their fugitives on the sidewalk. They started on foot with their charge to the Hammond Street station-house, where they secured their prisoners for the night.

The slaves claimed that they had been on this side of the river frequently, by consent of their masters.

About three o'clock application was made to Judge Burgoyne for a writ of *habeas corpus,* to bring the slaves before him. This was put in the hands of Deputy Sheriff Buckingham to serve, who, accompanied by several assistants, proceeded to Hammond Street station-house, where the slaves were lodged. Mr. Bennett, Deputy United States Marshal, was unwilling to give them up, and a long time was spent parleying between the marshal and the sheriff's officers. The sheriff being determined that the writ should be executed, Mr. Bennett went out to take counsel with his friends. Finally, through the advice of Mayor Faran, Mr. Bennett agreed to lodge the slaves in the jail, ready to be taken out at the order of Judge Burgoyne. Mr. Buckingham obtained the complete control of the slaves.

On the morning of the 29th, Sheriff Brashears, being advised by lawyers that Judge Burgoyne had no right to issue his writ for the slaves, and remembering Judge McLean's decision in the Rosetta case, made a return on the writ of *habeas corpus,* that the slaves were in the custody of the United States Marshal, and, therefore, without his jurisdiction. This returned the slaves to the custody of the Marshal. By agreement, the parties permitted the slaves to remain in the county jail during that day, with the understanding that their examination should commence the next morning, before Commissioner Pendery. An inquest had been held on the body of the child which was killed, and a verdict was found by the jury charging the death of the child upon the mother, who it was said would be held under the laws of Ohio to answer the charge of murder. An examination took place on Wednesday, before the United States Commissioner. Time was allowed their counsel to obtain evidence to show that they had been brought into the State at former times by their masters. A meeting of citizens was held on Thursday evening, to express sympathy with the alleged fugitives.

The *Cincinnati Commercial* of January 30, said:—The mother is of an interesting appearance, a mulatto of considerable intelligence of manner, and with a good address. In reply to a gentleman who yesterday complimented her upon the looks of her little boy, she said, "You should have seen my little girl that—that—[she did not like to say, was killed]—that died, that was the bird."

The *Cincinnati Gazette,* of January 30, said: We learn that the mother of the dead child acknowledges that she had killed it, and that her determination was to have killed all the children, and then destroy herself, rather than return to slavery. She and the others complain of cruel treatment on the part of their master, and allege that as the cause of their attempted escape.

The coroner's jury, after examining the citizens present at the time of the arrest, went to the jail last evening, and examined the grandmother of the child—one of the slaves. She testified that the mother, when she saw they would be captured, caught a butcher knife and ran to the children, saying she would kill them rather than to have them return to slavery, and cut the throat of the child, calling on the grandmother to help her kill them. The grandmother said she would not do it, and hid under a bed.

The jury gave a verdict as follows:—That said child was killed by its mother, Margaret Garner, with a butcher knife, with which she cut its throat.

Two of the jurors also find that the two men arrested as fugitives were accessories to the murder.

"The murdered child was almost white, and was a little girl of rare beauty."

The examination of witnesses was continued until Monday, February 4, when the commissioner listened to the arguments of counsel until February 7th. Messrs. Jolliffe and Gitchell appeared for the fugitives, and Colonel Chambers, of Cincinnati, and Mr. Finnell, of Covington, Kentucky, for the claimants of the slaves. A great number of assistants, (amounting very nearly to five hundred,) were employed by the United States Marshal, H. H. Robinson, from the first, making the expenses to the United States

Government very large; for their twenty-eight days' service alone, at $2.00 per day, amounting to over $22,000. February 8th, the case was closed, so far as related to the three slaves of Mr. Marshall, but the decision was postponed. The examination in regard to MARGARET and her children was farther continued. It was publicly stated that Commissioner Pendery had declared that he "would not send the woman back into slavery while a charge or indictment for murder lay against her." Colonel Chambers, counsel for the slave-claimants, in his argument, "read long extracts from a pamphlet entitled, 'A Northern Presbyter's Second Letter to Ministers of the Gospel of all Denominations, on Slavery, by Nathan Lord, of Dartmouth College,' approving and recommending Dr. Lord's views." Colonel Chambers having alluded, in his remarks, to Mrs. Lucy Stone Blackwell, and said that she had sought to give a knife to Margaret Garner, the Court gave permission to Mrs. Blackwell to reply to Colonel C. Mrs. B preferred not to speak at the bar, but addressed the crowded court-room directly after the adjournment. Her eloquent remarks will be found in the papers of the day. At the close of the hearing, February 14th, the commissioner adjourned his court to the 21st, afterwards to the 26th, when, he said, he would give his decision.

Meantime the case was making some progress in the State courts. Sheriff Brashears having made return to the Common Pleas Court that the fugitives were in the custody of the United States Marshal, Judge Carter said this could not be received as a true return, as they were in the County jail, under the sheriff's control. The sheriff then amended his return, so as to state that the prisoners were in his custody, as required in the writ, and this was received by the Court. The fugitives now came fully into the charge of the State authorities. The sheriff held them "by virtue of a *capias* issued on an indictment by the grand jury for murder."

The slaves declared they would go dancing to the gallows rather than to be sent back into slavery.

On the 26th February, Commissioner Pendery gave his decision. First, he refused to discharge Margaret and three others from the custody of the United States Marshal and deliver them to the Sheriff of Hamilton County, although held to answer, under the laws of Ohio, to the charge of murder. He then proceeded to consider the claim of Marshall to three of the slaves, decided it to be valid, and ordered them into Marshall's custody. He then considered Gaines's claim to Margaret and her three surviving children, decided that also to be good and valid, and ordered them to be delivered into the possession of said Gaines.

The case of the rightful custody, as between the United States Marshal and the Ohio Sheriff also came on, February 26th, before Judge Leavitt, of the United States District Court, and was argued by counsel on both sides. On the 28th, Judge Leavitt decided that the custody was with the United States Marshal. The substance of Judge L.'s argument and decision is found in the following extract.

"Judge McLean says: 'Neither this nor any other Court of the United States, nor Judge thereof, can issue a *habeas corpus* to bring up a prisoner who is in custody under the sentence or execution of a State Court, for any other purpose than to be used as a witness. And it is immaterial whether the imprisonment be under *civil or criminal process.'* If it be true, as there asserted, that no Federal Court can interfere with the exercise of the proper jurisdiction of a State Court, either in a civil or criminal case, the converse of the proposition is equally true. And it results that a State Court cannot take from an officer of the United States, even on a criminal charge, the custody of a person in execution on a civil case.

"It is said in argument that if these persons cannot be held by the arrest of the Sheriff under the State process, the rights and dignity of Ohio are invaded without the possibility of redress. I cannot concur in this view. The Constitution and laws of the United States provide for a reclamation of these persons, by a demand on the Executive of Kentucky. It is true, if now remanded to the claimant and taken back to Kentucky as slaves, they cannot be said to have fled from justice in Ohio; but it would clearly be a case within the spirit and intention of the Constitution and the Act of Congress, and I trust nothing would be hazarded by the prediction that upon demand properly made upon the Governor of Kentucky, he would order them to be surrendered to the authorities of Ohio to answer to its violated law. I am sure it is not going too far to say that if the strictness of the law did not require this, an appeal to comity would not be in vain."

Mr. Chambers said his client, Mr. Gaines, authorized him to say that he would hold the woman Margaret, who had killed her child, subject to the requisition of the Governor of Ohio, to answer for any crime she might have committed in Ohio.

Judge Leavitt's decision covered the cases of the four adult fugitives. Another legal process was going on, at the same time, before Judge Burgoyne, of the Probate Court, viz.—a hearing under a writ of *habeas corpus* allowed by Judge Burgoyne, alleging the illegal detention, by the United States Marshal, of the three negro children, Samuel, Thomas, and Silla Garner, which took place in the Probate Court, before Judge B., on the afternoon of February 27.

Mr. Jolliffe said he represented the infants at the request of their father and mother, who had solicited him to save the children, if possible.

Messrs. Headington and Ketchum appeared for the United States Marshal.

Judge Burgoyne intimated that, in view of the serious and important questions involved, he should require some time to render a decision. He intimated, however, that a majority of the Judges of the Supreme Court having passed on the constitutionality of the Fugitive Slave Law was no reason why he should not take up the Constitution and read it for himself, being sworn to support the Constitution of the United States and the Constitution of the State of Ohio.

Mr. Ketchum suggested that his Honor was as much bound in conscience to regard the decision of the majority of the Judges of the United States Courts as the express provisions of the Constitution itself.

Judge Burgoyne said, that however the decisions of the Judges of the United States Courts might aid him in coming to a conclusion, where the obligations of his conscience were involved, he could not screen himself behind a decision made by somebody else.

Judge Burgoyne subsequently decided that, in as far as the Fugitive Slave Law was intended to suspend the writ of *habeas corpus*—and he believed that it was so intended—it clearly transcended the limits prescribed by the Constitution, and is "utterly void." Judge B. required the United States Marshal to answer to the writ on the following Friday; and on his neglect to do so, fined and imprisoned him. Judge Leavitt, of the United States Court, soon released the Marshal from prison.

The *Cincinnati Columbian,* of February 29, gave the following account:— The last act of the drama of the fugitives was yesterday performed by the rendition of the seven persons whose advent into the city, under the bloody auspices of murder, caused such a sensation in the community. After the decision of Judge Leavitt, Sheriff Brashears surrendered the four fugitives in his custody, under a *capias* from an Ohio court, to United States Marshal Robinson. An omnibus was brought to the jail, and the fugitives were led into it—a crowd of spectators looking on.

Margaret was in custody of Deputy-Marshal Brown. She appeared greatly depressed and dispirited. The little infant, Silla, was carried by Pic. Russell, the door-keeper of the United States Court, and was crying violently. Pollock, the reporter of the proceedings in the United States Court, conducted another of the fugitives, and all were safely lodged in the omnibus, which drove down to the Covington ferry-boat; but, although a large crowd followed it, no hootings or other signs of excitement or disapprobation were shown.

On arriving at the Kentucky shore, a large crowd was in attendance, which expressed its pleasure at the termination of the long proceedings in this city by triumphant shouts. The fugitives were escorted to the jail, where they were safely incarcerated, and the crowd moved off to the Magnolia Hotel, where several toasts were given and drank. The crowd outside were addressed from the balcony by H. H. Robinson, Esq., United States Marshal for the Southern District of Ohio, who declared that he had done his duty and no more, and that it was a pleasure to him to perform an act that added another link to the glorious chain that bound the Union. [What a *Union!* For what "glorious" purposes!]

Mr. Finnell, attorney for the claimants, said he never loved the Union so dearly as now. It was proved to be a substantial reality.

Judge Flinn also addressed to the crowd one of his peculiar orations; and was followed by Mr. Gaines, owner of Margaret and the children. After hearty cheering the crowd dispersed.

Further to signalize their triumph, the slaveholders set on the Covington mob to attack Mr. Babb, reporter for one of the Cincinnati papers, on the charge of being an abolitionist, and that gentleman was knocked down, kicked, trampled on, and would undoubtedly have been murdered, but for the interference of some of the United States Deputy Marshals.

A legal irregularity on the part of the Sheriff was brought to the notice of Judge Carter on the morning of February 29. It was passed over lightly.

On the Sunday after the delivery of the slaves, they were visited in the Covington jail by Rev. P. C. Bassett, whose account of his interview, especially with Margaret, was published in the *American Baptist,* and may also be found in the *National Antislavery Standard* of March 15, 1850. Margaret confessed that she had killed the child. "I inquired," says Mr. Bassett, "if she were not excited almost to madness when she committed the act!" 'No,' she replied, 'I was as cool as I now am; and would much rather kill them at once, and thus end their sufferings, then have them taken back to slavery and be murdered by piece-meal.' She then told the story of her wrongs. She spoke of her days of suffering, of her nights of unmitigated toil, while the bitter tears coursed their way down her cheeks."

Governor Chase, of Ohio, made a requisition upon Governor Morehead, of Kentucky, for the surrender of Margaret Garner, charged with murder. The requisition was taken by Joseph Cooper, Esq. to Gov. Morehead, at Frankfort, on the *6th of March*—an unpardonable delay in the circumstances. Gov. Morehead issued an order for the surrender of Margaret.

On taking it to Louisville, Mr. Cooper found that Margaret, with her infant child, and the rest of Mr. Gaines's slaves had been sent down the river in the steamboat Henry Lewis, to be sold in Arkansas. Thus it was that Gaines kept his pledged word that Margaret should be surrendered upon the requisition of the Governor of Ohio! On the passage down the Ohio, the steamboat, in which the slaves were embarked, came in collision with another boat, and so violently that Margaret and her child, with many others, were thrown into the water. About twenty-five persons perished. A colored man seized Margaret and drew her back to the boat, but her babe was drowned! "The mother," says a correspondent of the *Louisville Courier,* "exhibited no other feeling than joy at the loss of her child." So closed another act of this terrible tragedy. The slaves were transferred to another boat, and taken to their destination. (*See* Mr. Cooper's letter to Gov. Chase, dated Columbus, March 11, 1856.) Almost immediately on the above tragic news, followed the tidings that Gaines had determined to bring Margaret back to Covington, Kentucky, and hold her subject to the requisition of the Governor of Ohio. Evidently he could not stand up under the infamy of his conduct. Margaret was brought back, and placed in Covington jail, to await a requisition. On Wednesday, Mr. Cox, the prosecuting-attorney, received the necessary papers from Gov. Chase, and the next day (Thursday), two of the Sheriff's deputies went over to Covington for Margaret, but did not find her, as she had been taken away from the jail the night before. The jailor said he had given her up on Wednesday night, to a man who came there with a written order from her master, Gaines, but could not tell where she had been taken. The officers came back and made a return 'not found.'

The *Cincinnati Gazette* said,—"On Friday our sheriff received information which induced him to believe that she had been sent on the railroad to Lexington, thence via. Frankfort to Louisville, there to be shipped off to the New Orleans slave market.

He immediately telegraphed to the sheriff at Louisville (who holds the original warrant from Gov. Morehead, granted on the requisition of Gov. Chase,) to arrest her there, and had a deputy in readiness to go down for her. But he has received no reply to his dispatch. As she was taken out on Wednesday night, there is reason to apprehend that she has already passed Louisville, and is now on her way to New Orleans.

Why Mr. Gaines brought Margaret back at all, we cannot comprehend. If it was to vindicate his character, he was most unfortunate in the means he selected, for his duplicity has now placed this in a worse light than ever before, and kept before the public the miserable spectacle of his dishonor.

We have learned now, by experience, what is that boasted comity of Kentucky on which Judge Leavitt so earnestly advised Ohio to rely."

The assertion of the *Louisville Journal,* that Margaret was kept in Covington jail "ten days," and that the Ohio authorities had been notified of the same, is pronounced to be untrue in both particulars by the *Cincinnati Gazette,* which paper also declares that prompt action was taken by the governor of Ohio, and the attorney and sheriff of Hamilton County, as soon as the fact was known.

Here we must leave MARGARET, a noble woman indeed, whose heroic spirit and daring have won the willing, and extorted the unwilling, admiration of hundreds of thousands. Alas for her! after so terrible a struggle, so bloody a sacrifice, so near to deliverance once, twice, and even a third time, to be, by the villainy and lying of her "respectable" white owner again engulphed in the abyss of Slavery! What her fate is to be, it is not hard to conjecture. But friendless, heart-stricken, robbed of her children, outraged as she has been, not wholly without friends,

> "Yea, three firm friends, more sure than day and night,
> Herself, her Maker, and the angel Death."

EXTRACT from a sermon recently delivered in Cleveland, Ohio, by REV. H. BUSHNELL, from the following text: "And it was so, that all that saw it, said, There was no such deed done nor seen from the day that the children of Israel came up out of the land of Egypt unto this day: CONSIDER OF IT, TAKE ADVICE, AND SPEAK YOUR MINDS."—JUDGES XIX: 30.

A few weeks ago, just at dawn of day, might be seen a company of strangers crossing the winter bridge over the Ohio River, from the State of Kentucky, into the great city of our own State, whose hundred church-spires point to heaven, telling the travellers that in this place the God of Abraham was worshipped, and that here Jesus the Messiah was known, and his religion of love taught and believed. And yet, no one asked them in or offered them any hospitality, or sympathy, or assistance. After wandering from street to street, a poor laboring man gave them the shelter of his humble cabin, for they were strangers and in distress. Soon it was known abroad that this poor man had offered them the hospitalities of his home, and a rude and ferocious rabble soon gathered around his dwelling, demanding his guests. With loud clamor and horrid threatening they broke down his doors, and rushed upon the strangers. They were an old man and his wife, their daughter and her husband with four children; and they were of the tribe of slaves fleeing from a bondage which was worse than death. There was now no escape—the tribes of Israel had banded against them. On the side of the oppressor there is power. And the young wife and mother, into whose very soul the iron had entered, hearing the cry of the master: "Now we'll have you all!" turning from the side of her husband and father, with whom she had stood to repel the foe, seized a knife, and with a single blow nearly severed the head from the body of her darling daughter, and throwing its bloody corpse at his feet, exclaimed, "Yes, you *shall* have us all! take that!" and with another blow inflicted a ghastly wound upon the head of her beautiful son, repeating, "Yes, you *shall* have us all! take that!" meanwhile calling upon her old mother to help her in the quick work of emancipation—for there were two more. But the pious old grandmother could not do it, and it was now too late—the rescuers had subdued and bound them. They were on their way back to the house of their bondage—a life more bitter than death! On their way through that city of churches whose hundred spires told of Jesus and the good Father above; on their way amid the throng of Christian men, whose noble sires had said and sung, "Give me *liberty,* or give me *death."*

But they all tarried in the great Queen City of the West—in chains, and in a felon's cell. There our preacher visited them again and again. There he saw the old grandfather and his aged companion, whose weary pilgrimage of unrequited toil and tears was nearly at its end. And there stood the young father and the heroic wife "Margaret." Said the preacher, "Margaret, why did you kill your child?" "It was my own," she said, "given me of God, to do the best a mother could in its behalf. *I have done the best I could!* I would have done more and better for the rest! I knew it was better for them to go home to God than back to slavery." "But why did you not trust in God—why not wait and hope?" "I did wait, and then we dared to do, and fled in fear, but in hope; hope fled—God did not appear to save—*I did the best I could!"*

And who was this woman? A noble, womanly, amiable, *affectionate mother.* "But was she not deranged?" Not at all—calm, intelligent, but resolute and determined. "But was she not fiendish, or beside herself with passion?" No, she was most tender and affectionate, and all her passion was that of a *mother's fondest love.* I reasoned with her, said the preacher; tried to awaken a sense of guilt, and lead her to repentance and to Christ. But there was no remorse, no desire of pardon, no reception of Christ or his religion. To her it was a religion of *slavery,* more cruel than death. And where had she lived? where thus taught? Not down among the rice swamps of Georgia, or on the banks of Red River. No, but within sixteen miles of the Queen City of the West! In a nominally Christian family—whose master was most liberal in support of the Gospel, and whose mistress was a communicant at the

Lord's table, and a professed follower of Christ! Here, in this family, where slavery is found in its mildest form, she had been kept in ignorance of God's will and word, and learned to know that the mildest form of American slavery, at this day of Christian civilization and Democratic liberty, was worse than death itself! She had learned by an experience of many years, that it was so bad she had rather take the life of her own dearest child, without the hope of Heaven for herself, than that *it* should experience its unutterable agonies, which were to be found even in a Christian family! But here are her two little boys, of eight and ten years of age. Taking the eldest boy by the hand, the preacher said to him, kindly and gently, "Come here, my boy; what is your name?" *"Tom,* sir." "Yes, *Thomas."* "No sir, *Tom."* "Well, Tom, how old are you?" "Three *months."* "And how old is your little brother?" "Six *months,* sir!" "And have you no other name but Tom?" "No." "What is your father's name?" "Haven't got any!" "Who made you, Tom?" "Nobody!" "Did you ever hear of God or Jesus Christ?" "No, sir." And this was slavery in its best estate. By and by the aged couple, and the young man and his wife, the remaining children, with the master, and the dead body of the little one, were escorted through the streets of the Queen City of the West by a *national guard of armed men,* back to the great and chivalrous State of old Kentucky, and away to the shambles of the South—back to a life-long servitude of hopeless despair. It was a long, sad, silent procession down to the banks of the Ohio; and as it passed, the death-knell of freedom tolled heavily. The sovereignty of Ohio trailed in the dust beneath the oppressor's foot, and the great confederacy of the tribes of modern Israel attended the funeral obsequies, and made ample provision for the necessary expenses! "And it was so, that all that saw it, said, *There was no such deed done, nor seen from the day that the children of Israel came up out of the land of Egypt unto this day;* CONSIDER OF IT, TAKE ADVICE, AND SPEAK YOUR MINDS!"

Daughters Signifyin(g) History

The Example of
Toni Morrison's Beloved

ASHRAF H. A. RUSHDY

◆ ◆ ◆

ESPITE THE DANGERS OF remembering the past, African-American artists have insistently based a large part of their aesthetic ideal on precisely that activity. John Edgar Wideman prefaces his novel *Sent for You Yesterday* with this testament: "Past lives in us, through us. Each of us harbors the spirits of people who walked the earth before we did, and those spirits depend on us for continuing existence, just as we depend on their presence to live our lives to the fullest." This insistence on the interdependence of past and present is, moreover, a political act, for it advocates a re-visioning of the past as it is filtered through the present. Wideman elsewhere has asked, "What is history except people's imaginary recreation?" Racial memories, he suggests, "exist in the imagination." They are in fact a record of "certain collective experiences" that "have been repeated generation after generation."[1]

As Toni Morrison has said, "[I]f we don't keep in touch with the ancestor . . . we are, in fact, lost." Keeping in touch with the ancestor, she adds, is the work of a reconstructive memory: "Memory (the deliberate act of remembering) is a form of willed creation. It is not an effort to find out the way it really was—that is research. The point is to dwell on the way it appeared and why it appeared in that particular way." This concern with the appearance, with the ideology of transmission, is, though, only part of the overall trajectory of her revisionary project. Eventually her work, she states, must "bear witness and identify that which is useful from the past and that which ought to be discarded."[2] It must, that is, signify on the past and make it palatable for a present politic—eschewing that part of the past which has been constructed out of a denigrative ideology and reconstructing that part which will serve the present.

Morrison is both participant and theorist of this black aesthetic of remembering, and she has recently set out some of the mandates for establishing a form of literary theory that will truly accommodate African-American literature—a theory based on an inherited culture, an inherited "history," and the understanding of the ways that any given artistic work negotiates between those cultural/historical worlds it inhabits. Moreover, not only does Morrison, following the line of Pauline Hopkins, delineate the "dormant inmost feelings in that history"; she takes up, delicately yet resolutely, the task of reviving the very figures of that history.[3]

By taking a historical personage—a daughter of a faintly famous African-American victim of racist ideology—and constructing her as a hopeful presence in a contemporary setting, Morrison offers an introjection into the fields of revisionist historiography and fiction. She makes articulate a victim of a patriarchal order in order to criticize that order. Yet she portrays an unrelenting hopefulness in that critique. She does not inherit, as Deborah McDowell maintains some writers do, "the orthodoxy of victimage," nor does she reduce her narrative to anything resembling what Henry Louis Gates, Jr., has called a "master plot of victim and victimizer."[4] She, like Ralph Ellison, returns to history not to find claims for reparation or reasons for despair, but to find "something subjective, willful, and complexly and compellingly human"—to find, that is, something for her art. She does so, moreover, by doing what Hortense Spillers claims Ishmael Reed does with the discursive field of slavery in his *Flight to Canada*: "construct[ing] and reconstruct[ing] repertoires of usage out of the most painful human/historical experience."[5] In articulating a reconstructive—critical and hopeful—feminist voice within the fields of revisionist historiography and contemporary fiction, what Morrison does is create daughters signifyin(g) history.

Raising *Beloved:* A Requiem That Is a Resurrection

Morrison thought that her most recent book would be the least read of her novels because it would be perceived to be a work dealing with slavery, an institution that is willingly placed under erasure by what she calls a "national amnesia": "I thought this has got to be the least read of all the books I'd written because it is about something the characters don't want to remember, I don't want to remember, black people don't want to remember, white people don't want to remember." But *Beloved* is not about slavery as an institution; it is "about those *anonymous* people called slaves."[6]

Morrison's sense of ambivalence, of wishing to forget and remember at the same time, is enacted in her attitude toward the story and its characters. Speaking about the writing of *Beloved,* she declares her wish to invoke all those people who are "unburied, or at least unceremoniously buried," and go about "properly, artistically, burying them." However, this burial's purpose, it would appear, is to bring them back into "living life." This tension between needing to bury the past and needing to revive it, between a necessary remembering and an equally necessary forgetting, exists in both the author and her narrative. We might better understand that tension by attending to the author's construction of the scenes of inspiration leading her to write this novel.

Morrison has said that the idea of *Beloved* was inspired by "two or three little fragments of stories" that she had "heard from different places."[7] The first was the story of Margaret Garner, a slave who in January 1856 escaped from her owner Archibald K. Gaines of Kentucky, crossed the Ohio River, and attempted to find refuge in Cincinnati. She was pursued by Gaines and a posse of officers. They surrounded the house where she, her husband Robert, and their four children were harbored. When the posse battered down the door and rushed in, Robert shot at them and wounded one of the officers before being overpowered. According to Levi Coffin, "at this moment, Margaret Garner, seeing that their hopes of freedom were vain, seized a butcher knife that lay on the table, and with one stroke cut the throat of her little daughter, whom she probably loved the best. She then attempted to take the life of the other children and to kill herself, but she was overpowered and hampered before she could complete her desperate work."[8] Margaret Garner chose death for both herself and her most beloved rather than accept being forced to return to slavery and have her children suffer an institutionalized dehumanization. The story of Margaret Garner was eventually to become the historical analogue of the plot of *Beloved.*[9]

Morrison said that what this story made her realize was that "the best thing that is in us is also the thing that makes us sabotage ourselves" ("Conversation" 585). The story of Margaret Garner stayed with Morrison, representing, albeit unclearly, something about feminine selflessness. It took another story to clarify more precisely what Margaret Garner and her story meant.

Morrison found that story in Camille Billops's *The Harlem Book of the Dead*—an album featuring James Van Der Zee's photographs of Harlem funerals. These were photographs, Morrison has said, that had a "narrative quality." One photograph and its attendant story in particular caught her attention:

> In one picture, there was a young girl lying in a coffin and he [Van Der Zee] says that she was eighteen years old and she had gone to a party and that she was dancing and suddenly she slumped and they noticed there was blood on her and they said, "What happened to you?" And she said, "I'll tell you tomorrow. I'll tell you tomorrow." That's all she would say. And apparently her ex-boyfriend or somebody who was jealous had come into the party with a gun and a silencer and shot her. And she kept saying, "I'll tell you tomorrow" because she wanted him to get away. And he did, I guess; anyway, she died. ("Conversation" 584)

After reading the narrative of Margaret Garner, Toni Morrison had thought she glimpsed an opaque truth that she had always known, somehow: "But that moment, that decision was a piece, a tail of something that was always around, and it didn't get clear for me until I was thinking of another story."

When Van Der Zee provided that next story, Morrison saw clearly what she'd glimpsed through a darker glass: "Now what made those stories connect, I can't explain, but I do know that, in both instances, something seemed clear to me. A woman loved something other than herself so much. She had placed all of the value of her life in something outside herself. That the woman who killed her children loved her children so much; they were the best part of her and she would not see them sullied" ("Conversation" 584). In 1978, nine years before the publication of *Beloved,* Morrison started attempting to formulate the terms of that tension between remembering and forgetting, burying and reviving. In the foreword to *The Harlem Book of the Dead* she writes: "The narrative quality, the intimacy, the humanity of his photographs are stunning, and the proof, if any is needed, is in this collection of photographs devoted exclusively to the dead about which one can only say, 'How living are his portraits of the dead.' So living, so 'undead,' that the prestigious writer, Owen Dodson, is stirred to poetry in which life trembles in every metaphor."[10] One of Owen Dodson's "living" poems is on the page facing the picture of the young girl as she lies in her coffin:

They lean over me and say:
"Who deathed you who,
who, who, who, who. . . .
I whisper: "Tell you presently . . .
Shortly . . . this evening . . .
Tomorrow . . ."
Tomorrow is here
And you out there safe.
I'm safe in here, Tootsie. (52–53)

If Van Der Zee's photographs give renewed life to the dead, so does Dodson's poetry give renewed voice. Across from a picture of a girl in a coffin resides her living voice, her expression of the safety of death. As early as 1973, Morrison had been concerned with making the dead articulate. When Sula dies, she feels her face smiling: "'Well, I'll be damned,' she thought, 'it didn't even hurt. Wait'll I tell Nell.'"[11]

In 1987, with *Beloved,* Morrison goes further in giving the dead voice, in remembering the forgotten. *Beloved* is, in effect, a requiem that is a resurrection. The most obvious example of this commemoration is Beloved herself, the ghost of Margaret Garner's unnamed child: "So I just imagined the life of a dead girl which was the girl that Margaret Garner killed, the baby girl that she killed. . . . And I call her Beloved so that I can filter all these confrontations and questions that she has in that situation" ("Conversation" 585). Beloved is more than just a character in the novel, though. She is the embodiment of the past that must be remembered in order to be forgotten; she symbolizes what must be reincarnated in order to be buried, properly: "Everybody knew what she was called, but nobody anywhere knew her name. Disremembered and unaccounted for, she cannot be lost because no one is looking for her."[12]

In the end, though, Beloved is not the most important character in Morrison's revisionist strategy. That character is Denver, the other daughter. Morrison's original intent in the novel, she said in 1985, was to develop the narrative of Beloved into the narrative of Denver. First she would imagine the life of the murdered child, "to extend her life, you know, her search, her quest, all the way through as long as I care to go, into the twenties where it switches to this other girl." This "other girl," Denver, is the site of hope in Morrison's novel. She is the daughter of history. Nonetheless, as Morrison emphasizes, even when Denver becomes the focus of the narrative's attention, "Beloved will be there also" ("Conversation" 585). Before turning to the novel, and determining how Morrison inscribes hope into a critical revision of history, let us return briefly to the narrative of Margaret Garner in order to see the history that she revises.

Toward *Beloved:* Margaret Garner

It was sometime in January 1856 that Margaret Garner attempted her escape and killed her daughter. The story and the ensuring court case were reported in the Cincinnati newspapers and reported again in *The Liberator* in March 1856. Another detailed narrative appeared in the *Annual Report of the American Anti-Slavery Society* in 1856.[13] The newspaper coverage may have been motivated by a variety of reasons, some of them, one intuits, having to do with the exoticism of the story. In much the same way, Jim Trueblood of Ralph Ellison's *Invisible Man* becomes the focus of white attention after he commits incest with his daughter:

> The white folks took up for me. And the white folks took to coming out here to see us and talk with us. Some of 'em was big white folks, too, from the big school way across the State. Asked me lots 'bout what I thought 'bout things, and 'bout my folks and the kids, and wrote it all down in a book. . . . That's what I don't understand. I done the worse thing a man could ever do in his family and instead of chasin' me out of the country, they gimme more help than they ever give any other colored man, no matter how good a nigguh he was.[14]

In *Beloved* Morrison has Paul D respond to the media attention Sethe gets for infanticide in much the same way as the "invisible man" responds to Trueblood's story:

> Because there was no way in hell a black face could appear in a newspaper if the story was about something anybody wanted to hear. A whip of fear broke through the heart chambers as soon as you saw a Negro's face in a paper, since the face was not there because the person had a healthy baby, or outran a street mob. Nor was it there because the person had been killed, or maimed or caught or burned or jailed or whipped or evicted or stomped or raped or cheated, since that could hardly qualify as news in a newspaper. It would have to be something out of the ordinary—something whitepeople would find interesting, truly different, worth a few minutes of teeth sucking if not gasps. And it must have been hard to find news about Negroes worth the breath catch of a white citizen of Cincinnati. (155–56)[15]

As Levi Coffin noted, the Margaret Garner case "attracted more attention and aroused deeper interest and sympathy" than any other he had known (I'll return to the importance of this critique of print media later).

The case became a forum for "that noble anti-slavery lawyer" John Jolliffe, counsel for the defence, to argue that the 1850 Fugitive Slave Law was unconstitutional. Lucy Stone, who visited Garner in jail, spoke to the crowd outside her trial, describing Garner as a quintessentially American hero: "I thought the spirit she manifested was the same with that of our ancestors to whom we had erected a monument at Bunker Hill—the spirit that would rather let us all go back to God than back to slavery." A year and a half after her trial, Garner had become a symbol for what Frederick Douglass called his "philosophy of reform." Addressing an assembly celebrating the twenty-third anniversary of West Indian Emancipation, Douglass proclaimed:

> The whole history of the progress of human liberty shows that all concessions yet made to her august claims, have been born of earnest struggle. The conflict has been exciting, agitating, all-absorbing, and for the time being, putting all other tumults to silence. It must do this or it does nothing. If there is no struggle there is no progress. . . . This struggle may be a moral one, or it may be a physical one, but it must be a struggle. Power concedes nothing without a demand. It never did and it never will. Find out what any people will quietly submit to and you have found out the exact measure of injustice and wrong which will be imposed upon them. . . . The limits of tyrants are prescribed by the endurance of those whom they oppress. . . . If we ever get free from the oppressions and wrongs heaped upon us, we must pay for their removal. We must do this by labor, by suffering, by sacrifice, and if needs be, by our lives and the lives of others.
>
> Hence, my friends, every mother who, like Margaret Garner, plunges a knife into the bosom of her infant to save it from the hell of our Christian Slavery, should be held and honored as a benefactress.[16]

As late as 1892, the story of Margaret Garner could be used to signify the extreme measures a person would take to escape what the lawyer Jolliffe called the "seething hell of American slavery" and Douglass the "hell of our Christian Slavery."

In Frances E. W. Harper's *Iola Leroy,* Margaret Garner's case symbolized in the heroine's life what the author calls "school-girl notions." Iola is the daughter of the slaveowner Eugene Leroy and his wife, Marie, who has "negro blood in her veins"; Iola, when she attends school in the North, does not yet know her maternal racial background. In discussion with her fellow schoolgirls in the Northern school, Iola defends the institution of slavery, claiming that their slaves are "content." One of her schoolfriends disagrees: "'I don't know,' was the response of her friend, 'but I do not think that that slave mother who took her four children, crossed the Ohio River on the ice, killed one of the children and attempted the lives of the other two, was a contented slave.'"[17] Significantly, when Iola does discover her racial heritage she begins a mission of education, the biggest part of which is the paper she reads to the Council Meeting at Mr. Stillman's house, a paper entitled "Education of Mothers." Nameless now, Margaret Garner had become a political symbol for discontent. By 1948, Herbert Aptheker would cite the Margaret Garner case to argue why "the Negro woman so often urged haste in slave plottings." By 1981, Angela Y. Davis would echo him in arguing that the Margaret Garner case demonstrated not only the willingness of slave women to organize insurrections but also the unique desperation of the slave mother.[18]

By 1987, Margaret Garner's story would inspire a Pulitzer Prize–winning novel. Morrison has said that she does not know what eventually happened to Margaret Garner.[19] There are conflicting reports. According to Coffin and *The Liberator,* while Garner was being shipped back to Kentucky she jumped overboard with her baby; she was saved but her baby drowned. According to a report in the *Cincinnati Chronicle* and the *Philadelphia Press,* Margaret and her husband Robert worked in New Orleans and then on Judge Bonham's plantation in Mississippi until Margaret died of typhoid fever in 1858.[20] Whatever her fate, at Morrison's hands she has been buried in order to be resurrected into a new life, and she has been remembered in order that the institution she suffered may be forgotten.

Signifyin(g) on History

Beloved, according to Stanley Crouch, one of its harshest reviewers, "means to prove that Afro-Americans are the result of a cruel determinism."[21] This criticism is a good place to start our discussion of the novel, not because Crouch has hit upon some truth regarding *Beloved* or Morrison (he has not) but because he demonstrates the sort of conclusion a reader may reach if unburdened by knowledge of the historical place of *Beloved's* writing, its historical analogue, and its critical position in the African-American aesthetic and politics of remembering history.

Beloved is the product of and a contribution to a historical moment in which African-American historiography is in a state of fervid revision. The debate currently rages between those who argue that slavery led to the "infantilization" of adult Africans because the most significant relationship in any slave's life was that between the slave and the master, and those who argue that slaves formed viable internal communities, family structures, and protective personae that allowed them to live rich, coherent lives within their own system of values.[22] One premise underlying this debate is the question of whether slaves were acquiescent or resistant to the institution, whether they conformed to the "Sambo" or "Mammy" stereotypes who accepted their stations or whether they were in perpetual opposition to them—both in daily resistance and in sensational insurrections.[23] It is within this revisionary fray that *Beloved* may profitably be examined. As I hope to demonstrate below, the novel both remembers the victimization of the ex-slaves who are its protagonists and asserts the healing and wholeness that those protagonists carry with them in their communal lives. Crouch, unfortunately, reads the novel as if it were a rendition only of victimization, only of determinism; in other words, he misreads it.

Morrison has on more than one occasion asserted that she writes from a double perspective of accusation and hope, of criticizing the past and caring for the future. She claims that this double perspective is the perspective of a "Black woman writer," that is, "one who look[s] at things in an unforgiving/loving way . . . , writing to repossess, re-name, re-own." In *Beloved,* this perspective is described as "the glare of an outside thing that embraces while it accuses" (271). It is on precisely this issue of a dual vision that she marks the distinction between black men's writing and black women's: "[W]hat I found so lacking in most black writing by men that seems to be present in a lot of black women's writing is a sense of joy, in addition to oppression and being women or black or whatever."[24]

Morrison writes out of a dual perspective in order to re-possess, as I have suggested earlier, by remembering the ancestor, not only an aesthetic act but also an act of historical recovery: "[R]oots are less a matter of geography than sense of shared history; less to do with place, than with inner space."[25] Each act of writing a novel is for her an act of discovering deep within herself some relationship to a "collective memory." Memory itself, write Mary Frances Berry and John Blassingame, is for African-Americans "an instrument of survival." It is an instrument, writes Morrison, that can be traced back to an African heritage: "[I]t's true what Africans say: 'The Ancestor lives as long as there are those who remember.'"[26]

In the novel this truth is expressed by Sethe's mother-in-law. Baby Suggs knows that "death was anything but forgetfulness" (4). That remembering is both a resurrection and a pain is testified to by Amy Denver, who assisted in the birthing of Sethe's daughter: "Anything dead coming back to life hurts." The daughter Amy delivered testifies to that: "A truth for all times, thought Denver" (35). Let us now turn our attention to the novel in which all the double perspectives of this black woman writer are expressed—remembering and forgetting, accusing and embracing, burying and reviving, joy and oppression.

Reading *Beloved*

The obvious place to begin a reading tracing Morrison's signifyin(g) on the story of Margaret Garner is the site of infanticide. One of the recurrent tropes of the African-American novel of slavery is the possible response to an institution attempting to render meaningless the mother-child relationship. In William Wells Brown's *Clotelle*, the slave mother Isabella would rather commit suicide than face slavery for herself and her children. Hunted by a crowd of dogs and slavecatchers, Isabella leaps into the Potomac as an act symbolizing the "unconquerable love of liberty which the human heart may inherit." The chapter is entitled "Death Is Freedom."[27] In Zora Neale Hurston's *Moses, Man of the Mountain*, slavery is described as an institution in which only death can give freedom. As Amram tells Caleb, "[Y]ou are up against a hard game when you got to die to beat it."[28] It is an even harder game, Morrison would add, when you have to kill what you love most.

Coffin explicitly states Margaret's motivation: "[T]he slave mother . . . killed her child rather than see it taken back to slavery" (557). Like Harriet Jacobs, Margaret, in Coffin's reading of her history, sees death as a better alternative than slavery. "It seemed to me," writes Jacobs, "that I would rather see them [her children] killed than have them given up to his [the slaveowner's] power. . . . When I lay down beside my child, I felt how much easier it would be to see her die than to see her master beat her about."[29]

Sethe killed Beloved, according to Stamp Paid, because she "was trying to outhurt the hurters." "She love those children" (243). Loving as a slave, according to Paul D (whom Stamp Paid is trying to persuade with his assessment of Sethe's motivation), meant loving small, loving in an unobvious way so that whatever was loved did not become part of a technique of punishment. Paul D's advice, and his credo, was to "love just a little bit" so that when the slave owners took whatever or whoever the slave loved and "broke its back, or shoved it in a croaker sack, well, maybe you'd have a lit-tle love left over for the next one" (45). Ella, another ex-slave who was loved by no one and who considered "love a serious disability" (256), lived by the simple dictim "Don't love nothing" (92). When Paul D learns of Sethe's infanticide, he tells her that her love is "too thick." She responds by telling him, "Love is or it ain't. Thin love ain't love at all" (164). Although Paul D lives by his philosophy of loving small as a protective measure, he knows what Sethe means. "He knew exactly what she meant: to get to a place where you could love anything you chose—not to need permission for desire—well now, *that* was freedom" (162). Although Paul D knows the conditions of freedom and Sethe knows the conditions of love, each has to learn to claim that freedom, to claim that love, and thereby to claim gen-uine community and begin the process of healing.

Sethe's process of healing occurs when she acknowledges her act and accepts her responsibility for it while also recognizing the reason for her act within a framework larger than that of individual resolve. Here, per-haps, is Morrison's most powerful introjection into the Margaret Garner story—the establishing of a context for Sethe's act. Sethe's own mother kills all the children fathered by the whites who raped her. As Nan, Sethe's grandmother tells her, "She threw them all away but you. The one from the crew she threw away on the island. The others from more whites she also threw away. Without names, she threw them" (62). Another impor-tant person helping Sethe through the exorcising of her painful memories is Ella, who, it is hinted, has also committed infanticide. By placing such a frame around Sethe's story, Morrison insists on the impossibility of judg-ing an action without reference to the terms of its enactment—the wrongness of assuming a transhistorical ethic outside a particular histori-cal moment. Morrison is not justifying Sethe's actions; she is writing about them in the only way she knows how—through eyes that accuse and em-brace, through a perspective that criticizes while it rejoices. Toward the end, she has constructed two daughterly presences in her novel who help Sethe remember and forget her personal history, who embody the dual perspective of critique and rejoicing.

Beloved, the incarnation of the ghost of the murdered daughter, is the most obvious revisionist construction in Morrison's novel. Through Beloved, she signifies on history by resurrecting one of its anonymous victims. When Beloved comes back to haunt Sethe for murdering her, Beloved becomes the incarnated memory of Sethe's guilt. Moreover, she is nothing but guilt, a symbol of an unrelenting criticism of the dehumaniz-ing function of the institution of slavery. In this, she is the daughter representing a severe critique, demonstrating the determinism in slave history. She represents, however, only half of Morrison's work: the accusing glare, the unforgiving perspective, the need to forget—"It was not a story to pass on." There is another daughter in the novel, another daughter of history—representing the embracing glance, the loving view, the need to remember.

When Sethe first sees the reincarnated Beloved, her "bladder filled to capacity." She runs immediately to the outhouse but does not make it: "Right in front of its door she had to lift her skirts, and the water she voided was endless. Like a horse, she thought, but as it went on and on she thought, No, more like flooding the boat when Denver was born. So much water Amy said, 'Hold on, Lu. You going to sink us you keep that up.' But there was no stopping water breaking from a breaking womb and there was no stopping now" (51). She would later, in a retrospective moment, remember this scene in trying to discover who Beloved could be (132). What is worth noticing, though, is that at that precise moment she does not remember the birth of Beloved but the birth of Denver. Denver is the fictional recreation of Margaret Garner's other daughter, the daughter who survives. Coffin describes Garner and this daughter in the courtroom: "The babe she held in her arms was a little girl, about nine months old, and was much lighter in color than herself, light enough to show a red tinge in its cheek" (562–63).[30] In *Beloved,* Denver becomes the daughter of hope.

Denver is the first to recognize that Beloved is the incarnation of the ghost that had haunted 124; and she is also the first who lives through that recognition and develops the understanding necessary for an affirmative return to life. Like everyone else in the novel, she must learn to confront the past in order to face the future. She, too, must deal with what she has been repressing for most of her life: "the hurt of the hurt world" (28). Denver begins, like her mother, by attempting to prevent the past from intruding upon her life: "[S]he had her own set of questions which had nothing to do with the past. The present alone interested Denver" (119). Denver is not able to avoid the past for long, though, because the past becomes an immediate pain to her present life and an incipient danger to her future. What Denver must do is remember, and she must do so by revising her memory—her history and her mother's history—in a collective anamnesis.[31] Denver is preeminently in this novel the signifyin(g) daughter.

The first recognition Denver has of the danger Beloved represents to Sethe—the danger of the past's taking over the present—occurs in the Clearing. When Sethe goes to the Clearing to commune with her dead mother-in-law Baby Suggs, a spiritual force begins to choke her. Sethe reflects on the moment: "But one thing for sure, Baby Suggs had not choked her as first she thought. Denver was right, and walking in the dappled tree-light, clearer-headed now—away from the enchantment of the Clearing—Sethe remembered the touch of those fingers that she knew better than her own" (98). Denver will later accuse Beloved, who is the incarnated memory of her own murder, of choking her mother:

> "You did it, I saw you," said Denver.
> "What?"
> "I saw your face. You made her choke."
> "I didn't do it."
> "You told me you loved her."
> "I fixed it, didn't I? Didn't I fix her neck?"
> "After. After you choked her neck."
> "I kissed her neck. I didn't choke it. The circle of iron choked it."
> "I saw you." Denver grabbed Beloved's arm.
> "Look out, girl," said Beloved and, snatching her arm away, ran ahead as
> fast as she could along the stream that sang on the other side of the woods.
> (101)

For Denver, this is the first of her two crucial moments. She has not gone to the other side of the woods in years because she has willfully isolated herself in the house and the yard: "124 and the field behind it were all the world she knew or wanted." There had been a time when "she had known more and wanted to."

Reflecting on what she thinks she has just witnessed—Beloved's attempt to choke her mother—and looking out at Beloved's flight, Denver remembers the moment that caused her willful isolation. When she was seven she had wandered beyond the confines of the house and yard and entered the children's class Lady Jones conducted. For a full year, she learned to write and read: "She was so happy she didn't even know she was being avoided by her classmates—that they made excuses and altered their pace not to walk with her. It was Nelson Lord—the boy as smart as she was—who put a stop to it; who asked her the question about her mother that put chalk, the little *i* and all the rest those afternoons held, out of reach forever." Denver never went back to Lady Jones's, but she also did not ask anybody whether Nelson Lord's question was true. Reflecting now both on the latest incident in the Clearing and on the moment Nelson Lord had ended her adventurousness forever, Denver begins to confront questions regarding the ways the past shapes the present—she begins to ask herself whether she has a complicitous role in her mother's history: "Walking toward the stream, beyond her green bush house, she lets herself wonder what if Beloved really decided to choke her mother. Would she let it happen? Murder, Nelson Lord had said. 'Didn't your mother get locked away for murder? Wasn't you in there with her when she went?'" (104). It was "the second question that made it impossible for so long to ask Sethe about the first." Because Denver knows her mother's loving care, she finds it impossible to ask about the moment Sethe might have expressed her love murderously.

At age seven, Denver chose not to ask Sethe to explain; she preferred the comfort she received from the ghost haunting 124: "Now it held for her all the anger, love and fear she didn't know what to do with" (103). It is Denver who hears and identifies her dead sister's presence in the ghost. And by recognizing the ghost's identity, Denver begins the process of confronting the ramifications of the past: "The return of Denver's hearing, cut off by an answer she could not bear to hear, cut on by the sound of her dead sister trying to climb the stairs, signaled another shift in the fortunes of the people of 124. From then on the presence was full of spite" (103–4). For ten years, Denver prefers to live in the ambivalence wrought of suspicion without desiring any explanation.

At age fifteen, confronted with the incarnated memory of her mother's crime, Denver again chooses the ghost: "The display she witnessed at the Clearing shamed her because the choice between Sethe and Beloved was without conflict." Ironically, although Denver thinks that the present alone is what interests her, she luxuriates in the past, in dwelling in a shadowy history that she is unwilling to confront or confirm. Now, though, she has realized that she must make a choice—a choice she defers for now but must eventually make.

She makes an initial choice based on her fear for her own life: "I love my mother but I know she killed one of her own daughters, and tender as she is with me, I'm scared of her because of it" (205). Because of this, Denver feels the onus of protecting Beloved: "It's all on me, now, but she can count on me. I thought she was trying to kill her that day in the Clearing. Kill her back. But then she kissed her neck and I have to warn her about that. Don't love her too much. Don't. Maybe it's still in her the thing that makes it all right to kill her children. I have to tell her. I have to protect her" (206). There is only so long Denver can nurture this resentment; there is only so much the past can inform her living present. Beloved becomes demanding: "Anything she wanted she got, and when Sethe ran out of things to give her, Beloved invented desire" (240). It takes an act of seeing how this memory is literally consuming her mother for Denver to realize that her initial choice must be altered: "Then Sethe spit up something she had not eaten and it rocked Denver like gunshot. The job she started out with, protecting Beloved from Sethe, changed to protecting her mother from Beloved" (243).

This is the second crucial moment in Denver's life, when she must assume responsibility for having nurtured resentment, for having kept the past alive for selfish reasons. She will now have to leave 124 and face the larger community. She will have to stop dwelling on her mother's history and recognize the larger communal history of slavery's suffering. In doing so, she must understand her mother's act in light of a larger narrative. Beloved had responded to Denver's accusation of choking Sethe's neck by referring to an institution: "I didn't choke it. The circle of iron choked it." Slavery, Beloved is saying in a lower frequency, is the thing to blame. Denver will have to learn to listen to that lower frequency.

As she stands on the steps, Denver remembers her grandmother's final words: "Lay down your sword. This ain't a battle; it's a rout." Standing uneasily on the steps she has not left since Nelson Lord asked her that painful question, Denver is visited by Baby Suggs's ghost:

> Denver stood on the porch in the sun and couldn't leave it. Her throat itched; her heart kicked—and then Baby Suggs laughed, clear as anything. "You mean I never told you nothing about Carolina? About your daddy? You don't remember nothing about how come I walk the way I do and about your mother's feet, not to speak of her back? I never told you all that? Is that why you can't walk down the steps? My Jesus my."
> But you said there was no defense.
> "There ain't."
> Then what do I do?
> "Know it, and go on out the yard. Go on." (244)

"Know it": historical knowledge, if it isn't the defense, *is* at least the only way to integrity. It is a knowledge of the larger collective—of her father, her mother, her grandmother, Carolina, Sweet Home, slavery. It is understanding the forces of slavery that compelled her mother to do what she did. There is another story besides Beloved's, a larger narrative besides her family's, a deeper pain than suspicion and fear and spite. She follows her grandmother's advice and leaves the yard. By leaving the house, she enables herself to know.

She is first of all initiated into maturity and then understanding. The first place she goes is to Lady Jones's. When Lady Jones recognizes her and says, "Oh, baby . . . Oh, baby," Denver passes an indefinable threshold:

"Denver looked up at her. She did not know it then, but it was the word 'baby,' said softly and with such kindness, that inaugurated her life in the world as a woman. The trail she followed to get to that sweet thorny place was made up of paper scraps containing the handwritten names of others" (248). Those paper scraps represent her place in history—both within the family as a literate daughter of an unlettered mother and within the culture as a remembering being.

A woman now, Denver begins to glean the inner meaning of a larger reality, to comprehend the dangers that dwelling on the past holds. Denver's discovery, though, occurs when she becomes imbricated into a story Sethe is telling Beloved. The passage in which Sethe's relationship to Beloved is delineated must be quoted in full:

> *Denver thought* she understood the connection between her mother and Beloved: Sethe was trying to make up for the handsaw; Beloved was making her pay for it. But there would never be an end to that, and seeing her mother diminished shamed and infuriated her. Yet she knew Sethe's greatest fear was *the same one Denver had in the beginning*—that Beloved might leave. That before Sethe could make her understand what it meant—what it took to drag the teeth of that saw under the little chin; to feel the baby blood pump like oil in her hands; to hold her face so her head would stay on; to squeeze her so she could absorb, still, the death spasms that shot through that adored body, plump and sweet with life—Beloved might leave. Leave before Sethe could make her realize that worse than that—far worse—was what Baby Suggs died of, what Ella knew, what Stamp saw and what made Paul D tremble. That anybody white could take your whole self for anything that came to mind. Not just work, kill, or maim you, but dirty you. Dirty you so bad you couldn't like yourself anymore. Dirty you so bad you forgot who you were and couldn't think it up. And though she and others lived through and got over it, she could never let it happen to her own. The best thing she was, was her children. Whites might dirty *her* all right, but not her best thing, her beautiful, magical best thing—the part of her that was clean. . . . This and much more, *Denver heard* her say from her corner chair, trying to persuade Beloved, *the one and only person she felt she had to convince,* that what she had done was right because it came from true love. (251, emphasis added)

This moment of understanding, the moment when Sethe articulates her recognition of the reasons she killed Beloved, is filtered through Denver's hearing and understanding; it begins with Denver's thinking and ends with her hearing. Although Sethe thinks she is attempting to convince only one daughter of her love, in reality she is convincing the other daughter too. Denver had, "in the beginning," wished Beloved to stay because Beloved represented the ambiguity she felt about her mother—because Beloved was an accusation always readily available. Denver has since understood that because of a larger communal history, her mother's deed might not be so heinous as she had at first thought. That is not to say that Morrison is trying to negate the guilt Sethe feels, or even attempting to palliate it by reference to an institutional context. Rather, by having both of the daughters listen to Sethe's realization, Morrison represents for us the ambivalent duality of what she considers primarily the black woman writer's way of looking at the world—as she puts it, "in an unforgiving/loving way." Each daughter in this novel represents one way. Beloved accuses while Denver embraces; Beloved is unforgiving while Denver is loving; Beloved will be "Disremembered and unaccounted for" while Denver is the source of re-membering. Two things occur when Denver finally follows Baby Suggs's advice and steps out of 124—one that leads to a personal healing and another that leads to a communal.

First, she tells the community that Beloved, the murdered baby, has returned to punish Sethe. It is a story that must be narrated for its subjects to be cured: "Nobody was going to help her unless she told it—told all of it" (253). The community responds in three ways: "those that believed the worst; those that believed none of it; and those, like Ella, who thought it through" (255). It is Ella, finally, who initiates the exorcism of Beloved; and it is significant that Ella is the one to do this. First of all, Ella, like the matured Denver, has outgrown the need to dwell on the past: "Whatever Sethe had done, Ella didn't like the idea of past errors taking possession of the present. Sethe's crime was staggering and her pride outstripped even that; but she could not countenance the possibility of sin moving on in the house, unleashed and sassy. Daily life took as much as she had. The future was sunset; the past something to leave behind. And if it didn't stay behind, well, you might have to stomp it out" (256). Moreover, Ella too has a place in the larger narrative of slavery. Her puberty was spent "in a house where she was shared by father and son, whom she called 'the lowest yet.' It was the 'lowest yet' who gave her a disgust for sex and against whom she measured all atrocities" (256). And Ella's personal history has hints of infanticide in it too: "Ella had been beaten every way but down. She remembered the bottom teeth she had lost to the brake and the scars from the bell were thick as rope around her waist. She had delivered, but would not nurse, a hairy white thing, fathered by 'the lowest yet.' It lived five days never making a sound. The idea of that pup coming back to whip her too set her jaw working" (258–59). By registering her narrative within a framework of determinism and forgiveness, Ella has learned how to free herself. She offers that possibility to Sethe. For twenty-eight days, Sethe had been free—the time between crossing the Ohio River and the time she killed her baby daughter. Sethe had known then that "freeing yourself was one thing; claiming ownership of that freed self was another" (95). In that twenty-eight days, she had claimed herself. After murdering Beloved, she lost that claim. Ella, by exorcising Beloved, by not allowing the past to consume the present, offers Sethe the opportunity to reclaim herself. In the end Sethe does, and does so by an act of community. In this her life is following the pattern established by her daughter Denver.

Denver's personal healing is attested to when she meets Nelson Lord for the first time since he had asked her the question that had deafened her. This is the second thing that happens when she leaves 124. She sees Nelson: "All he did was smile and say, 'Take care of yourself, Denver,' but she heard it as though it were what language was made for. The last time he spoke to her his words blocked up her ears. Now they opened her mind" (252). This encounter demonstrates Denver's growth. She knows now her shared history—her family's, her community's, her culture's. As much as Nelson's original question had been the closure of language for her, so now is his amiable comment a renewal of communication.

Sethe, after Denver, will make a successful return to life in the same way. When she told Paul D how she killed Beloved, he made a comment that caused a forest to spring up between them (165). It will take Paul D's own education, and Sethe's attempts to understand herself and make Beloved understand her actions, before they are able to reunite. Paul D finally realizes that he "wants to put his story next to hers." Not only is this an act of a shared narrative, but it is also an affirmation that Sethe has a claim to herself:

> "Sethe," he says, "me and you, we got more yesterday than anybody. We need some kind of tomorrow."
>
> He leans over and takes her hand. With the other he touches her face. "You your best thing, Sethe. You are." His holding fingers are holding hers.
>
> "Me? Me?" (273)

Like Denver, who finds the ability to discover herself in Nelson Lord's words, Sethe finds the ability to reclaim, to recover, herself in Paul D's. Before she told Paul about Beloved, she had thought that theirs was a shared narrative: "Her story was bearable because it was his as well—to tell, to refine, and tell again. The things neither knew about the other—

the things neither had word shapes for—well, it would come in time" (99). The full story does come in time, but it is a product of extreme stress and pain, of the effort to remember what each desires to forget. It is a story told in a language that deafens while it enlightens: "This was not a story to pass on."

Hearing *Beloved*

It is a story, however, that does get passed on—and it is passed on through the ear. While Sethe thinks she is trying to convince only Beloved of the reasons she committed murder, Denver is *listening*. As I suggested earlier, Denver is the filtering ear for Sethe's process of self-discovery: "This and much more Denver heard her say. . . ." It is important that Denver, the signifyin(g) daughter, *hears* what Sethe has to say. It alerts us to how this novel situates itself in the African-American literary tradition. *Beloved* belongs to that class of novels Gates characterizes as "speakerly texts"— those texts "whose rhetorical strategy is designed to represent an oral literary tradition" and to produce the "illusion of oral narration."[32] Within the structure of the broadest frame of *Beloved*'s "speakerly text" there exists what we might call the "aural being." It is this being who represents our belonging to this novel, and this being is represented within the novel by the signifyin(g) daughter.

Peter Brooks has suggested that meaning in novels resides in the dialogical relationship between "tellers and listeners," in the transmission of the "'horror,' the taint of knowledge gained." The reader of narratives, that is, is "solicited not only to understand the story, but to complete it."[33] That reader—when constructed within the novel, that aural being—is, like Marlowe's auditor, a creation of the speakerly text. Moreover, and this is distinctly an aspect of the African-American literary tradition, the voice of the speakerly text is a product of a generational memory. We may find the protocols for this sort of generational memory represented in at least two other novels written by African-American women: Hurston's *Their Eyes Were Watching God* (1937)—the prototype, Gates tells us, of the speakerly text—and Sherley Anne Williams's *Dessa Rose* (1986).

Beloved is also a novel that constructs its ideal "listener." Denver will tell and retell the story that she now understands. Like Pheoby in *Their Eyes Were Watching God,* Denver uses the knowledge of "horror," transmitted to her aurally, to perform a healing narrative—orally. And, like Pheoby, Denver represents the implied community of ideal readers, the "aural being." What, finally, Denver is to *Beloved* is the space for hearing the tale of infanticide with a degree of understanding—both as the sister of the murdered baby and as the living daughter of the loving mother. Denver, that is, is a site of participation.

Morrison has said on various occasions that she writes into her narratives the "places and spaces so that the reader can participate."[34] It is a dialogic form that she has suggested is akin to music and to black preaching. These are art forms that, she suggests, are part of the repertoire of "Black art," which is difficult to define but does have "major characteristics,"

> [o]ne of which is the ability to be both print and oral literature: to combine those two aspects so that the stories can be read in silence, of course, but one should be able to hear them as well. It should try deliberately to make you stand up and make you feel something profoundly in the same way that a Black preacher requires his congregation to speak, to join him in the sermon, to behave in a certain way, to stand up and to weep and *to cry and to accede or to change and to modify*—to expand on the sermon that is being delivered. In the same way that a musician's music is enhanced when there is a response from the audience. Now in a book . . . I have to provide the places and spaces so that the reader can participate. (Emphasis added)[35]

She intends her novels to be healing, belonging to a form she calls "village literature"—literature that should "clarify the roles that have become obscured," literature that is able to "identify those things in the past that are useful and those things that are not," a literature, finally, that is able to "give nourishment."[36] The novel as a form of "Black art" works with history as its subject in order to criticize and to revise—to cry and to modify.

Morrison claims that it is precisely because the black oral historical tradition is now a thing of the past that the African-American novel is so necessary: "the novel is needed by African Americans now in a way that it was not needed before. . . . We don't live in places where we can hear those stories anymore; parents don't sit around and tell their children those classical, mythological, archetypal stories that we heard years ago."[37] Those stories must have a place in African-American culture, and they have found their place in the novel. The novel becomes for Morrison what Aunt Sue was for Langston Hughes—the site of an oral history passed from generation to generation:

> And the dark-faced child, listening,
> Knows that Aunt Sue's stories are real stories.
> He knows that Aunt Sue never got her stories

Out of any book at all,
But that they came
Right out of her own life.[38]

Because all those ancestors, like Aunt Sue, are no longer available, there must evolve within the African-American tradition an art form that gives them voice. *Beloved* is but one more novel in a tradition doing just that. But it also does one more thing: it situates itself not only theoretically but also performatively as an oral literature.

I noted earlier that Morrison provides a criticism of print media through Paul D's assessment of what newspapers will or will not write about black people. Like other novels in the tradition of African-American letters, Morrison criticizes the ideological imperative of print media in order to establish the value of oral historical relation. This criticism of print media is very much part of the overall revisionist motive in criticizing the historiography of slavery. It is, after all, only when slave narratives and slave accounts began to be taken seriously as historical documents that the other side of slavery could be articulated. The contemporary novel of signifyin(g) history, or the speakerly text, represents this struggle for the validation of orality. In Williams's *Dessa Rose,* for instance, the slave Dessa is given two voices—one as the white pro-slavery polemicist Adam Nehemiah "reconstructs" her voice in his journal, and the other as she orally tells her story to her grandchildren in her own voice. Dessa, that is, can save herself only by telling a story different from the one she is written to fit, by refusing to be written and asserting herself in voice.[39] In *Beloved* it is schoolteacher who uses writing in a detrimental way. Schoolteacher attempts to read and write Sethe as a subhuman thing by listing what he calls her "animal" characteristics alongside her human ones. Sethe resolved that "no one, nobody on this earth, would list her daughter's characteristics on the animal side of the paper" (251). Like Dessa, Sethe refuses to allow the written to usurp her humanity, and she finds that her humanity is best represented by the spoken word. To discover how *Beloved* is constructed to represent its own orality, we must first of all delineate the variety of oral communities in the novel.

Paul D belonged to a chain gang that had its own language, signifying nothing to those who did not belong to its community: "They sang it out and beat it up, garbling the words so they could not be understood; tricking the words so their syllables yielded up other meanings" (108). Like the chain gang described by Frederick Douglass, the slaves would sing songs that "to many would seem unmeaning jargon, but which, nevertheless, were full of meaning to themselves."[40] But when he enters the community of Sethe and her two daughters, Paul D finds himself unable to comprehend their language: "Hearing the three of them laughing at something he wasn't in on. The code they used among themselves that he could not break" (132). When Sethe first converses with Ella, after escaping from the Sweet Home plantation, what Sethe says yields up a surplus of meaning to Ella because of her ear for the silences: "she listened for the holes— the things the fugitives did not say; the questions they did not ask. Listened too for the unnamed, unmentioned people left behind" (92). When Ella initiates the exorcism with a holler, language becomes wholly oral: "In the beginning was the sound, and they all knew what that sound sounded like" (259).

Finally, though, the most important oral community in this novel is composed of those able to understand the mode of discourse necessary to relating the crux of this story—the murder of Beloved:

> Sethe knew that the circle she was making around the room, him, the subject, would remain one. That she could never close in, pin it down for anybody who had to ask. If they didn't get it right off—she could never explain. Because the truth was simple, not a long drawn-out record of flowered shifts, tree cages, selfishness, ankle ropes and wells. Simple: she was squatting in the garden and when she saw them coming and recognized the schoolteacher's hat, she heard wings. Little hummingbirds stuck their needle beaks right through her headcloth into her hair and beat their wings. And if she thought anything, it was No. No. Nono. Nonono. Simple. She just flew. Collected every bit of life she had made, all the parts of her that were precious and fine and beautiful, and carried, pushed, dragged them through the veil, out, away, over there where no one could hurt them. Over there. Outside this place, where they would be safe. And the hummingbird wings beat on. (163)

Paul D has trouble understanding this discourse, just as he had trouble understanding the code existing between Sethe and her daughters. "At first he thought it was her spinning. Circling him the way she was circling the subject. . . . Then he thought, No, it's the sound of her voice; it's too near" (161). Eventually, Paul D understands only that Sethe murdered Beloved; he suggests that it was because her love was "too thick." It will take him the rest of the novel to understand that, for Sethe, "Love is or it ain't. Thin love ain't love at all" (164).

It takes memory and articulation for Sethe to understand her own action. What she had to remember is another oral community between her grandmother and herself; "she was remembering something she forgot she knew" (61):

> Nan was the one she knew best, who was around all day, who nursed babies, cooked, had one good arm and half of another. And who used different words. Words Sethe understood then but could neither recall nor repeat now. She believed that must be why she remembered so little before Sweet Home except singing and dancing and how crowded it was. What Nan told her she had forgotten, along with the language she told it in. The same language her ma'am spoke, and which would never come back. But the message—that was and had been there all along. Holding the damp white sheets against her chest, she was picking meaning out of a code she no longer understood. (62)

The story Nan tells her is that of Sethe's mother killing those children fathered by whites. The story is remembered when Beloved returns and asks about Sethe's mother. It is a story that has a progressive effect on Sethe, exactly as the story of Sethe's murder of Beloved has on Denver: "As small girl Sethe, she was unimpressed. As grown-up woman Sethe she was angry, but not certain at what." Now, in remembering her own relationship to her two daughters, she is able to understand her mother's acts and her grandmother's code. By situating herself within a communal narrative of grandmother-mother-daughter relationships, Sethe is able to understand herself. The code becomes unlocked and available for her hearing.

I have suggested that part of the significance of Denver's "hearing" her mother explain to Beloved the reasons for her action is that she becomes the "aural being" of this speakerly text. Moreover, the act of hearing symbolizes Denver's overcoming her deafness—wrought, as it was, of her first hearing of her mother's act. For Sethe, telling her story allowed her to understand *her* mother's history. For Denver, telling her mother's story allows her to understand the communal history and her place in it. As we saw, Sethe's final healing occurs in imitation of Denver—as Denver places her story next to Nelson Lord's, Sethe places hers next to Paul D's. Denver is, then, in a very real sense, completing her mother's story. That, finally, is what an aural being is to the speakerly text's unfolding—both the space for the reader's participation and, as Brooks suggests, a symbol of the illusion of completeness, of closure.

It is worth nothing the differences between aural beings and their roles in the novels we can designate as speakerly texts. *Their Eyes Were Watching God* gives us a framed story, with the hearer—Pheoby—being presented at the beginning and end of the relation. She is the gauge of our understanding of

Janie's tale and the source of Janie's justification in the eyes of the community: "Nobody better not criticize yuh in mah hearin."[41] In Hurston's novel, then, in the scene in which the grandmother relates her story to her granddaughter is part of the overall enactment of the telling of the tale. Much as Nanny attempted to justify her life in an oral story to her granddaughter, so does Janie—that very granddaughter—attempt to justify her life by telling it to her friend. In *Dessa Rose,* we find out only in the epilogue that the aural beings are Dessa's grandchildren. By exposing the fact that this is an enactment of the grandmother's oral narration at the very end, Williams forces us to reconsider our relation to textual history. "Afro-Americans," she writes in her prefatory note, "having survived by word of mouth—and made of that process a high art—remain at the mercy of literature and writing" (ix). In a bold gesture, Williams makes Dessa's orality the foundation of any textual record of her. The white Nehemiah's records become illegible and blank sheets; Dessa's story is recorded by her son and *said* back to her. The oral transmission, then, is the enactment of part of this novel's polemical trajectory: the establishing of the primacy of a told tale.

Beloved differs from these two means of organizing orality within the speakerly text in that it is based on a variety of discrete oral linguistic communities, and its story is about the establishment of a communal narrative. The critique of the newspaper's report and the condemnation of schoolteacher's racist anthropology attest to the ex-slaves' refusal to be written. They are, nonetheless, discrete individuals prevented by various deafnesses from *hearing* the communal story to which they belong. Paul D must learn to understand the community of mother and daughters, just as he must learn to hear Sethe's story of her infanticide (he had felt her *voice* was too close, we recall). Denver must understand Sethe's story, as well, because she is the one who must go out and tell it—tell it in order to save her mother. Likewise, Sethe learns to understand how to claim herself as her own best thing only after she is able to understand what her grandmother told her, only after she is able to understand her mother's actions as part of a larger framework of experience.

The scenes of hearing the mother's tongue, understanding the mother's code, knowing the mother's history—these are themselves the very enactment of an ongoing generational oral transmission. In themselves, they represent the organization of this novel's speakerliness. Unlike *Dessa Rose* and *Their Eyes Were Watching God,* each of which enacts a single scene of oral transmission of one person's story to her grandchildren or to her friend, *Beloved* is concerned with demonstrating the variety and continuousness of oral transmissions necessary for any person to understand her own story. In this, each of the major characters in the novel signifies on the story of each of her or his fellow characters in order to establish a communal narrative—*Beloved* itself. The best figure for this (internal) formal revision is Paul D's desire to place his story next to Sethe's. The novel is, finally, about putting stories together and putting them to rest.

Putting to rest, of course, for Morrison means giving renewed and energetic life. From this rest, she gives her characters resurrection. In the end, perhaps the greatest achievement of Morrison's novel is that she gives the murdered victim of history *voice;* she resurrects the unjustly killed and allows that daughter to have renewed historical life by criticizing the sort of history that has hitherto excluded her and her rebellious spirit. In the end, this impetus is best expressed in one of W. E. B. Du Bois's most lyrical moments, in a passage that can almost act as a commentary on the novel, which would be published nearly eighty-five years later: "It is a hard thing to live haunted by the ghost of an untrue dream; to see the wide vision of empire fade into real ashes and dirt; to feel the pang of the conquered, and yet to know that with all the Bad that fell on one black day, something was vanquished that deserved to live, something killed that in justice had not dared to die."[42] In giving that "ghost" a renewed voice and life, Morrison not only criticizes the institution responsible for *Beloved's* death but also shows the healing knowledge that accrues to those attentive to the ghost's presence. What Morrison does in *Beloved* is to remember in order to revive, to survive, to rename, to re-possess. At the end of *The Color Purple*, Alice Walker, signing herself as author and medium, writes, "I thank everybody in this book for coming." In the preface to *Dessa Rose*, Williams claims to have the feeling of "owning" a summer in the nineteenth century. Resuscitating historical figures may indeed give one the feeling of belonging to a larger community, of being at one with the ancestors—in Walker's metaphor, of being in the temple of the familiar; in Morrison's metaphor, of burying the dead to revive them. Nothing serves more persuasively to delineate how an author feels when she has revised and revived history than Morrison's own commentary on her novel. At the end of her conversation with Gloria Naylor, Toni Morrison reflects on what her creative act continues to mean to her:

> It was a conversation. I can tell, because I said something I didn't know I knew. About the "dead girl." That bit by bit I had been rescuing her from the grave of time and inattention. Her fingernails maybe in the first book; face and legs, perhaps, the second time. Little by little bringing her back into liv-

ing life. So that now she comes running when called—walks freely around the house, sits down in a chair; looks at me. . . . She is here now, alive. I have seen, named and claimed her—and oh what company she keeps.

Notes

1. John Edgar Wideman, *Sent for You Yesterday* (1983; rpt., New York: Random House, 1988), prefatory half-page; Wideman, *Interviews with Black Writers,* ed. John O'Brien (New York: Liveright, 1973), 220–21.

2. Toni Morrison, "Rootedness: The Ancestor as Foundation," in *Black Women Writers (1950–1980): A Critical Evaluation,* ed. Mari Evans (New York: Doubleday, 1984), 339–45, esp. 344; Morrison, "Memory, Creation, and Writing," *Thought: A Review of Culture and Idea* 59 (Dec. 1984): 385–90, esp. 385, 389. Cf. Morrison, "City-Limits, Village Values: Concepts of the Neighborhood in Black Fiction," in *Literature and the Urban Experience: Essays on the City and Literature,* ed. Michael C. Jaye and Ann Chalmers Watt (New Brunswick: Rutgers Univ. Press, 1980), 35–43.

3. Toni Morrison, "Unspeakable Things Unspoken: The Afro-American Presence in American Literature," *Michigan Quarterly Review* 28 (Winter 1989): 1–34, esp. 11; cf. 25, where she describes how in the writing of *Tar Baby* she had to deal with "the nostalgia, the history, the nostalgia for the history; the violence done to it and the consequences of that violence." See Pauline Hopkins, *Contending Forces: A Romance Illustrative of Negro Life North and South* (Boston: The Colored Cooperative Publishing Co., 1900), 13–14.

4. Deborah E. McDowell, "Boundaries: Our Distant Relations and Close Kin," in *Afro-American Literary Study in the 1900s,* ed. Houston A. Baker, Jr., and Patricia Redmond (Chicago: Univ. of Chicago Press, 1989), 51–70, esp. 70; Henry Louis Gates, Jr., "Introduction," *Reading Black, Reading Feminist: A Critical Anthology,* ed. Gates (New York: Meridian, 1990), 1–17, esp. 16.

5. Hortense J. Spillers, "Changing the Letter: The Yokes, the Jokes of Discourse, or Mrs. Stowe, Mr. Reed," in *Slavery and the Literary Imagination,* ed. Deborah E. McDowell and Arnold Rampersad (Baltimore: Johns Hopkins Univ. Press, 1989), 25–61, esp. 52. See also Ralph Ellison, "A Very Stern Discipline," in *Going to the Territory* (New York: Random House, 1986), 275–307, esp. 276, 287–88. The term, theory, and typographical notation of "signifyin(g)" are all derived from the work of Henry Louis Gates, Jr., from his two formative essays, "Literary Theory and the Black Tradition" and "The 'Blackness of Blackness': A Critique of the Sign and the Signifying Monkey," both in *Figures in Black: Words, Signs, and the 'Racial' Self* (New York: Oxford Univ. Press, 1987), 3–58, 235–76, and especially from his consummate book, *The Signifying Monkey: A Theory of African-American Literary Criticism* (New York: Oxford Univ. Press, 1988).

6. Bonnie Angelo, "The Pain of Being Black" [An Interview with Toni Morrison], *Time,* May 22, 1989, 68–70, esp. 68. Morrison also expressed the difficulty of her chosen subject matter in *Beloved* to Sandi Russell in March 1986; see Russell, "'It's OK to Say OK,'" *Women's Review* [London] 5 (Mar. 1986): 22–24; reprinted in *Critical Essays on Toni Morrison,* ed. Nellie Y. McKay (Boston: G. K. Hall, 1988), 43–54, esp. 45: "It was an era I didn't want to get into—going back into and through grief."

7. Gloria Naylor and Toni Morrison, "A Conversation," *Southern Review* 21 (1985): 567–93, esp. 584–85. Hereafter I will cite all quotations from this article parenthetically in the body of the essay.

8. Levi Coffin, *Reminiscences of Levi Coffin* (Cincinnati: Western Tract Society, 1876), 557–67, esp. 559–60. Portions of Coffin's narrative have been reprinted in *Black Women in White America: A Documentary History,* ed. Gerda Lerner (New York: Random House, 1971), 60–63; and Charles L. Blockson, *The Underground Railroad* (New York: Berkeley, 1987), 195–200.

9. The story of Margaret Garner's escape will seem familiar to some readers as a historical event replicating (four years after) the literary event of Eliza's escape in Harriet Beecher Stowe's *Uncle Tom's Cabin,* chaps. 7 and 8. Eliza, too, crosses the semifrozen Ohio River from Kentucky to escape Shelby. For the sources for the Eliza episode, see Stowe, *The Key to Uncle Tom's Cabin* (1853; rpt., Port Washington, N.Y.: Kennikat Press, 1968), 21–23.

10. Toni Morrison, Foreword, Camille Billops, *The Harlem Book of the Dead* (New York: Morgan & Morgan, 1978). The photographs are by James Van Der Zee, the poetry by Owen Dodson, and the text by Camille Billops.

11. Toni Morrison, *Sula* (New York: Knopf, 1973), 149.

12. Toni Morrison, *Beloved* (New York: Knopf, 1987), 274. Subsequent quotations from *Beloved* will be taken from this edition and will be cited parenthetically in the body of the essay.

13. The story was reported in *The Liberator,* Mar. 21, 1856, 47, reprinted from the *Cincinnati Commercial;* see Lerner, *Black Women in White America,* 62–63. It was also reported in the *Philadelphia Press,* Mar. 14, 1870, reprinted from the *Cincinnati Chronicle;* see Blockson, *The Underground Railroad,* 199–200. For the *Annual Report of the American Anti-Slavery Society* (New York, 1856), 44–47, see Frederick Douglass, *The Life and Writings of Frederick Douglass,* 5 vols., ed. Philip S. Foner (New York: International Publishers, 1950–1975), 2:568 n. 30.

14. Ralph Ellison, *Invisible Man* (New York: Random House, 1952), 53, 67.

15. While hearing Trueblood relate this story to him and the white Mr. Norton, the "invisible man" thinks to himself, "How can he tell this to white men . . . when he knows they'll say that all Negroes do such things?" (57).

16. For Levi Coffin, John Jolliffe, and Lucy Stone, see Coffin, *Reminiscences,* 557, 548, 561–62, 564–65. Frederick Douglass, "WEST INDIA EMANCIPATION, speech deliv-

ered at Canandaigua, New York, 4 August 1857," *The Life and Writings*, 2:426–39, esp. 437.

17. Frances E. W. Harper, *Iola Leroy, or Shadows Uplifted* (1892; rpt., Boston: Beacon, 1987), 65, 98.

18. Herbert Aptheker, "The Negro Woman," *Masses and Mainstream* 11 (Feb. 1948): 10–17, esp. 11–12; Angela Y. Davis, *Women, Race & Class* (New York: Random House, 1981), 21, 29, 205.

19. Naylor and Morrison, "A Conversation," 584: "I'm not even sure what the denouement is of her story." Cf. Barbara Christian, "'Somebody Forgot to Tell Somebody Something': African-American Women's Historical Novels," in *Wild Women in the Whirlwind: Afra-American Culture and the Contemporary Literary Renaissance*, ed. Joanne M. Braxton and Andrée Nicola McLaughlin (New Brunswick: Rutgers Univ. Press, 1990), 326–41, esp. 336. Christian is quoting Morrison's "Distinguished University of California Regents' Lecture," University of California, Berkeley, Oct. 13, 1987.

20. See note 13 above; cf. Coffin, *Reminiscences*, 567.

21. Stanley Crouch, "Aunt Medea," *New Republic*, Oct. 19, 1987, 38–43, esp. 42.

22. See, for instance, Stanley M. Elkins, *Slavery: A Problem in American Institutional and Intellectual Life*, 3rd rev. ed. (1959; Chicago: Univ. of Chicago Press, 1976), esp. 223–310; and those who have responded to his arguments, especially John W. Blassingame, *The Slave Community: Plantation Life in the Antebellum South*, 2nd rev. ed. (1972; Oxford: Oxford Univ. Press, 1979); George P. Rawick, *From Sundown to Sunup: The Making of the Black Community* (Westport, Conn.: Westport Publishing Co., 1972); Willie Lee Rose, *Slavery and Freedom*, ed. William H. Freehling (Oxford: Oxford Univ. Press, 1982), esp. 188–200; Mary Frances Berry and John H. Blassingame, *Long Memory: The Black Experience in America* (Oxford: Oxford Univ. Press, 1982); Eugene D. Genovese, *Roll, Jordan, Roll: The World the Slaves Made* (New York: Random House, 1974); Herbert Gutman, *The Black Family in Slavery and Freedom, 1750–1925* (New York: Random House, 1976); and Lawrence W. Levine, *Black Culture and Black Consciousness: Afro-American Folk Thought from Slavery to Freedom* (Oxford: Oxford Univ. Press, 1977).

23. For the debate concerning Herbert Aptheker's *American Negro Slave Revolts*, 5th rev. ed. (1943; New York: International Publishers, 1987), see Rawick, *From Sundown to Sunup*, 53–75.

24. Robert B. Stepto, "'Intimate Things in Place': A Conversation with Toni Morrison," in *Chant of Saints: A Gathering of Afro-American Literature, Art, and Scholarship*, ed. Michael S. Harper and Robert B. Stepto (Urbana: Univ. of Illinois Press, 1979), 213–29, esp. 225.

25. Russell, "'It's OK to say OK,'" *Critical Essays on Toni Morrison*, 43–47, esp. 46, 44.

26. Claudia Tate, "Toni Morrison [An Interview]," in *Black Women Writers at Work*, ed. Claudia Tate (New York: Continuum, 1984), 118–31, esp. 130–31; Berry and Blassingame, *Long Memory*, x; Morrison, Foreword, *The Harlem Book of the Dead*.

27. William Wells Brown, *Clotelle; or, The Colored Heroine. A Tale of the Southern States* (Boston: Lee & Shepherd, 1867), 50–52. In the first edition of this novel, entitled *Clotel; or, The President's Daughter. A Narrative of Slave Life in the United States* (1853), Clotel herself jumps into the Potomac. This novel, too, it is worth mentioning, uses a historical daughter as its protagonist, Clotelle being (as legend has it) the mulatto daughter of Thomas Jefferson and his slave housekeeper Sally Hemings. For a discussion of the Jefferson legend in relation to Brown's novels, see Bernard W. Bell, *The Afro-American Novel and Its Traditions* (Amherst: Univ. of Massachusetts Press, 1987), 39–40, 354 nn. 1, 4. For a more recent treatment of the Jefferson connection, see Barbara Chase-Riboud's wonderful novel, *Sally Hemings* (1979; rpt., New York: Avon, 1980).

28. Zora Neale Hurston, *Moses, Man of the Mountain* (1939; rpt., Urbana: Univ. of Illinois Press, 1984), 16.

29. Harriet A. Jacobs, *Incidents in the Life of a Slave Girl, Written by Herself,* ed. Jean Fagan Yellin (Cambridge: Harvard Univ. Press, 1987), 80, 86; cf. 16, 31, 35, 47, 55–56, 61–52, 109, 141, 166, 173.

30. As I pointed out earlier, in one account, Margaret Garner's second daughter is drowned; in others, we know nothing of her future.

31. I have discussed the ways that collective anamnesis informs three of Morrison's novels in another paper, "'Rememory': Primal Scenes and Constructions in Toni Morrison's Novels," *Contemporary Literature* 31 (Fall 1990): 300–23.

32. Gates, *The Signifying Monkey,* 170–216, esp. 181; cf. 22. Gates suggests an analogy between the "speakerly text" and the Russian Formalist idea of *skaz;* see Victor Erlich, *Russian Formalism: History-Doctrine* (The Hague: Mouton, 1969), 238; cited in Gates, 276 n. 19; cf. 112.

33. Peter Brooks, *Reading for the Plot: Design and Intention in Narrative* (Oxford: Oxford Univ. Press, 1984), 260; cf. 236.

34. Morrison, "Rootedness," 341. Cf. Naylor and Morrison, "A Conversation," 582; and Tate, "Toni Morrison [An Interview]," 125.

35. Morrison, "Rootedness," 341. For her comparison of the black novel to music, see Russell, "'It's OK to Say OK,'" 46; and Robert B. Stepto, "'Intimate Things in Place': A Conversation with Toni Morrison," 228.

36. Thomas LeClair, "The Language Must Not Sweat': A Conversation with Toni Morrison," *New Republic,* Mar. 21, 1981, 25–29, esp. 26.

37. Morrison, "Rootedness," 340.

38. Langston Hughes, "Aunt Sue's Stories," *Collected Poems* (New York: Random House, 1959), 6.

39. Sherley Anne Williams, *Dessa Rose* (1986; New York: Berkeley, 1987), 10, 250, 260. Much of my reading of *Dessa Rose* is indebted to two recent studies: Gwendolyn Mae Henderson, "Speaking in Tongues: Dialogics, Dialectics, and the Black Woman Writer's Literary Tradition," in *Changing Our Own Words: Essays on Criticism, Theory, and*

Writing by Black Women, ed. Cheryl A. Wall (New Brunswick: Rutgers Univ. Press, 1989), 16–37, esp. 25–26, 32; and Deborah E. McDowell, "Negotiating between Tenses," *Slavery and the Literary Imagination*, 144–63, esp. 150, 156–57.

40. Frederick Douglass, *Narrative of the Life of Frederick Douglass, an American Slave*, ed. Houston A. Baker Jr., rev. ed. (1845; Harmondsworth: Penguin, 1982), 57. On other slave songs that specifically were meant to exclude the slaveholding community from understanding their intent, see Levine, *Black Culture and Black Consciousness*, 11, 51.

41. Zora Neale Hurston, *Their Eyes Were Watching God* (1937; rpt., Urbana: Univ. of Illinois Press, 1978), 284.

42. W. E. B. Du Bois, *The Souls of Black Folk*, *W. E. B. Du Bois: Writings*, ed. Nathan Huggins (New York: Library of America, 1986), 357–547, esp. 415.

Beloved

A Spiritual

KARLA F. C. HOLLOWAY

❖   ❖   ❖

> I have to cast my lot with those
> who age after age, perversely,
> with no extraordinary power,
> reconstitute the world.
> —Adrienne Rich,
> "Natural Resources"

THE LITERARY AND LINGUISTIC devices that can facilitate the revision of the historical and cultural texts of black women's experiences have perhaps their most sustained illustration in Toni Morrison's *Beloved*. Here, narrative structures have been consciously manipulated through a complicated interplay between the implicit orature of recovered and (re)membered events and the explicit structures of literature. The reclamation and revision of history function as both a thematic emphasis and textual methodology. The persistence of this revision is the significant strategic device of the narrative structures of the novel.

Myth dominates the text. Not only has Morrison's reclamation of this story from the scores of people who interviewed Margaret Garner shortly after she killed her child in 1855 constituted an act of recovery, it has accomplished a mythic revisioning as well. Morrison refused to do any further research on Margaret Garner beyond her reviewing of the magazine article that recounted the astonishment of the preachers and journalists who found her to be "very calm . . . very serene" after murdering her child (Rothstein). The imagination that restructures the initial article Morrison read into her novel *Beloved* is the imagination of a myth-maker. The mythological dimensions of her story, those that recall her earlier texts, that rediscover the altered universe of the black diaspora, that challenge the Western valuations of time and event (place and space) are those that, in various quantities in other black women writers and in sustained quantities in Morrison's works, allow a critical theory of text to emerge.[1]

Morrison revisions a history both spoken and written, felt and submerged. It is in the coalescence of the known and unknown elements of slavery—the events, minuscule in significance to the captors but major disruptions of black folks' experience in nurturing and loving and *being*— where Morrison's reconstruction of the historical text of slavery occurs. Morrison's reformulation propels a backlog of memories headlong into a postemancipation community that has been nearly spiritually incapacitated by the trauma of slavery. For Morrison's novel, what complicates the physical and psychic anguish is the reality that slavery itself defies traditional historiography. The victim's own chronicles of these events were systematically submerged, ignored, mistrusted, or superceded by "histori ans" of the era. This novel positions the consequences of black invisibility in both the records of slavery and the record-keeping as a situation of primary spiritual significance. Thus, the "ghostly"/"historical" presence that intrudes itself into this novel serves to belie the reportage that passes for historical records of this era as well as to reconstruct those lives into the spiritual ways that constituted the dimensions of their living.

Because slavery effectively placed black women outside of a historical universe governed by a traditional (Western) consideration of time, the *aspect* of their being—the quality and nature of their "state" of being—becomes a more appropriate measure of their reality. In historian Joan Kelly's essays, the exclusion of women throughout "historical time" is discussed in terms that clarify how the activities of civilization were determined by and exclusive to males. In defining a "feminist historiography" (a deconstruction of male-centered formulations of historical periods), Kelly focuses on the ways in which history is "rewritten and periodized" according to issues that affect women (6).[2] In black women's writing, this deperiodization is more fully articulated because of the propensity of this literature to strategically place a detemporalized universe into the centers of their texts. Not surprisingly, black women have experienced the universe that Kelly's essays on women's history theoretically discuss.

It is perhaps the insistence of this alternative perspective in regards to black women's experiences that explains some dimension of the strident element in the critical response to *Beloved*. Stanley Crouch, who wrote in *The New Republic* that "[i]t seems to have been written in order to enter American slavery into the big-time martyr ratings contest," missed the point entirely. Morrison wrote *Beloved* precisely because:

It was not a story to pass on.

They forget her like a bad dream.
After they made up their tales, shaped
and decorated them . . . in the end,
they forgot her too. Remembering seemed
unwise. . . .

It was not a story to pass on. . . .

This is not a story to pass on. (274, 275)

Like the litany of repetition that is a consistent narrative device in black
women's literature, these closing phrases of the novel echo between the
seeming contradiction of the initial "it was/this is not . . ." and the final
words "pass on." The phrase becomes a directive. Its message reveals that
this was not a story to die. Morrison revisions "Pass on," inverting it to
mean go on through . . . continue . . . tell. She privileges the consequences of the sustained echo and in this way forces the sounds of these
words (orature) to contradict the appearance of the visual (literate) text.
Morrison has "passed on" this story in defiance of those who would diminish the experience she voices back into presence.

The final pages of the novel, where these lines appear, illustrate what I
see as the interplay between structures that are implicitly orate but explicitly literate in black women's writing. In Morrison, this contrapuntal
structure dominates the novel and appears as a device that mediates
speech and narrative, the visual and the cognitive, and time and space.
These paired elements of text and philosophy are central to my discussion
in this essay.

Mediation such as the contrapuntal interplay sustains the text and res-
cues it from formlessness. Even when the narrative structure, for example,
dissolves into the eddying recollection of Beloved's memory, the text survives and the reader, almost drowning in the sheer weight of her over-
whelmingly tactile recollection, survives this immersion into text because
of Morrison's comforting mediation. In a discussion with a group of Virginia Polytechnic Institute students in 1988, Morrison explained to them
that one of her goals for this work was to acknowledge the reader's presence and participation in what she admitted was a difficult and painful
story. Her strategy was in part an assurance of her mediative narrative
presence. She spoke of writing with the sense that she was inviting the
reader to "Come on in," and that she would assure safe passage. As I listened to her, I was reminded of the pie-ladies in the basement churches

Son remembers in *Tar Baby,* whose "Come on in, you honey you" echoed through his adult memories. A similar guide, ancestral and essentially beneficent, also mediates the story of *Beloved.*

The signals of "telling" as a survival strategy—dialect, narrative recursion, suspension of time and place—are all in this text, especially in the compact and powerful passages where Sethe's, Denver's, and Beloved's voices are prosopopeic (re)memory.[3] Morrison introduces this section with a particularly beautiful and haunting recollection of the elements of speech and the devices of narrative that black women writers have used so effectively. Morrison's blending of voice and text privileges neither. Instead, they both collapse into the other and emerge as an introspective that enfolds the dimensions of both the mind and history in a visually rich and dazzling projection of a revisioned time and space. The narrative streams that (re)member and chronicle these events are prefigured in an episode when Denver, Sethe, and Beloved are ice-skating in a place where the "sky above them was another country. Winter stars, close enough to lick, had come out before sunset" (174). It is at this moment that Beloved sings the song that fulfills her mother's intimation that this is indeed the spirit of her dead daughter. At that time, Morrison writes, "Outside, snow solidified itself into graceful forms. The peace of winter stars seemed permanent" (176). In this way of removing hours from their reality (Sethe tells her daughters that it's "time to sleep") and placing them into a seasonal metaphor (they stumbled over the snow, but—and Morrison uses the following recursive, repeated structure—"nobody saw them falling" at least three times), the text prepares itself, the reader, and these three women for its temporal lapse. The chapter just prior to Sethe's discursive monologue ends in this way:

> When Sethe locked the door, the women inside were free at last to be what they liked, see whatever they saw and say whatever was on their minds.
>
> Almost. Mixed in with the voices surrounding the house . . . were the thoughts of the women of 124, unspeakable thoughts, unspoken. (199)

But they are spoken, for the next voice is Sethe's. And her first statement is in dialect—a sign that the text is about to embrace recursion and signify upon itself:[4] "Beloved, she my daughter. She mine" (200).

Sethe's version of her awareness of Beloved, and each of the three passages that follows hers are indeed "versions" of the same story with a different narrator. This is not particularly structurally ambiguous even though it is instead crowded with information that makes any attention to time or place simply inappropriate. French theorist and philosopher

Cathérine Clément, in a dialogue with Hélène Cixous about the nature of their discourse in *La Jeune Née*, accepts that "there can be two women in the same space who are *differently* engaged, speaking of almost exactly the *same things*, investing in two or three different kinds of discourse and going from one to the other and then on to the spoken exchange" (136). Cixous replies how she basically "distrust[s] the identification of a subject with a single discourse" (136).[5]

At this space in *Beloved*, Morrison cannot entrust this story to the single, individual discourse of any of the three women who are implicated in the myth. Instead, it is their collective telling that accomplishes the creative process of their task—to tell, (re)member, and validate their own narratives and to place them, full-bodied and spoken, into the space they share. Each of their voices is distinct, examples of the "different kind of discourse" Clément refers to, even though the three women are in the same dissolved space of Beloved's ephemeral presence.

Sethe's discourse is dense—interwoven with dialect and poetry and complicated with the smells and touches and colors that are left to frame her reality.

> Think what the spring will be for us! I'll plant carrots just so she can see them, and turnips . . . white and purple with a tender tail and a hard head. Feels good when you hold it in your hand and smells like the creek when it floods . . . we'll smell them together. (201)

Hers is a discourse vibrant and redolent—almost as if the vitality of her description would defy the dying and killing she acknowledges with her wintry declaration that, "Beloved, she my daughter."

Denver's discourse, in the same space as Sethe's, for she too uses her "unspeakable thoughts" to acknowledge Beloved, is the "different engagement" but "same thing" that Cixous and Clément discuss. Morrison highlights this "same difference" with the technique of repetition that functions as a recursion strategy—a means of accessing memory and enabling its domination of the text. Denver's first words, "Beloved is my sister," take us back to Sethe's. Her discourse also recollects her first memories and then propels her into her current dilemma. It (re)members her sister's death from a variety of perspectives—what she did (went to her secret house in the woods), what she tasted (her mother's milk along with her sister's blood), what she was told (by Grandma Baby). But it is the final repetition of her opening claim of Beloved as "my sister" that encircles her narrative discourse and encloses it within the safety of kinship acknowledged—"She's mine, Beloved. She's mine."

Beloved's discourse is the Derridean trace element—the one that dislocates the other two by challenging—disrupting what semblance of narrative structure or sense there had been in Sethe's or Denver's thinking.[6] But
her discourse also supports the narrative because her dialogue accomplishes the same kind of disruption that her presence actualized. It was she
who denied them their space in a secure and memoryless present. So her
discourse opens with an elliptical "I am Beloved and she is mine." That
opening pronouncement is the last structure syntactically marked as a
sentence. The rest evidences a fully divested text. Western time is obliter-
ated, space is not even relevant because Beloved's presence is debatable,
and the nature of her being is a nonissue because her belonging ("she is
mine") has been established by her mother and sister.

> I am not dead   I am not   there is a house
> there is what she whispered to me   I am where
> she told me   the sun closes my eyes   when I
> open them I see the face I lost. (213)

Emptied of the values that mark and specify dimension in a Western
tradition, Morrison's narrative now belongs to itself—the text claims its
text. Voice ("I am where she told me") is the only certain locus that remains. Her next chapter verifies the creation of this oracular space. It col-
lapses all their voices into a tightened poetic chant. Finally the identity of
the speaker is absolutely unclear and singularly irrelevant. Sethe's, Denver's, and Beloved's voices blend and merge as text and lose the distinction
of discourse as they narrate:

> You are my face; I am you.
> Why did you lave me who am you?
> I will never leave you again
> Don't ever leave me again
> You went in the water
> I drank your blood
> I brought your milk . . .
> I waited for you
> You are mine
> You are mine
> You are mine. (215, 216)

When Zora Neale Hurston described dialect as the "urge to adorn"—
an oral "hieroglyph"—she probably was not prefiguring the dimensions
that Morrison has brought to the glyph of black language. However,

Hurston certainly recognized the potential in black language to dissolve the artificial constructs of time that confine it to a tradition that belies its origin. What Morrison does with language is an act of liberation. The consequences of this freedom is that the text, which seems to be literate (i.e., written), is revealed as an oracular (i.e., a spoken) event. This is a blend that Walter Ong explicitly acknowledges when he writes that orality is "never completely eradicable; reading a text oralizes it" (175). Morrison enriches Ong's observation. Her texts are a constant exchange between an implicit mythic voice, one that struggles against the wall of history to assert itself and an explicit narrator, one that is inextricably bound to its spoken counterpoint.

The structures within African and African-American novels consistently defy the collected eventualities of time "past, present, and future," and in consequence a consideration of *aspect* may be a more appropriate frame through which to consider the chronicle of events in this story.[7] Temporal time represents a narrow specific moment of occurrence. The relatively limited idea of time as being in either the past, the present, or the future is inadequate for a text like *Beloved,* where the pattern of events crisscrosses through these dimensions and enlarges the spaces that they suggest. This novel immediately makes it clear that a traditional (Western) valuation of time is not definitive of the experience it (re)members; instead it is an intrusion on a universe that has existed seemingly without its mediation. Weeks, months, and years become irrelevant to the spite of 124—the house that Beloved's spirit inhabits. Baby Suggs, Morrison writes, was "suspended between the nastiness of life and the meanness of the dead" (3–4). This suspension was shared by more than Baby Suggs. Living itself is suspended in this story because of the simultaneous presence of the past.

In "Toward the Solstice" Adrienne Rich writes:

> if I could know
> in what language to address
> the spirits that claim a place
> beneath these low and simple ceilings,
> tenants that neither speak nor stir
> yet dwell in mute insistence
> till I can feel utterly ghosted in this house. (69)

When spirits "claim a place," there must be a simultaneous disruption of the spaces occupied not only by others but also by their aspects—their beings. The "tenants" in Rich's poem who "neither speak nor stir" still manage to pull her into their places until she feels "utterly ghosted." Morrison's spirit is a tug as well, and yet it is not only the dimensions of being that Beloved has claimed as her own, it is dimensionality itself—including the fourth dimension, time. Once time is implicated in Beloved's "insistence," a pattern familiar to Morrison's work asserts itself.

Sula's time "ends" on earth with her death, and yet, after she has died we hear her remark that it didn't even hurt—and her urge to tell her best friend Nel of that revelation. Her voice survived, suspended through the dimensions, or across them, as did her urge to share her knowledge, to continue to "tell." Circe, in Morrison's *Song of Solomon,* clearly defies time. How old is she? It is immaterial. What is critical is that she has lived past (and through) time to assure that the myth Milkman needed to reclaim his legacy would one day be his. She alone is able to retell the story he must hear if he is to solve the riddle that is his life. Milkman, who tells her, "They think you're dead," is easily claimed by her mythic dimensions. The fruity, ginger odor of her house that smells like Pilate's and her dark embracing presence draw him into her fabric. Time is suspended long enough for him to lose his place in the dangerous present that threatens his spirituality and find his place in a nurturing past.[8] *Tar Baby,* Morrison's sustained mythic text, begins with a water lady, a goddess reminiscent of the African water goddesses, nudging Son to an island where reclamation is the only surety. On Isles des Chevaliers, the mythology of ancestral blind horsemen dominates the present, and everyone there is waiting for the past to renew itself through them. For Morrison, myth becomes a metaphorical abandonment of time because its function is to reconnect the poetry that the development in languages has shifted away from the word.[9] The sense of a metaphor is represented as origin in myth—the two are not separable, and therefore to be metaphorical is to abandon the dissonance of time. Within such a cosmology, the potential of *Beloved* is freed from the dominance of a history that would submerge this story. This liberation is perhaps the most critical issue of Morrison's novel.

If Beloved is not only Sethe's dead daughter returned but also the return of all the faces, all the drowned but remembered faces of mothers and their children who have lost their being because of the force of that Euro-American slave-history, then she has become a cultural mooring place, a moment for reclamation and for naming. Morrison's epigraph to her novel cites the Old Testament: "I will call her Beloved who was not Beloved." I will *call.* I will name her who was not named. "I need to find a place to be," Beloved's discourse insists. Her being depended on not losing her self again. "Say my name," Beloved insists to Paul D. She demands to be removed from her nothingness, to be specified, to be "called."

If history has disabled human potential, then assertion, the ghostly insistence that Rich writes of in "Toward the Solstice," must come outside of history. Beloved's existence is liminal. Between worlds, being neither "in" nor "of" a past or a present, she is a confrontation of a killing history and a disabling present. Since neither aspect allows the kind of life that a post-emancipation black community would have imagined for itself because at the very least, "not a house in the county ain't packed to the rafters with some dead Negro's grief" (5), *Beloved* becomes a text collected with the textures of living and dying rather than with a linear movement of events. Morrison has written novels marked by seasons (*The Bluest Eye*) and years (*Sula*), but this story is marked by the shifting presence of the house, number 124 on Bluestone Road, that was introduced in Book One as "spite[ful]," in Book Two as "loud," and in Book Three as finally "quiet." This shift allows the focus of the novel to ignore the possible time frames. Neither distance nor years mattered to the white house where Beloved insisted herself back into reality. For Sethe, "the future was a matter of keeping the past at bay" (42), and since this story (not a story to "pass on") demystifies time, allowing it to "be" where/whenever it must be, we know, even before the story assumes this "text," that there was neither future nor present in the woman who walked fully dressed out of the water.

The recursion of this text, its sublimation of time and its privileging of an alternative not only to history, but to reality, places it into the tradition of literature by black women because of its dependence on the alternative, the inversion that sustains the "place" that has re-placed reality.[10] Certainly not all recursive texts sublimate time, but temporal displacement is clearly a possibility of such technique. This is why Hurston's note that black folk think in glyphs rather than writing is not only an acknowledgment of another cosmology but also an acknowledgment of the necessity of evolution in the basic design of the ways we think about thought. Thomas Kuhn's discussion in *The Structure of Scientific Revolutions* considers "evolution from the community's state of knowledge at any given time" (171) as the appropriate visual dimension of progress. It is evolution, that is, a changing and shifting conceptualization that identifies the aspective nature of recursion, rather than temporicity as the operative narrative space of Morrison's text. In her re-visioning of the history of slavery, Morrison proposes a paradigm of that history that privileges the vision of its victims and that denies the closure of death as a way of sidestepping any of that tragedy. The houses of the counties held grief; Sethe practiced, without success, holding back the past; and Beloved held not only her own history, but those of "sixty million and more." In these ways, the vision of this novel is innervision, the cognitive reclamation of our spiritual histories.

Notes

1. My position is that a critical theory of black *women*'s writing emerges as the dimensions of a cultural expression within an African-American literary tradition and specifies, through an interpretation of literary style and substance and its formal modes and figurations, certain textual modes of discourse. Such a specification underscores my primary argument that black women's literature reflects its community—its cultural ways of knowing as well as its ways of framing that knowledge in language. The figures of language that testify to that cultural mooring place—the inversive, recursive, and sometimes even subversive structures that layer the black text—and give it a dimension only accessed when the cultural and gendered points of its initiation are acknowledged.

2. I think it is interesting that when Kelly mentions black women in the frame of her discussion, it is a way of "help[ing] us [I presume she means white feminists] appreciate the social formation of 'feminity' as an internalization of ascribed inferiority which serves, at the same time, to manipulate those who have the authority women lack" (6). The "usefulness" of black women's experience to the feminist movement among white women is a demeaning part of its "history." Her comments about history are probably correct even though they point up a more critical issue for the critic of black women's literature in terms of understanding the distance between the issues of "feminism" in white and black communities. Alice Walker has acknowledged this distance in her stated preference for "womanist" as opposed to "feminist" discourse.

3. I use "(re)memory" as a means of bringing attention to the inner-vision of the world—its approximation of consciousness and its way of interpreting the literary revisioning of the mythic principle in black women writers' texts. By assuming this theoretical posture, I am able to stress the semiographic qualities of the word and its potential for mythologizing things in both the present and the past. Within this framework, the word is a dynamic entity that (re)members community and connects it back to the voices from which it has been severed, effectively forcing it out of its silence. Of course, it is also used here as an acknowledgment of Morrison's description of this event as what has made it so difficult for Sethe to "believe in time." A "rememory" is one of those "things [that] just stay[s] . . . there for you, waiting" (36, 7).

4. Henry Louis Gates's term is "free indirect discourse" for the narrative techniques that privilege dialect. One of his many discussions on this is in *Figures in Black*, where he notes that Hurston's "oral hieroglyphic" is a "spoken or mimetic voice,

cast in dialect, yet marked as a written one—a mimetic voice masking as a diegetic voice, but also a diegetic voice masking as a mimetic one . . . a free indirect 'narrative of division'" (243). The masking that Gates describes is equivalent to what I discuss in this essay as the shift between the elliptical interplay between implicit structures of orature and explicit structures of literature. See also his discussion in *The Signifying Monkey* (198–200).

5. There is a noticeable lack of tension in the discourse of Sethe, Denver, and Beloved—testimony to their spiritual relationship.

6. Derrida identifies "trace" as "not a presence but rather the sumulacrum of a presence that dislocates, displaces and refers beyond itself" (142–43).

7. Aspect describes action in terms of its duration without a consideration of its place in time. In *Caribbean and African Languages,* Morgan Dalphinis's discussion explores how aspect is a better descriptor of such basic cultural concepts than those traditionally measured by a "(past/present/future) time-based yardstick" (87). The implications of such a measure for literature that reflects its culture in the arrangement and use of language is clearly relevant to literatures of the African diaspora.

8. See Holloway. "The Lyrics of Salvation" in Holloway and Demetrakopoulos, esp. 112.

9. The discussion of the mythology in words most compatible with my own thinking can be found in Owen Barfield's *Poetic Diction,* esp. the chapters "Meaning and Myth" and "The Making of Meaning".

10. Black literary theory's interest in the nature of inversion in the black text provides some rich critical discussion and speculation. Houston Baker has provided one of the most interesting comments on this strategy. He writes, in *Blues, Ideology, and Afro-American Literature,* that "mythic and literary acts of language are not intended or designed for communicative ends. Rather than informational or communicative utterances that assure harmonious normalcy in human cultures such linguistic acts are radically contingent events whose various readings or performances occasion *inversive* symbolic modes of cognition and other extra- ordinary human responses" (my emphasis, 122). Baker's comment formulates a particularly important rubric for the discussion in this essay. The dissolution of "normalcy" would seem to predicate the "inversive" cognitive and narrative strategies in *Beloved.* However, the importance of inversion signaling *subversion* in black women's writing is the dimension that is distinct to a feminist canon. In *The Signifying Monkey,* Gates identifies the "mystery type of narrative discourse" as one "characterized by plot inversions." These, he notes, function "of course as temporal inversions." His point is to illustrate Ishmael Reed's texts as a "sort of indeterminacy" that predicates the use of inversion as textual "impediment." Impediment is somewhat closer to the subversion I describe, but it implies a blockage that is not a feature of the black woman writer's use of this technique.

Works Cited

Baker, Houston A., Jr., *Blues, Ideology, and Afro-American Literature.* Chicago: Univ. of Chicago Press, 1984.

Barfield, Owen. *Poetic Diction.* 1928. Rpt. Middletown, Conn.: Wesleyan Univ. Press, 1973.

Cixous, Hélène, and Catherine Clément. *The Newly Born Woman.* Trans. B. Wing. Minneapolis: Univ. of Minnesota Press, 1986.

Crouch, Stanley. "Aunt Medea: *Beloved* by Toni Morrison." New Republic, Oct. 19, 1987, Univ. Press, 38–43.

Dalphinis, Morgan. *Caribbean and African Languages.* London: Karia Press, 1985.

Derrida, Jacques. *Speech and Phenomenon.* Trans. David Allison. Evanston: Northwestern Univ. Press, 1973.

Gates, Henry Louis. *Figures in Black.* Oxford: Oxford Univ. Press, 1987.

———. *The Signifying Monkey.* Oxford: Oxford Univ. Press, 1988.

Holloway, Karla, and S. Demetrakopoulos. *New Dimensions of Spirituality: A BiRacial and BiCultural Reading of the Novels of Toni Morrison.* Westport, Conn.: Greenwood Press, 1987.

Kelly, Joan. *Women, History and Theory.* Chicago: Univ. of Chicago Press, 1984.

Kuhn, Thomas. *The Structure of Scientific Revolutions.* Chicago: Univ. of Chicago Press, 1962.

Morrison, Toni. *Beloved.* New York: Alfred A. Knopf, 1987.

———. *Song of Solomon.* New York: Alfred A. Knopf, 1977.

———. *Sula.* New York: Alfred A. Knopf, 1973.

———. *Tar Baby.* New York: Alfred A. Knopf, 1981.

Ong, Walter. *Orality and Literacy: The Technology of the Word.* New York: Methuen, 1983.

Rich, Adrienne, "Natural Resources" and "Toward the Solstice." *The Dream of a Common Language: Poems 1974–1977.* New York: Norton, 1979.

Rothstein, Mervyn. "Morrison Discusses New Novel." *New York Times,* Aug. 26, 1987.

Toni Morrison's *Beloved*

Re-Membering the Body
as Historical Text

MAE G. HENDERSON

◆　◆　◆

Now, women forget all those things they don't want
to remember. The dream is the truth. Then they act
and do things accordingly. . . . So the beginning
of this was a woman and she had come back from
burying the dead.
　　　　　　　　—Zora Neale Hurston, *Their Eyes*
　　　　　　　　　　　　　　Were Watching God

We tell stories because in the last analysis human
lives need and merit being narrated. This remark
takes on its full force when we refer to the necessity
to save the history of the defeated and the lost. The
whole history of suffering cries out for vengeance
and calls for narrative.
　　　　　　　　—Paul Ricoeur, *Time and Narrative*

Upon the death of the other we are given to memory, and thus to interiorization . . . since Freud,
this is how the "normal" "work of mourning" is
often described. It entails a movement in which an
interiorizing idealization takes in itself or upon itself the body and voice of the other, the other's vis-
age and person, ideally and quasi-literally devouring them. This mimetic interiorization is not fictive;
it is the origin of fiction, of apocryphal figuration. It

takes place in a body. Or rather, it makes for a body, voice, and a soul which, although "ours," did not exist and had no meaning *before* this possibility that one *must* always begin by remembering, and whose trace must be followed.

—Jacques Derrida, *Memories for Paul de Man*

I had brought not a child but suffering into the world and it, suffering, refused to leave me, insisted on coming back, on haunting me, permanently. One does not bear children in pain, it's pain that one bears: the child is pain's representative and once it is delivered moves in for good. . . . [A] mother is . . . marked by pain, she succumbs to it.

—Julia Kristeva, "Stabat Mater"

There is an "uncanniness" about his past that a present occupant has expelled (or thinks it has) in an effort to take its place. The dead haunt the living. The past: it "re-bites" [*il remord*] (it is a secret and repeated biting). History is "cannibalistic," and memory becomes the closed arena of conflict between two contradictory operations: forgetting, which is not something passive, a loss, but an action directed against the past; and the mnemic trace, the return of what was forgotten. . . . More generally speaking, an autonomous order is founded upon what it eliminates; it produces a "residue" condemned to be forgotten. But what was excluded . . . reinfiltrates the place of its origin—It resurfaces, it troubles, it turns the present's feeling of being "at home" into an illusion, it lurks—this "wild," this "obscene," this "filth," this "resistance" of "superstition"—within the walls of the residence, and behind the back of the owner (the ego), or over its objections, it inscribes there the law of the other.

—Michel de Certeau, *Heterologies: The Discourse of the Other*

DESCRIBING NINETEENTH-CENTURY slave narratives, Toni Morrison observes, "No slave society in the history of the world wrote more—or more thoughtfully—about its own enslavement." Yet, for Morrison, the narratives, with their "instructive" and "moral" force, are incomplete:

> Over and over, the writers pull the narrative up short with a phrase such as, "but let us drop a veil over these proceedings too terrible to relate." In shaping the experience to make it palatable to those who were in a position to alleviate it, they were silent about many things, and they "forgot" many other things . . .[1]

"Things too terrible to relate" were most often the sexual exploitation of slave women by white men. Convention allowed, indeed almost demanded, that these violations be named but not described. Morrison continues, "But most importantly—at least for me—there was no mention of their *interior life*" (emphasis added). The writer's "job"—as Morrison sees it—"becomes how to rip that veil drawn over proceedings too terrible to relate," to "find and expose a truth about the interior life of people who didn't write it," to "fill in the blanks that the slave narratives left, to part the veil that was so frequently drawn," and, finally, "to implement the stories that [she has] heard" (110–13).

Morrison's image of the veil revises a Du Boisian metaphor that was originally intended to suggest the division between blacks and whites in American society.[2] Rather than measuring a division *between* the races, however, Morrison's veil measures a division *within* the race, a psychic and expressive boundary separating the *speakable* from the *unspeakable* and the *unspoken*.[3] Her task as a writer, therefore, is to transgress these discursive boundaries by setting up a complementary and dialogic relationship between the "interiority" of her own work and the "exteriority" of the slave narrative.

Morrison, then, aims to restore a dimension of the repressed personal in a manifestly political discourse. In some ways, the texts of the slave narratives can be regarded as classic examples of the "return of the repressed," primarily because the events relating to violence and violation (which are self-censored or edited out) return again and again in "veiled allusions." To the degree that her work is intended to *resurrect* stories *buried* and *express* stories *repressed*, Morrison's relation to the slave narrators, as well as the relation of her text to its precursor narratives, can be profitably compared to not only the relation of the historian to informant but also that of the analyst to analysand.

Dedicating her novel *Beloved* to the "Sixty Million and more" who failed to survive the Middle Passage, Morrison sets out to give voice to the "disremembered and unaccounted for"—the women and children who left no written records. The epigraph from Romans 9:25 prefigures the writer's purpose of reclaiming this "lost tribe":

> I will call them my people, which were not my people; and her beloved which was not beloved.

By citing a New Testament passage that echoes a passage from the Old Testament, the author not only problematizes the nature of the relation between the past and the present but also thematizes the importance of historical reclamation and repossession. As Jehovah reclaimed the Israelites after their apostasy (figured in Hosea as spiritual adultery), so Morrison seeks to repossess the African and slave ancestors after their historic violation (figured in *Beloved* as physical rape).

Further, Morrison reinscribes the tension between Old Testament law and New Testament spirit. Significantly, it is the epistles of Paul (Romans and Galatians, in particular) that announce that the doctrine of justification by deeds under the Old Dispensation of the Law is revised through justification by grace under the New Dispensation of the Spirit.[4] Engaging the Scriptures as a kind of intertext, Morrison enacts in her novel an opposition between the law and the spirit, redeeming her characters from the "curse of the law" as figured in the master's discourse. In her rewriting of Scripture, Morrison ushers in an ironic new dispensation figured not by the law of the (white) Father but by the spirit of the (black and female) child, Beloved. Thus, Morrison challenges the hegemonic status of the (primarily male) slave narratives as well as the "canonical" history embodied in the master('s) narratives in a project that holds both more accountable to the "disremembered and unaccounted for."

Like several of her contemporaries, Morrison seeks to achieve these ends in a novel that both historicizes fiction and fictionalizes history.[5] In the following passage she recollects the events on which the novel was based:

> I . . . remember being obsessed by two or three little fragments of stories that I heard from different places. One was a newspaper clipping about a woman named Margaret Garner in 1851. It said that the Abolitionists made a great deal out of her case because she had escaped from Kentucky . . . with her four children. She lived in a little neighborhood just outside of Cincinnati and she had killed her children. She succeeded in killing one; she

tried to kill two others. The interesting thing, in addition to that, was the interviews that she gave. She was a young woman. In the inked pictures of her she seemed a very quiet, very serene-looking woman and everyone who interviewed her remarked about her serenity and tranquility. She said, "I will not let those children live how I have lived." She had run off into a little wood shed right outside her house to kill them because she had been caught as a fugitive. And she made up her mind that they would not suffer the way that she had and it was better for them to die. They put her in jail for a little while and I'm not even sure what the denouement is of her story. But that moment, that decision was a piece, a tail of something that was always around.[6]

Morrison links the above story fragment to another related in James Van der Zee's *The Harlem Book of the Dead:*

> In one picture, there was a young girl lying in a coffin and he says that she was eighteen years old and she had gone to a party and that she was dancing and suddenly she slumped and they noticed there was blood on her and they said, "what happened to you?" And she said, "I'll tell you tomorrow. I'll tell you tomorrow. . . ." That's all she would say. And apparently her ex-boyfriend or somebody who was jealous had come to the party with a gun and a silencer and shot her. And she kept saying, "I'll tell you tomorrow" because she wanted him to get away. And he did, I guess; anyway she died. (584)

These newspaper clippings and Van der Zee's photostory provided the historical or "real-life" bases for the novel. "Now what made those stories connect, I can't explain," says Morrison, "but I do know that, in both instances, something seemed clear to me. A woman loved something other than herself so much, she had placed all of the value of her life in something outside herself." Morrison's project, then, is twofold: the exploration of the black woman's sense of self and the imaginative recovery of black women's history.

Describing her narrative strategy as a "kind of literary archeology," Morrison explains that, for her, "the approach that's most productive and most trustworthy . . . is the recollection that moves from the image to . . . text." Her task, as she defines it, is to "[move] that veil aside" in order to penetrate the "memories within." Although these memories—personal and collective—constitute the "subsoil of [her] work," she believes that these alone cannot give "total access to the unwritten interior life." For Morrison, "only the act of the imagination" can provide such access:

[O]n the basis of some information and a little bit of guesswork you journey to a site to see what remains were left behind and to reconstruct the world that these remains imply. What makes it fiction is the nature of the imaginative act: my reliance on the image—on the remains—in addition to recollection, to yield up a kind of truth. By "image," of course, I don't mean "symbol"; I simply mean "picture" and the feelings that accompany the picture.[7]

Elaborating on the relationship between picture and meaning, Morrison contrasts her own literary method (to move from image to text) to that of writers who move "from event to the image that it left": "My route is the reverse: the image comes first and tells me what the 'memory' is about."[8]

The notion of "literary archeology"—the imaginative and reconstructive recovery of the past that characterizes Morrison's fictive process—can be usefully compared with R. G. Collingwood's description of the historical process: If the novelist relies upon the a priori imagination to construct the *possible* story in which characters and incidents develop "in a manner determined by a necessity internal to themselves," the historian relies upon the same inferential process to construct "his" story of the *past*. In the following passage, Collingwood demonstrates that "as works of imagination, the historian's work and the novelist's do not differ":

Each of them makes it his business to construct a picture which is partly a narrative of events, partly a description of situations, exhibition of motives, analysis of characters. Each aims at making his picture a coherent whole, where every character and every situation is so bound up with the rest that this character in this situation cannot but act in this way, and we cannot imagine him as acting otherwise. The novel and the history must both of them make sense; nothing is admissible in either except what is necessary and the judge of this necessity is in both cases the imagination. Both the novel and the history are self-explanatory, self-justifying, the product of an autonomous or self-authorizing activity; and in both cases this activity is the *a priori* imagination.[9]

The present essay will examine Morrison's novel in the context of contemporary historical theory on discourse and narrativity and suggest a reading that links historiography and psychoanalysis.

Like Morrison, the principal character in *Beloved* struggles with a past that is part of white/male historical discourse. Lacking a discourse of her own, Sethe must transform the residual images ("rememories") of her past into a historical discourse shaped by narrativity. These images, however, remain for a time disembodied—without form, sequence, or meaning. The challenge of the illiterate slave is similar to that of the highly literate contemporary historian or novelist: to discover a way of organizing memory, of contriving a narrative configuration in the absence of written records. If it is true, as Henry Louis Gates, Jr., argues, that the sense of self as defined in the West since the Enlightenment "turns in part upon written records," if "our idea of the self . . . is . . . inextricably interwoven with our ideas . . . of [writing]," then what are the consequences of an absence of written records? Quite simply and perhaps startlingly, as a slave "one's sense of one's existence . . . depended upon memory." "It was memory, above all else," according to Gates, "that gave shape to being itself."[10] What these remarks do not address, however, is how one formally shapes and derives meaning from disparate memories. In other words, how does one extract a configuration from a cluster of images or diversity of events? How does one, finally, transpose memories from a visual to a diagetic, or narrative, register? Like Morrison, Sethe must learn to represent the unspeakable and unspoken in language—and, more precisely, as narrative.

Morrison figures both the interiority and the exteriority of memory, that is, memory as thought and memory as material inscription.[11] In the novel, "Beloved" is the public inscription of a private memorial—seven letters chiseled into the pink headstone of a child-victim of "mother-love," a word Sethe had remembered from the preacher's funeral eulogy. If the inscription of Beloved is the trace ("the mark left behind") that initiates the novel's plot, it is also an image that haunts the text in the multiple guises of the character Beloved. Besides designating an object of affection, the term *beloved* occurs in matrimonial and eulogistic discourse. Both are commemorative, linguistic events: the former prefiguring the future, the latter refiguring the past. The action of the novel, however, attends to the novelistic present—a present problematized by an unresolved past and an unanticipated future, a present that the past does not prefigure and the future does not refigure.

At the outset of the novel, Sethe's "future was a matter of keeping the past at bay" (42).[12] Her aim has been to protect her children from "rememory," which she describes as follows:

> Someday you be walking down the road and you hear something or see something going on. So clear . . . It's when you bump into a rememory that belongs to somebody else. Where I was before I came here, that place [Sweet Home] is real. It's never going away. Even if the whole farm—every

tree and grass blade of it dies. The picture is still there and what's more, if you go there—you who never was there—if you go there and stand in the place where it was, it will happen again; it will be there for you, waiting for you. (36)

"Rememory," it seems, is something that possesses (or haunts) one rather than something that one possesses. It is, in fact, that which makes the past part of one's present. Yet, despite her best efforts to "[beat] back the past," Sethe remains, in her words, "full of it." "Every mention of her past life hurt. Everything in it was painful or lost" (58). Hayden White's description of Ibsen's Hedda Gabler also seems apt for Morrison's Sethe: she "suffers [from] the incubus [or, in this case, the succubus] of the past—a surfeit of history compounded by, or reflected in, a pervasive fear of the future."[13]

Thus, unable to contrive a meaningful or appropriate configuration for her memories, Sethe finds herself tyrannized by unconfigured and literally disfiguring images. As a consequence of an attempted escape, she receives a savage beating, which leaves her back "a clump of scars." The scars function as signs of ownership inscribing her as property, while the mutilation signifies her diminishment to a less-than-human status. Traces of the past that Sethe represses (but can neither remember nor forget) have been gouged into her back by the master's whip and bear the potential burden of both *history* and *herstory*. Like the inscription of Beloved and the pictorial images of the past, the scars function as an archaeological site or memory trace.

If the master has inscribed the master('s) code on Sethe's back, a white woman and a black man offer her alternative readings of it. Although initially "struck dumb" at the sight of Sethe's scars, Amy, a runaway white girl who saves the fugitive's life and midwifes the delivery of her second daughter, sees Sethe's back as a "chokecherry tree":

> See, here's the trunk—it's red and split wide open, full of sap, and this here's the parting for the branches. . . . Leaves, too, look like, and dern if these ain't blossoms. Tiny little cherry blossoms, just as white. Your back got a whole tree on it. In bloom. (79)

Amy describes an image that prompts her to wonder "what God have in mind." In her reverie, Sethe's back remains the trace of an event whose meaning, motivation, and consequence are largely unreadable. Alternative readings are provided by Baby Suggs (Sethe's mother-in-law) and by Paul D, the last survivor of the men from Sweet Home, the Kentucky plantation where he and Sethe had met before the war. Baby Suggs perceives her daughter-in-law's back as a pattern of "roses of blood," stenciled onto the bedsheet and blanket. Paul D, who arrives after the open wounds have healed, remarks on "the sculpture [Sethe's] back had become, like the decorative work of an ironsmith too passionate for display." The distance between these suggestively gendered readings—the chokecherry tree and blood roses, on the one hand, and the wrought-iron maze, on the other—signifies the distance between so-called natural and culturally inscribed meanings attributed to the sign.

It is the white man who inscribes; the white woman, the black man, and the black woman may variously read but not write. Because it is her back (symbolizing the *presence* of her *past*) that is marked, Sethe has only been able to read herself through the gaze of others. Her challenge is to learn to read herself—that is, to configure the history of her body's text. If, as Paul Ricoeur contends, "the past survives by leaving its trace," then Sethe must learn how to link these traces (marks of her passage through slavery) to the construction of a personal and historical discourse.[14] Her dilemma is that, as an illiterate female slave, she finds herself the written object of a white male discourse and the spoken subject of a black male and white female discourse. Significantly, Baby Suggs does not speak of the wounds on Sethe's back ("Baby Suggs hid her mouth with her hand" [93]). Instead, she concentrates on the ritual of healing: "[*W*]*ordlessly*, the older woman greased the flowering back and pinned a double thickness of cloth to the inside of the newly stitched dress" (93, emphasis added). The presumption is, of course, that black women have no voice, no text, and consequently no history. They can be written and written upon precisely because they exist as the ultimate Other, whose absence or (non)being only serves to define the being or presence of the white or male subject. The black woman, symbolizing a kind of double negativity, becomes a tabula rasa upon which the racial/sexual identity of the other(s) can be positively inscribed.

Sethe's back is numb ("the skin on her back had been dead for years"), signifying her attempts to repress the past. (But the return of Paul D, and later of Beloved, signals the return of the repressed.) For Sethe, these scars constitute traces of past deeds too horrible and violent either to forget or to remember, a situation that Morrison describes elsewhere as "a perfect dilemma." The brutal whipping she receives as punishment for her attempt to run away is only part of a cluster of events that Sethe vainly seeks to forget.

If Morrison formalizes and thematizes the operation of imaginative construction, she also dramatizes, in the character of "schoolteacher" (as he is called by the slaves), the consequences of an alternative approach. The scenes with schoolteacher offer a paradigm for reading the methodology of the white male as scholar and master. Arriving at Sweet Home after the death of its previous owner, schoolteacher announces himself "with a big hat and spectacles and a coach full of paper" and begins to "watch" his subjects. His methodology—based on numbering, weighing, dividing—suggests the role of the cultural historian (or ethnologist) who is concerned with sizes, densities, details, appearances, externalities, and visible properties ("Schoolteacher'd wrap that string all over my head, 'cross my nose, around my behind. Number my teeth").[15] Schoolteacher possesses the master('s) text, and as a data collector, cataloger, classifier, and taxonomist concerned with matters of materiality and empiricism, he divides or dismembers the indivisibility of the slaves' humanity to reconstruct (or perhaps deconstruct) the slave in his text. His physical measurements recall those of Hawthorne's Custom's House Surveyor, whose careful and accurate measurements disclose little except that "each limb [of the letter A] proved to be precisely three inches and a quarter in length." In both cases, putatively scientific techniques prove altogether inadequate. Yet unlike Hawthorne's Surveyor, who discovers himself confronted with a "riddle which . . . [he] sees little hope of resolving," Morrison's historical investigator remains hopelessly unconscious "of his own infirmity."[16] Sethe tells us,

> He was talking to one of his pupils and I heard him say, "Which one are you doing?" And one of the boys said, "Sethe." That's when I stopped because I heard my name, and then I took a few steps to where I could see what they was doing. Schoolteacher was standing over one of them with one hand behind his back. He licked a forefinger a couple of times and turned a few pages. Slow. I was about to turn around and keep on my way. . . . when I heard him say, "No, no. That's not the way. I told you to put her human characteristics on the left; her *animal* ones on the right. And don't forget to line them up." (193, emphasis added)

Schoolteacher's historiography encodes the notion and forms of "wildness" and "animality." As Hayden White explains, this notion is a "culturally self-authenticating device" intended to "confirm the value of [the] dialectical antithesis between 'civilization' . . . and 'humanity.'"[17] Like Nehemiah Adams, the historical investigator in Sherley Anne Williams's *Dessa Rose*, Morrison's schoolteacher espouses a concept of "otherness" as a form of subhumanity that serves, through a process of negative self-identification, to confirm his own sense of superiority. Sethe's "savagery" confirms schoolteacher's "civilization"; her "bestiality" assures his "humanity." Schoolteacher's sense of history is defined by the struggle between culture and nature, and questions of meaning and interpretation turn upon this opposition.[18]

The dismemberment of schoolteacher's method is the discursive analog to the dismemberment of slavery. Just as his pupils measure and divide Sethe according to schoolteacher's instructions, so schoolteacher himself, speaking with the slave catchers, reveals to Paul D "his worth." Overhearing the men talking, Paul D, who "has always known, or believed he did, his value—as a hand, a laborer who could make profit on a farm . . . now [discovers] his worth, which is to say he learns his price. The dollar value of his weight, his strength, his heart, his brain, his penis, and his future" (226). As both slaveholder and scholar, schoolteacher is involved with the *dismembering* of slaves from their families, their labor, their selves. Against these forms of physical, social, and scholarly dismemberment, the act of (re)memory initiates a reconstitutive process in the novel. If dismemberment deconstitutes and fragments the whole, then rememory functions to re-collect, re-assemble, and organize the various discrete and heterogeneous parts into a meaningful sequential whole through the process of narrativization discussed below.

The scenes of Paul D's figurative dismemberment both refigure the earlier scene of schoolteacher's anatomical dismemberment of Sethe and prefigure a later scene that Sethe vainly attempts to forget: "I am full God damn it of two boys with mossy teeth, one sucking on my breast the other holding me down, their book-reading teacher watching and writing it up" (70). Like Paul D, who is forced to go around with a horse's bit in his mouth, Sethe is forced to submit to the bovinelike humiliation of "being milked." In this grotesque parody of Madonna and child, Sethe's milk, like her labor and the fruits of her womb, is expropriated. But the theft of her "mother's milk" suggests the expropriation of her future—her ability to nurture and ensure the survival of the next generation. Ironically, Sethe herself has mixed schoolteacher's ink:

> [Schoolteacher liked] how [she] mixed it and it was important to him because at night he sat down to write in his book. It was a book about [the slaves] . . . He commenced to carry round a notebook and write down what we said. (37)

The image of schoolteacher's ink converges with the expropriation of Sethe's milk in a symbol that evokes Hélène Cixous's metaphor for "écriture féminine"—women writing a language of the body in the white ink of the mother's milk. Not only the pages of his notebook but also the literal inscription of Sethe's back with schoolteacher's whip (pen) constitute the perverse fulfillment of Cixous's call.[19] Appropriating Sethe's "milk" through a process of phallic substitution, schoolteacher uses the pen—for Sandra Gilbert and Susan Gubar the symbol and instrument of masculine "authority"—to "re-mark" the slave woman with the signature of his paternity.[20] Sethe must discover some way of regaining control of her story, her body, her progeny, her milk, her ability to nurture the future.

Schoolteacher's association with "the prison-house of language," figured not only in his private ledger but in the public slave codes as well, refigures the New Testament's personification of the Decalogue. St. Paul tells the churches in Galatia that "the law was our schoolmaster," or (alternatively translated) "we were held prisoners by the law."[21] It is this white/male construction of the law according to the authority of the master discourse that Sethe must first dismantle in order to construct her own story.

For schoolteacher, history is a confining activity; for Sethe, it must become a liberating one. She must "free retrospectively, certain possibilities that were not actualized in the historical past" and detect "possibilities buried in the . . . past,"[22] just as Morrison does by historicizing fiction. As historian, Sethe must liberate her present from the "burden of the past" constructed in history. She must learn to remap the past so that it becomes a blueprint for the future. Her job is to reconstitute the past through personal narrative, or storytelling. Collingwood has argued that the historian is primarily "a story teller," suggesting that "historical sensibility is manifested in the capacity to make a plausible story out of congeries of 'facts' which, in their unprocessed form, made no sense at all."[23] Like Morrison, Sethe uses the memory of personal experience and what Collingwood calls the "constructive imagination" as a means of re-membering a dis-membered past, dis-membered family, and community.

If Morrison moves "from image to text," Sethe, too, begins with the image and shapes "rememories" of the past, endowing them with form, drama, and meaning through a process of narrativization described by Ricoeur as *configuration* and White as *emplotment*. Narrativization enables Sethe to construct a meaningful life-story from a cluster of images, to transform separate and disparate events into a whole and coherent story.[24]

For Sethe, the past has the power to make her either captive or free. Her feelings, hopes, desires, perceptions—all colored by past incidents and events—culminate in what remain for her unspeakable acts and actions: physical violation and infanticide. "Freeing yourself was one thing," Sethe thinks, "claiming ownership of that freed self was another" (95). Her pre-occupation with the past makes it impossible for her to process new experiences except through the distant lens of the particular events in question. What Gates describes as "this brilliant substructure of the system of slavery"—the dependence of the slave upon her memory—had the potential to make the slave [and later the ex-slave], in some respects, "a slave to [her]self, a prisoner of [her] own power to recall."[25]

If certain events remain unconfigured, others are overly and inappropriately configured. Thus, an alternative reading of Sethe's dilemma, based on White's model, might be that she has "overemplotted" the events of her past; she has "charged them with a meaning so intense that . . . they continue to shape both [her] perceptions and [her] responses to the world long after they should have become 'past history.'" The problem for Sethe, then, is to configure or emplot, on the one hand, and to *re*configure or *re*emplot on the other. She must imaginatively reconstitute, or re-member, her history "in such a way as to change the *meaning* of those events for [her] and their *significance* for the economy of the whole set of events that make up [her] life."[26] If Gates can assert that "the act of writing for the slave [narrator] constitute[s] the act of creating a public . . . self," then the act of re-membering, for the unlettered slave, constitutes the act of constructing a private self.[27] As Ricoeur argues, the (re)configuration of the past enables one to refigure the future; such is Sethe's task.

If memory is *materialized* in Beloved's reappearance, it is *maternalized* in Sethe's (re)configuration. Sethe gives birth to her past and to her future: first to the baby with no name whose sad and angry spirit comes back to haunt 124 Bluestone Road and later to the incarnate Beloved, the young woman with "flawless skin and feet and hands soft and new." The return of Beloved, therefore, becomes not only a psychological projection but also a physical (rather than spiritual) manifestation. Her "rebirth" represents, as it were, the uncanny return of the dead to haunt the living, the return of the past to shadow the present.

Yet it is the notion of "self-distanciation" that intrigues Morrison in this as in other works: "What is it that really compels a good woman to displace the self, her self?" asks Morrison. What interests her is not only the nobility and generosity of these actions but also that such love ("the best thing that is in us") "is . . . the thing that makes us [as women] sabotage ourselves, sabotage in the sense [of perceiving] that our life ['the best part of ourselves'] is not as worthy." Her method of characterization is intended to suggest this process of displacement—"to project the self not into the way we say 'yourself' but to put a space between those words, as though the self were really a *twin* or a thirst or a friend or something that sits right next to you and watches you." Morrison has "[projected] the dead out into the earth" in the character of Beloved, so that Beloved becomes the twin self or mirror of Sethe and other women in the novel.[28] The author's critical reflections, however, point to another dimension of Sethe's dilemma, a dilemma that combines private and public functions of rememory. If the individual is defined as a conduit of communal consciousness, then (drawing on Teresa de Lauretis) the events of Sethe's life can be emplotted through historiography; conversely, if the community is defined as a conduit of individual consciousness, then the events of Sethe's psychic life can be encoded in psychoanalytic discourse.[29]

At the point of this intersection between the personal and the social, the psychic and the historical begin to merge. What I have been describing as social subjectivity emplotted by historiography can also be figured in terms of psychic subjectivity and represented in the discourse of psychoanalysis. Speaking to the relation between psychoanalytical and historical consciousness, Norman Brown observes that "the method of psychoanalytical therapy is to deepen the historical consciousness of the individual ('fill up the memory-gaps') till [she] awakens from [her] own history." Interpreting Freud's notion of "archaic heritage," Brown further develops the link between history and psychoanalysis by recalling that humankind is a "prisoner of the past in the same sense as [quoting Freud] 'our hysterical patients are suffering from reminiscences' and neurotics 'cannot escape the past.'" He concludes that not only are all cultures bound to the past but individuals are likewise bound to what Freud describes as "the memory-traces of the experiences of former generations."[30]

The link between history and psychoanalysis, then, permits the events in Sethe's life to be encoded in an alternate plot structure. The sources of her "complex" or "dis-ease" manifest themselves in her endless efforts to avoid the past and avert the future. The events in her past—namely, her own violation and the ensuing decision to take her daughter's life—have become sources of both repression and obsession. Sethe must "conjure up" her past—symbolized by Beloved—and confront it as an antagonist. As in Freud's "recommendations on the technique of psychoanalysis," one might say that Sethe must learn to regard her problematic past as an "enemy worthy of [her] mettle, a piece of [her] personality, which has solid ground for its existence and out of which things of value for [her] future life have to be derived." Her communication with Beloved—and the events of the past that Beloved both symbolizes and evokes—affords Sethe the opportunity "to become . . . conversant with this resistance over which [she] has now become acquainted, to *work through* it, to overcome it, by continuing, in defiance of it, the analytic work."[31] Thus, the psychoanalytic process becomes the means by which Sethe must free herself from the burden of her past and from the burden of *history*.

In fact, as Michel de Certeau's work suggests, psychoanalysis is itself based on the theme that dominates Morrison's novel: the return of the repressed. "This 'mechanism,'" writes de Certeau, "is linked to a certain conception of time and memory, according to which consciousness is both the deceptive *mask* and the operative *trace* of events that organize the present." "If the past . . . is *repressed*," he continues, "it *returns* in the present from which it was excluded." The figuration of this "detour-return" and its consequences in the lives of individual characters, as well as the community as a whole, structures Morrison's novel.[32]

In the "poetic" chapters of the novel the reader senses the full implications of Beloved (and the younger daughter, Denver) for Sethe. The retreat of Sethe and her daughters behind the closed doors of 124 Bluestone represents a familial figuration of what Alfred Schutz calls "the succession of generations: contemporaries, predecessors, and successors,"[33] associated with the present, past, and future, respectively. The connection of Sethe's present with her past is embodied in her relationship to Beloved, while the connection with her future is embodied in her relationship with Denver. The family thus becomes the site at which to explore notions of "time and being." As a historical field, it represents the complex and intimate interdependence of past, present, and future; as an ontological field, it represents the complexity of the relation between Self and Other. The family, in other words, becomes a historically constituted social site where individual subjectivity is constructed.

Further, Beloved symbolizes women in both the contemporaneous and historical black communities. She represents the unsuccessfully repressed Other of Sethe as well as other women in and associated with the community: Ella, whose "puberty was spent in a house where she was abused by a father and son"; Vashti, who was forced into concubinage by her young master; and the girl reportedly locked up by a "whiteman" who had used her to his own purpose "since she was a pup." Beyond this, however, Beloved is associated with her maternal and paternal grandmothers and the generation of slave women who failed to survive the Middle Passage. As trace of "the disremembered and unaccounted for," Beloved's symbolic function of otherness connects the individual to repressed aspects of the self, as well as to contemporaneous and historical others. In fact, Beloved's implication in the lives of the collectivity of women makes it necessary that all the women in the community later participate in the ritual to exorcise her.

The reconstitution of Self and Other through rememory in the act of storytelling is central to Morrison's vision. It is an act that imposes sequence and meaning on the welter of images that shape and define one's sense of self. Yet, Sethe must not only narrativize her life in White's sense of formulating her past into a coherent story; she must also be able to continue the process of metamorphosis by "metaphorizing" her experiences within narrative.[34] Morrison uses the metaphor of maternity to establish an alternative to the metaphor of paternity common in white/male historical discourse. This recurrent structuring metaphor complements and amplifies the images of the female body encoded in the text. In "Site of Memory," Morrison provides a *cognitive* metaphor for representing her reconstructive methods as a novelist. The images of interiority that she privileges are specifically female, associated with the interior rather than the exterior life, with the personal rather than the public representation of experience. Ultimately, such a metaphor suggests that the object of our understanding is inside rather than outside and can be reached only by what Morrison describes as "literary archeology."[35]

Moreover, Sethe's birthing of the past and future appropriately figures Morrison's use of *depictive* metaphor. If the act of birthing represents Sethe's life-story in a metaphor of maternity, then the womb functions as an image of corporeal interiority, the counterpart to Sethe's psychic interiority and Morrison's diagetic interiority. As a narrative metaphor, maternity privileges interiority and marks Sethe's entry into subjectivity. Perhaps the best example of this function is found in the scene describing Sethe's reaction upon seeing the incarnate Beloved for the first time:

> [F]or some reason she could not immediately account for, the moment she got close enough to see [Beloved's face], Sethe's bladder filled to capacity. . . . She never made the outhouse. Right in front of its door she had to lift her skirts, and the water she voided was endless. Like a horse, she thought, but as it went on and on she thought, No, more like flooding the boat when Denver was born. So much water Amy said, "Hold on . . . You going to sink us keep that up." But there was no stopping water breaking from a breaking womb and there was no stopping now. (51)

Significantly, Sethe, on second thought, rejects the equine metaphor. In a radical reconception of history and culture, her ritual of birthing figures motherhood as a primary metaphor of history and culture. The postdiluvian connotation of "breaking of the water" historicizes the event and, at the same time, signifies a maternal delivery that becomes a means of "deliverance" from the dominant conception of history as a white/paternal metaphor. Morrison seems to depict here a second immaculate conception, as it were, in which black motherhood becomes self-generative—a process that reconstitutes black womanhood. By shifting the dominant metaphor from white to black and from paternity (embodied in the slavemaster) to maternity (embodied in the black female slave), Morrison has shifted meaning and value. Through this process of destructuring and restructuring, of decoding and recoding, the author redefines notions of genesis and meaning as they have constituted black womanhood in the dominant discourse.

The images of motherhood function heuristically to explain or "trace" Sethe's history and that of the community along "motherlines." Her past, birthed from a womblike matrix, is read back through motherlines tracked through four generations of marked slave women. Beloved's "thirst" for these stories gives her mother "an unexpected pleasure" in *speaking* things that "she and Baby Suggs had agreed without saying so . . . [were] *unspeakable*" (emphasis added). In speaking, that is, in storytelling, Sethe is able to construct an alternate text of black womanhood. This power to fashion a counternarrative, thereby rejecting the definitions imposed by the dominant other(s), finally provides Sethe with a self—a past, present, and future.

Beloved's persistent questions enable Sethe to remember long-forgotten traces of her own mother, traces carried through memory as well as through the body. Sethe remembers that her own mother bore a mark, "a circle and a cross burnt right in the skin" on her rib. It was the mark of ownership by the master who had as much as written "property" under her breast. Yet like Sethe (as well as Hawthorne's Hester Prynne), her mother had transformed a mark of mutilation, a sign of diminished humanity, into a sign of recognition and identity. Sethe recalls her mother's words: "This is your ma'am . . . I am the only one got this mark now. The rest dead. If something happens to me and you can't tell me by my face, you can know me by this mark" (61). Indeed, her own markings help her to decode the meaning of her mother's remarks. Sethe tells her own daughters, Denver and Beloved, "I didn't understand it then. Not till I had a mark of my own."

Constructed and metaphorized along motherlines, Sethe's retelling of her childhood story also enables her to decipher and pass on to her own daughter meaning encoded in a long-forgotten "mother tongue." Although Sethe knows that the "language her ma'am spoke . . . would never come back," she begins to recognize "the message—that was and had been there all along," and she begins "picking meaning out of a code she no longer understood." Like the historian who seeks to configure a probable story out of a plethora of documents, Sethe seeks to reconfigure events based on "words. Words Sethe understood then but could neither recall nor repeat now" (62). Remembering the story told her by Nan— "the one she knew best, who was around all day, who nursed babies, cooked, had one good arm and half of another"—Nan, who spoke "the same language her ma'am spoke," Sethe is able to reconstruct her own story:

> Nighttime. Nan holding her with her good arm, waving the stump of the other in the air. "Telling you. I am telling you, small girl Sethe," and she did that. She told Sethe that her mother and Nan were together from the sea. Both were taken up many times by the crew. "She threw them all away but you. The one from the crew she threw away on the island. The others from more whites she also threw away. Without names, she threw them. You she gave the name of a black man. She put her arms around him. The others she did not put her arms around. Never. Never. Telling you. I am telling you, small girl Sethe." (62)

Sethe's name recalls the Old Testament Hebrew name "Seth," meaning "granted" or "appointed." (Eve named her third-born child Seth, saying, "God has granted me another child in the place of Abel.")[36] In this instance, Sethe seems to signify the child whose life was spared or "granted" by her mother, who did not keep the offspring of her white rapists.

The story about her own mother that she hears as a child from Nan, another mutilated mother, ironically prefigures Sethe's own actions but at the same time challenges her to some accountability. It is a story that enables Sethe to reread or reemplot her own experiences in the context of sacrifice, resistance, and mother-love. For although Beloved, like Sethe and her mother, bears a mark of mutilation, the scar across Beloved's throat is the mark of Sethe's own hand. And it is the fingerprints on Beloved's forehead as well as the scar under her chin ("the little curved shadow of a smile in the kootchy-koochy-coo place") that enables Sethe to recognize her daughter returned from "the other side."

In light of her recognition Sethe reconstitutes a family story of infanticide, a story of repetition but with a marked difference. Sethe's story of mother-love seems to overwrite a story of rejection, and her task as historian is to find a narrative form that speaks to that difference. But it is her mother's story that refamiliarizes her own story. Sethe receives from her mother that which she had hoped to discover with Paul D: "Her story was bearable"—*not* because it was Paul D's, but *her mother's*—"to tell, to refine and tell again" (99). The maternal discourse becomes a testimonial for Sethe. Mother and daughter share protection of their own children, the one by saving a life and the other by taking a life.

But there are competing configurations as well. The first full representation of the events surrounding the infanticide comes from a collective white/male perspective, represented by schoolteacher and the sheriff:

> Inside [the shed], two boys bled in the sawdust and dirt at the feet of a nigger woman holding a blood-soaked child to her chest with one hand and an infant by the heels in the other. She did not kill them; she simply swung the baby toward the wall planks, missed and tried to connect a second time . . . . Right off it was clear, to schoolteacher especially, that there was nothing there to claim. The three (now four—because she'd had the one coming when she cut) pickaninnies they had hoped were alive and well enough to take back to Kentucky, take back and raise properly to do the work Sweet Home desperately needed, were not. . . . . He could claim the baby struggling in the arms of the mewing old man, but who'd tend her? Because the woman—something was wrong with her. She was looking at him now, and if his other nephew could see that look he would learn the lesson for sure: you just can't mishandle *creatures* and expect success. (149–50, emphasis added)

In schoolteacher's narrative, Sethe is "the woman [who] . . . made fine ink, damn good soup, pressed his collars the way he liked besides having at least ten breeding years left." In his words, "[S]he's gone wild, due to mishandling of the nephew" (149). The white sheriff reads these events as a cautionary tale on "the results of a little so-called freedom imposed on people who needed every care and guidance in the world to keep them from the cannibal life they preferred" (151). Granting authority to the white newspaper's account, Stamp Paid concludes that "while he and Baby Suggs were looking the wrong way, a pretty little slavegirl had recognized [her former master's hat], and split to the woodshed to kill her children" (158). Paul D, who suddenly "saw what Stamp Paid wanted him to see," summarizes events by insisting, "You got two feet, Sethe, not four" (164–65).

Sethe must compete with the dominant metaphors of the master('s) narrative—wildness, cannibalism, animality, destructiveness. In radical opposition to these, constructions is Sethe's reconceptualized metaphor of self based on motherhood, motherlines, and mother-love—a love described by Paul D as "too thick." Convinced that "the best thing she was, was her children," Sethe wants simply to stop schoolteacher:

Because the truth was . . . [s]imple: she was squatting in the garden and when she saw them coming and recognized schoolteacher's hat, she heard wings. Little hummingbirds stuck their needle beaks right through her headcloth into her hair and beat their wings. And if she thought anything, it was No. No. Nono. Nonono. Simple. She just flew. Collected every bit of life she had made, all the parts of her that were precious and fine and beautiful, and carried, pushed, dragged them through the veil, out, away, over there where no one could hurt them. (163)

"I took and put my babies where they'd be safe," she tells Paul D (164). And in this way, she explains to Beloved, "[N]o one, nobody on this earth, would list her daughter's characteristics on the animal side of the paper" (251).

In effect, Sethe creates a counter-narrative that reconstitutes her humanity and demonstrates the requirements of mother-love. By shifting the dominant white male metaphor to a black maternal metaphor for self and history, Sethe changes the plot and meaning of the story—and, finally, the story itself. A story of oppression becomes a story of liberation; a story of inhumanity has been overwritten as a story of higher humanity. This process of destructuring and restructuring the dominant discourse and its organizing tropes enables Sethe (and Morrison) to subvert the master code of the master('s) text. By privileging specifically female tropes in her narrative, Sethe is able to reconstitute her self and herstory within the context of intergenerational black women's experiences as represented in memory and in narrative. By placing her life history within a maternal family history and, by implication, placing her family history within a broader tradition of racial history, Morrison demonstrates both the strength of motherlines in the slave community and the ways in which ontogeny followed black female phylogeny. (The absence of Sethe's two runaway sons leaves Denver as sole heir and guarantor of the family's future.)

In accordance with Collingwood's notion of "history as re-enactment" of past experience, Sethe is able, finally, to re-enact a critical moment in her life. Collingwood describes this process, in which knowledge of the self is recovered:

In thus re-thinking my past thought I am not merely remembering it. I am constructing the history of a certain phase of my life: and the difference between memory and history is that whereas in memory the past is a mere spectacle, in history it is re-enacted in present thought. So far as this thought is mere thought, the past is merely re-enacted; so far as it is thought about thought [or the thought underlying an action], this past is thought of as being re-enacted, and my knowledge of myself is historical knowledge.[37]

Like the historian, Sethe is able to re-enact or re-think a critical moment from the past and is consequently able to demonstrate her possession *of* rather than *by* the past and to alter her own life history. Sethe's actions, moreover, show that the present is bound to the past and the past to the future, and it is precisely the (re)configuration of the past that enables her to refigure the future.[38]

What has been enacted in the psychic field in the past is dramatically and therapeutically reworked in the social field. The bonds of the past are broken in a climactic scene in which thirty neighborhood women, unable to "countenance the possibility of sin moving on in the house," perform a ritual of exorcism, which frees Sethe from the burden of her past:

> Instantly the kneelers and the standers joined [Sethe]. They stopped praying and took a step back to the beginning. *In the beginning there were no words. In the beginning was the sound,* and they all knew what that sound sounded like. (259, emphasis added)

Invoking "the beginning" in which there were "no words"—only "the sound"—black women's voices revise Scripture ("In the beginning was the Word") in a way that associates the semiotic (rather than the symbolic) with creation and creativity. In its revision, this "key," this "code," this "sound that broke the back of words" challenges the dominant white male constitution of black womanhood. Sethe is, moreover, "born again" in her reclamation by the community ("[The voices] broke over Sethe and she trembled like baptized in its wash") as much as by the community's exorcism of Beloved. The communal voice of black women, then, possesses the power not only to destroy but also to create. In fact, Sethe's "re-birth" is predicated upon the rupture of the master('s) discourse. Thus, not only is Sethe "delivered" from the "errors" of her past, but her discourse is "delivered" from the constraints of the master('s) discourse.

During the communal exorcism Sethe espies

> [the] black hat wide-brimmed enough to hide [schoolteacher's] face but not his purpose. He is coming into her yard and he is coming for her best thing. She hears wings. Little hummingbirds stick needle beaks right through her headcloth into her hair and beat their wings. And if she thinks anything, it

is no. No No. Nonono. She flies. The ice pick is not in her hand; it is her hand. (262)

Sethe, in effect, re-enacts the original event—"remembering, repeating, and working-through" the "primal scene" in a process that emblematizes the psychoanalytic process. This time, however, Sethe directs her response to the threatening Other rather than to "her best thing"—her children. Yet it is not only Sethe but the community itself that re-enacts the earlier scene. Because the community had failed to send warning of the slave captors' approach the first time, its "sin of omission" makes it no less responsible for Beloved's death than Sethe's "sin of commission." In a scene of collective re-enactment, the women of the community intervene at a critical juncture, to save not Beloved but Sethe. Thus, by revising her actions, Sethe is able to preserve the community, and the community, in turn, is able to protect one of its own.

According to Ricoeur's model, prefiguration denotes the temporality of the world of human action; configuration, the world of the narrative emplotment of these events; and refiguration, the moment at which these two worlds interact and affect each other. Sethe's actions constitute the prefigurative aspect; her storytelling, the configurative aspect; and re-enactment, the refigurative aspect.[39] Moreover, Morrison enables the reader to connect with the otherness of these past generations—especially as it relates to the experiences of the slave women—in a process made possible by "the intersection of the world of the text with the world of the reader." Just as Nan's story of the generational mother enables Sethe to (re)configure her past, so Morrison's story of the historical m(other) enables the reader to do likewise. The reader, like Sethe, learns that she must claim and surrender the past in order to refigure the future.[40]

The question of Sethe's accountability, however, remains. Does Morrison, finally, indict or defend Sethe's "too quick" mother-love? Is Sethe truly redeemed from an unspeakable past? If so, by what means? Where does Sethe's "redemption" from the "sins" of the past—those perpetuated both *upon* her and *by* her—lie? Is grace achieved through the spirit of Beloved (the past generations she symbolizes) or by its exorcism? Characteristically, Morrison draws out the paradoxes and ambiguities of this "perfect dilemma." I suggest, in fact, that she neither condemns nor condones but rather "delivers" her protagonist. For Sethe achieves redemption through *possession* by the spirit as well as *exorcism* of the spirit. Significantly, for Morrison, it is not through the law ("Because the Law worketh wrath") but the spirit (its reclamation and relinquishment) that the individual achieves "deliverance" from the "sins" of the past.[41] *Beloved*, then, (re)in-scribes the conditions of the promise in the New Testament. What is im-portant for Morrison, however, is the mediation between remembering (possession) and forgetting (exorcism). It is the process of "working-through" that the author finally affirms. As in previous novels, Morrison focuses less on "what" and "why" and more on "how." She privileges the journey rather than the destination, the means rather than the end—a process that enables Sethe to achieve redemption by creating a cohesive psychoanalytical and historical narrative.

Like Sethe, Morrison herself seeks to achieve some mediation between "resurrecting" the past and "burying" it. Expressing her desire to provide a proper, artistic burial for the historical ancestors figured by *Beloved*, Morri-son says:

> There's a lot of danger for me in writing. . . . The effort, the responsi-bility as well as the effort, the effort of being worth it. . . . The responsi-bility that I feel for . . . all of these people; these unburied, or at least un-ceremoniously buried, people made literate in art. But the inner tension, the artistic inner tension those people create in me, the fear of not properly, artistically, burying them, is extraordinary.[42]

She apparently intends to pay the historian's debt to the past, in Ricoeur's sense of rendering to the past its due and, in the process, to put it to rest.

What, then, is Morrison's final legacy to readers, and what is her own relation to the past? Does Sethe become for the reader what Beloved is for Sethe—an embodiment of the past and the experiences of previous gener-ations? What of the haunting injunction at the end of the novel that it is NOT a story to "be passed on"—that is, to be remembered, to be retold? Must Morrison's story, along with Sethe's past, be put behind? Must the reader rid herself of the burdens of the past by exorcising from historical consciousness the violence and violation experienced by her ancestors? If this injunction is taken seriously, how can Morrison's own commitment to a project of recovery and "rememory" be explained? Clearly, such an in-junction threatens to contradict the motive and sense of the entire novel.

In a 1989 interview, Morrison called *Beloved* a book "about something that the characters don't want to remember, I don't want to remember, black people don't want to remember, white people don't want to remem-ber."[43] The author's remarks speak to the public desire to repress the per-sonal aspects of the story of slavery. Morrison's accomplishment as histo-rian and analyst in the novel, however, is precisely *not* to allow for the continuation of a "national amnesia" regarding this chapter in America's history. For her, the absent (like the historical) is only the "other" of the present—just as the repressed is only the "other" of the conscious. Read in this context, the narrator's final and thrice-repeated enjoinder resonates with ambivalence and ambiguity. Suggesting that what is absent is not necessarily "gone" (leaving behind no "name," no "print," no "trace"), the narrator's closing reflections ensure the novel's open-endedness and subvert any monologic reading of the final injunction. Is it possible that the narrator means, indeed must mean, that this is not a story to be PASSED ON—not in the sense of being retold but in the sense of being forgotten, repressed, or ignored? Morrison finally seems to vindicate, and is vindicated by, Richard Hofstadter's observation that "[m]emory is the thread of personal identity, history of public identity." If this is so, it would follow, then, that the importance of our private memories becomes, ultimately, the basis for a reconstructed public history.[44]

Notes

1. Toni Morrison, "Site of Memory," in *Inventing the Truth: The Art and Craft of Memoir*, ed. William Zinsser, (Boston: Houghton-Mifflin, 1987), 109–10.

2. See W. E. B. Du Bois, "The Forethought," *The Souls of Black Folk* (Chicago: A. C. McClurg, 1903), viii.

3. See Toni Morrison's "Unspeakable Things Unspoken," *Michigan Quarterly Review* 28, no. 1 (Winter 1989): 1–34.

4. "Therefore we conclude that a man is justified by faith without the deeds of the law" (Romans 3:28); "But that no man is justified by the law in the sight of God, *it is* evident: for, The just shall live by faith" (Galatians 3:11).

5. Contemporary black writers whose work fictionalizes history include, among others, Margaret Walker (*Jubilee*), Earnest Gaines (*The Autobiography of Miss Jane Pittman*), David Bradley (*The Chaneysville Incident*), Alice Walker (*The Color Purple*), Sherley Anne Williams (*Dessa Rose*), and Barbara Chase Riboud (*Sally Hemmings* and *The Echo of Lions*).

6. Gloria Naylor and Toni Morrison, "A Conversation," *Southern Review* 21 (Summer 1985): 583–84.

7. Morrison, "Site of Memory," 111–12.

8. Ibid., 113–14.

9. Collingwood argues that, like the novelist, the historian constructs an imaginary picture consistent with the historical data, testimony, memory, documentation, etc. In an attempt to explain a fragmentary or incomplete record of the historical past, Collingwood further argues that the historian must employ what he calls "the constructive imagination" to create a "coherent and continuous picture"

consistent with the available historical data. R. G. Collingwood, *The Idea of History* (London: University Press, 1946), 245–46.

10. Henry Louis Gates, Jr., "Frederick Douglass and the Language of Self," *Yale Review* 70, no. 4 (July 1981); 592–611.

11. See Jacques Derrida, *Memories for Paul de Man* (New York: Columbia University Press, 1986), 102–50 passim.

12. Toni Morrison, *Beloved* (New York: Alfred Knopf, 1987). Page references for this work are given in the text.

13. Hayden White, *Tropics of Discourse: Essays in Cultural Criticism* (Baltimore: Johns Hopkins University Press, 1979), 33–34.

14. Paul Ricoeur, *The Reality of Historical Past* (Milwaukee: Marquette University Press, 1984), 11.

15. See Waldo E. Martin, Jr., *The Mind of Frederick Douglass* (Chapel Hill: University of North Carolina Press, 1984), for a discussion of the relation between the ethnologist and the cultural historian in the context of nineteenth-century practice: "Practitioners of a broad and allegedly scientific discipline, ethnologists . . . attempted to uncover stages and meanings of human developments primarily in cultural and related physical and secondarily in historical terms" (225).

16. Nathaniel Hawthorne, *The Scarlet Letter* (New York: E. P. Dutton & Co. Inc., 1938), 42, 51.

17. See White, *Tropics of Discourse,* 151. Unlike the notion of historical reconstruction, which seeks to account for otherness by questioning the normative model, this method seeks to identify *difference* with *deviance* and/or *diminishment.*

18. Cf. Sherley Anne William's unnamed narrator in "Meditations in History" and Adam Nehemiah in *Dessa Rose.* Williams and Morrison share reservations concerning disciplinary behaviors. Their works constitute a critique of certain aspects of both the praxis and the practitioners of these activities. Like Williams's characters, Morrison's investigator (who might as appropriately be designated ethnographer as historian) represents the author's indictment of the kind of "scholarly" and "scientific" discourse in which the preconceptions of the inquirer lead to gross distortions. For critical treatments of Williams's work from this perspective see my "(W)Riting *The Work* and Working the Rites," in Linda Kauffman, ed., *Feminism and Institutions: Dialogues on Feminist Theory* (London: Basil Blackwell, 1989 and "Speaking in Tongues: Dialogics, Dialectics, and Black Women Writer's Literary Tradition," in Cheryl Wall, ed., *Changing Our Own Words: Essays on Criticism, Theory and Writing By Black Women* (New Brunswick: Rutgers University Press, 1989), pp. 16–37.

19. See Hélène Cixous, "The Laugh of the Medusa," in *New French Feminisms: An Anthology,* ed. Elaine Marks and Isabelle de Courtivron (Amherst: University of Massachusetts Press, 1980), 251.

20. See Sandra Gilbert and Susan Gubar, *Madwoman in the Attic: The Woman*

Writer and the Nineteenth-Century Literary Imagination (New Haven: Yale University Press, 1970).

21. These are alternative translations of Galatians 3:24.

22. See Paul Ricoeur, *Time and Narrative* (Chicago: University of Chicago Press, 1988).

23. See White on Collingwood, *Tropics of Discourse*, 83.

24. According to Ricoeur, emplotment "brings together diverse and heterogeneous story elements . . . agents, goals, means, interactions, [and] circumstances . . . [A]n event must be more than just a singular occurence. It gets its definition from its contribution to the development of the plot. A story, too, must be more than just an enumeration of events in serial order; it must organize them into an intelligible whole, of a sort such that we can always ask what is the 'thought' of this story. In short, emplotment is the operation that draws a configuration out of a simple succession." See Ricoeur, *Time and Narrative*, vol. 1 (1984), 65.

25. Gates, "Frederick Douglass and the Language of Self," 593.

26. See White, *Tropics of Discourse*, 87.

27. Gates, "Frederick Douglass and the Language of Self," 599.

28. Naylor and Morrison, "A Conversation," 585.

29. Teresa de Lauretis, *Alice Doesn't: Feminism, Semiotics, Cinema* (Bloomington: Indiana University Press, 1984).

30. Freud, according to Brown's reading, extends this to recapitulation theory (ontogeny recapitulates phylogeny) in which "each individual recapitulates the history of the race. . . . From this it follows that the theory of neurosis must embrace a theory of history; and conversely a theory of history must embrace a theory of neurosis." See Norman O. Brown, *Life against Death: The Psychoanalytical Meaning of History* (Middletown: Wesleyan University Press, 1959), 19, 12–13. Robert Guthrie elaborates further: "The recapitulation theory held that an individual organism, in the process of growth and development, passes through a series of stages representing those in the evolutionary development of the species. G. Stanley Hall, for example, believed 'that in its play activity the child exhibits a series of phases corresponding to the cultural phase of human society, a hunting period, a building period, and so on.' Hall's attempt to mold individual development (ontogeny) with racial characteristics (phylogeny) was supported by many leading behavioral scientists of this time [early twentieth century]. (John Mark Baldwin's *Mental Development in the Child in the Race*, for example, was a frequently quoted source.)" Robert V. Guthrie, *Even the Rat Was White: A Historical View of Psychology* (New York: Harper & Row, 1976, 82.

31. Sigmund Freud, "Remembering, Repeating and Working-Through," *Standard Edition of the Works of Sigmund Freud, vol. 12, ed. James Strachey* (London: Hogarth Press, 1914), 146–57.

32. Michel de Certeau, *Heterologies: Discourse on the Other*, vol. 17 (Minneapolis: University of Minnesota Press, 1986), 3.

33. Alfred Schutz as quoted in Ricoeur, *Time and Narrative*, vol. 3, 109.

34. Although White's work speaks eloquently to a "classification of discourses based on tropology" (*Tropics*, 22), Philip Stambovsky's work on metaphor and historical writings addresses my concerns more specifically in this instance. Using Maurice Mandelbaum's "three historical forms—explanatory, sequential, and interpretive" as a "context for determining the functioning . . . of . . . metaphor in historical discourse," Stambovsky identifies three functions of metaphor: heuristic, depictive, and cognitive. See Philip Stambovsky, "Metaphor and Historical Understanding," *History and Theory* 27, no. 2 (1988): 125–34.

35. See Kaja Silverman, *The Acoustic Mirror: The Female Voice in Psychoanalysis and Cinema* (Bloomington: Indiana University Press, 1988), for an interesting discussion of the notions of interiority and exteriority.

36. Genesis 5:25. Seth was also the name of the Egyptian god of confusion, described as a tricksterlike marginal figure located "beyond or between the boundaries of social definition . . . [who] gleefully breaks taboos and violates the limits that preserve order." See Anna K. Nardo, "Fool and Trickster," *Mosaic* 22 (Winter 1989): 2.

37. Continuing, Collingwood writes, "The history of myself is thus not memory as such, but a peculiar case of memory. Certainly a mind which could not remember could not have historical knowledge. But memory as such is only the present thought of past experience as such, be that experience what it may be; historical knowledge is that special case of memory where the object of present thought is past thought, the gap between present and past being bridged not only by the power of past thought to think of the past, but also by the power to reawaken itself in the present." R. G. Collingwood, *The Idea of History*, 293–94.

38. I use Collingwood's term advisedly, heeding with the admonitions of Ricoeur that although the "re-enactment" of the past in the present operates under the sign of the same, "to re-enact does not consist in reliving what happened," primarily because it involves the notion of "rethinking." And according to Ricoeur, "rethinking already contains the critical moment that requires us to detour by way of the historical imagination." See Ricoeur, *Time and Narrative*, vol. 3, 144–45. Rather than locate this process under the sign of the same, which implies repetition, I would rather locate it under both the same and other—repetition with a difference.

39. Ricoeur designates these modes alternatively as mimesis 1, mimesis 2, and mimesis 3. (His formulation of mimesis includes what we normally [after Aristotle] call diegesis—thus expanding the notion of the imitation of an action to include

description.) Ricoeur makes it clear that refiguration (or mimesis 3) is a stage that "marks the intersection of the world of the text and the world of the hearer or reader," thereby relating the world configured by the text to the world of "real action." I have modified and extended his model by using the term to describe both the intersection of the inner world of the character and the outer world of her actions as well as the intersection of the world of the text and the world of the reader. See Ricoeur, *Time and Narrative,* vol. 1, 54–76.

40. "The basic thesis [of refiguration] from which all the others are derived holds that the meaning of a literary work rests upon the dialogical relation established between the work and its public in each age. This thesis, similar to Collingwood's notion that history is but a reenactment of the past in the mind of the historian, amounts to including the effect produced by the work—in other words, the meaning the public attributes to it—within the boundaries of work itself." Ricoeur, *Time and Narrative,* vol. 3, 171.

41. See Romans 4:15.

42. Naylor and Morrison, "A Conversation," 585.

43. Toni Morrison, "The Pain of Being Black," *Time,* May 22, 1989, 120.

44. Richard Hofstader, *The Progressive Historian* (New York: Alfred A. Knopf, 1968), 3.

The Ghosts of Slavery

Historical Recovery in
Toni Morrison's Beloved

LINDA KRUMHOLZ

❖　❖　❖

> Your country? How came it yours? Before the Pil-
> grims landed we were here. Here we have brought
> our three gifts and mingled them with yours: a gift
> of story and song—soft, stirring melody in an ill-
> harmonized and unmelodious land; the gift of
> sweat and brawn to beat back the wilderness, con-
> quer the soil, and lay the foundations of this vast
> economic empire two hundred years earlier than
> your weak hands could have done it; the third, a
> gift of the Spirit. . . . Would America have been
> America without her Negro people?
> —W. E. B. Du Bois
> *The Souls of Black Folk*

Toni Morrison's *Beloved* reconceptualizes American history. Most apparent in the novel is the historical perspective: Morrison constructs history through the acts and consciousness of African-American slaves rather than through the perspective of the dominant white social classes.[1] But historical methodology takes another vital shift in *Beloved;* history-making becomes a healing process for the characters, the reader, and the author.[2]

In *Beloved,* Morrison constructs a parallel between the individual processes of psychological recovery and a historical or national process. Sethe, the central character in the novel, describes the relationship between the individual and the historical unconscious:

If a house burns down, it's gone, but the place—the picture of it—stays, and not just in my rememory, but out there, in the world. What I remember is a picture floating around out there outside my head. I mean, even if I don't think it, even if I die, the picture of what I did, or knew, or saw is still out there. Right in the place where it happened. (36)

If Sethe's individual memories exist in the world as fragments of a historical memory, then, by extension, the individual process of recollection or "rememory" can be reproduced on a historical level. Thus, Sethe's process of healing in *Beloved,* her process of learning to live with her past, is a model for the readers who must confront Sethe's past as part of our own past, a collective past that lives right here where we live.

Arnold Rampersad, in his discussion of W. E. B. Du Bois's *The Souls of Black Folk,* also describes the recovery of history as both a national and a personal necessity:

[Du Bois's] point of view is clear. Admitting and exploring the reality of slavery is necessarily painful for a black American, but only by doing so can he or she begin to understand himself or herself and American and Afro-American culture in general. The normal price of the evasion of the fact of slavery is intellectual and spiritual death. Only by grappling with the meaning and legacy of slavery can the imagination, recognizing finally the temporality of the institution, begin to transcend it. (123)

In Rampersad's description, the repression of the historical past is as psychologically damaging as the repression of personal trauma. In *Beloved* Morrison, like Du Bois in *Souls,* negotiates the legacy of slavery as a national trauma, and as an intensely personal trauma as well.[3] Both works challenge the notion that the end of institutional slavery brings about freedom by depicting the emotional and psychological scars of slavery as well as the persistence of racism. And both Morrison and Du Bois delve into the stories and souls of black folk to tap the resources of memory and imagination as tools of strength and healing.

Morrison uses ritual as a model for the healing process. Rituals function as formal events in which symbolic representations—such as dance, song, story, and other activities—are spiritually and communally endowed with the power to shape real relations in the world. In *Beloved,* ritual processes also imply particular notions of pedagogy and epistemology in which—by way of contrast with dominant Western traditions—knowledge is multiple, context-dependent, collectively asserted, and spiritually derived. Through her assertion of the transformative power of ritual and the incorporation of rituals of healing into her narrative, Morrison invests the novel with the potential to construct and transform individual consciousness as well as social relations.

To make the novel work as a ritual, Morrison adapts techniques from modernist novels, such as the fragmentation of the plot and a shifting narrative voice, to compel the reader to actively construct an interpretive framework. In *Beloved,* the reader's process of reconstructing the fragmented story parallels Sethe's psychological recovery: repressed fragments of the (fictionalized) personal and historical past are retrieved and reconstructed. Morrison also introduces oral narrative techniques—repetition, the blending of voices, a shifting narrative voice, and an episodic framework—that help to simulate the aural, participatory dynamics of ritual within the private, introspective form of the novel. In many oral traditions, storytelling and poetry are inseparable from ritual, since words as sounds are perceived as more than concepts; they are events with consequences. Morrison uses modernist and oral techniques in conjunction with specifically African-American cultural referents, both historical and symbolic, to create a distinctly African-American voice and vision that, as in Baby Suggs's rituals, invoke the spiritual and imaginative power to teach and to heal.

The central ritual of healing—Sethe's "rememory" of and confrontation with her past—and the reader's ritual of healing correspond to the three sections of the novel. In part one the arrival first of Paul D then of Beloved forces Sethe to confront her past in her incompatible roles as a slave and as a mother. Moving from the fall of 1873 to the winter, the second part describes Sethe's period of atonement, during which she is enveloped by the past, isolated in her house with Beloved, who forces her to suffer over and over again all the pain and shame of the past. Finally, part three is Sethe's ritual "clearing," in which the women of the community aid her in casting out the voracious Beloved, and Sethe experiences a repetition of her scene of trauma with a difference—this time she aims her murderous hand at the white man who threatens her child.

The three phases of the reader's ritual also involve a personal reckoning with the history of slavery. In part one, stories of slavery are accumulated through fragmented recollections, culminating in the revelation of Sethe's murder of her child in the last chapters of the section. In part two, the reader is immersed in the voices of despair. Morrison presents the internal voices of Sethe, Denver, and Beloved in a ritual chant of possession, while Paul D and Stamp Paid are also overwhelmed by the legacy of slavery. The last part of the novel is the reader's "clearing," achieved through the comic relief of the conversation of Paul D and Stamp Paid and the hopeful reunion of Sethe and Paul D. The novel concludes with Denver's emergence as the new teacher, providing the reader with a model for a new pedagogy and the opportunity for the reconstruction of slave history from a black woman's perspective.

Finally, while *Beloved* can be read as a ritual of healing, there is also an element of disruption and unease in the novel, embodied in the character of Beloved. As an eruption of the past and the repressed unconscious, Beloved catalyzes the healing process for the characters and for the reader; thus, she is a disruption necessary for healing. But Beloved also acts as a trickster figure who defies narrative closure or categorization, foreclosing the possibility of a complete "clearing" for the reader. Thus, as the reader leaves the book, we have taken on slavery's haunt as our own.[4]

Baby Suggs and Rituals of Healing

Two ghosts impel the healing process in *Beloved:* Baby Suggs, holy, acts as a ritual guide, and Beloved, the ghost-woman, acts as a psychological catalyst for the three central (living) characters. The healing ritual in *Beloved* can be broken down into three stages. The first stage is the repression of memory that occurs from the traumas of slavery; the second stage entails a painful reconciliation with these memories; and the third is the "clearing" process, a symbolic rebirth of the sufferer. Baby Suggs provides a moral background for the first stage and a ritual model for the last. Beloved embodies the second stage, compelling the characters in her "family" to face all the pain and shame of their memories.

In *Beloved* the ritual methods of healing, of initiating the participant/reader, and of interpreting the world are represented by the lessons of Baby Suggs, whose spiritual power has earned her the appellation *holy* among her people. Baby Suggs conducts rituals outdoors in the Clearing, a place that signifies the necessity for a psychological cleansing from the past, a space to encounter painful memories safely and rest from them. The day Baby Suggs becomes free, after more than sixty years of slavery, she notices her own heartbeat and is thrilled at owning her own body for the first time. Baby Suggs then "open[s] her great heart to those who could use it" by becoming an "unchurched preacher" (87). Baby Suggs creates a ritual, out of her own heart and imagination, to heal former slaves and enable them to seek a reconciliation with their memories, whose scars survive long (even generations) after the experience of slavery has ended.

Baby Suggs's rituals in the Clearing manifest the Freudian psychoanalytic process of healing as well as a spiritual process of healing that combines African and Christian religious elements. Morrison uses Freudian psychological constructs to depict the response of slaves to their psychological torment, thus putting the construction of the African-American psyche into the most ubiquitous model of the psyche in Western literature and philosophy. According to Freud, the repression of traumatic memories directs energy away from social and sexual satisfaction to the construction of symptoms.[5] The psychoanalytic treatment involves unedited associational speech that is meant to elude the unconscious censors, transference of emotions onto the analyst, and finally an acting out or narrativizing of the trauma in order to free the diverted energy and to reintegrate (to some extent) the ego and the libido. The metaphor of "clearing" suggests the process of bringing the unconscious memories into the conscious mind and, thus, negotiating and transcending their debilitating control.

Morrison also uses African and African-American rituals to facilitate the psychological cure, suggesting that African religious ritual provides an antecedent for the psychoanalytic method and that Freudian theories are modern European derivations from long-standing ritual practices of psychic healing. The healing ritual combines Christian symbolism and African ritual expressions, as is common in the African-American church. In the spiritual context, the metaphor of "clearing" suggests a process of cleansing and rebirth.[6]

Baby Suggs's preaching and her spiritual vision invest the world with meaning without making that meaning static or rule-bound. In *Beloved,* as in all of Morrison's novels, meaning is multiple; contradictions stand intact. For example, black people and white people are essentially and irrevocably different; they are also essentially and eternally the same. Both statements are true at once, confounding the logical, objective ideology that forms the basis of Western culture.

The spiritual and subjective basis of ritual also has pedagogical implications. In ritual, the cultural specificity of knowledge and the multiple possibilities of interpretation, as well as the implied spiritual sanction, make ritual education different, at least conceptually, from the objective, scientific model of knowledge that is prevalent in American educational institutions. Baby Suggs's ritual methods of healing, teaching, and interpreting challenge basic pedagogical and epistemological premises of the United States' social system. Thus Morrison demonstrates how the reconstruction of the past makes possible a reconceptualization of the future, which is the power of history-making.

Baby Suggs is the moral and spiritual backbone of *Beloved*. Her morality is based on a method of engagement and interpretation rather than on static moral dictates. The most significant difference between Baby Suggs's version of spirituality and that of the white religions depicted in the novel is her disdain for rules and prohibitions to define morality, as well as her rejection of definitions in general. Her actions contrast with those of white men like Mr. Bodwin's father, a "deeply religious man who knew what God knew and told everybody what it was" (260).

Baby Suggs rejects the definitions of formal religions, definitions which, as the history of slavery has shown, can be easily manipulated to justify anything.[7] Baby Suggs preaches instead the guidance of a free heart and imagination:

> She did not tell them to clean up their lives or to go and sin no more.
> She did not tell them they were the blessed of the earth, its inheriting meek
> or its glorybound pure.
> She told them that the only grace they could have was the grace they
> could imagine. That if they could not see it, they would not have it. (88)

Baby Suggs represents an epistemological and discursive philosophy that shapes Morrison's work, in which morality is not preset in black and white categories of good and evil; "good" or "evil" spring from the *methods* of categorizing and judging, of understanding and distributing knowledge.

The only character in *Beloved* who represents a moral absolute of evil—the unnamed "schoolteacher"—is an embodiment of the wrong *methods*. Schoolteacher, the cruel slaveholder who takes over Sweet Home after the death of the "benevolent" slaveholder, Mr. Garner, has interpretive methods that are the opposite of Baby Suggs's. Rather than an engagement of the heart and imagination, schoolteacher's pedagogical tools are linguistic objectivity and scientific method.

His methods are shown to have devastating effects. For example, it is only when Sethe overhears schoolteacher teaching the nephews—and she is the subject of the lesson—that she fully comprehends her status as a slave. He says to the nephews, "I told you to put her human characteristics on the left; her animal ones on the right. And don't forget to line them up" (193). Schoolteacher's educational method adopts the clarity of Manichean oppositions and scientific discourse. The notebooks and neat lines verify his definitions as facts for his students. From our cultural position we can see that these "facts" are the product of a preset organization of categories and suppositions made invisible by the use of "objective" methods.

Nonetheless, the social authority of the schoolteacher and the logical clarity of his methods give his words the power of "truth."

Morrison depicts schoolteacher's pedagogical and interpretive methods as morally bereft, and through him she condemns not only slavery but also the United States' educational system. Schoolteacher's practices are basic to the institutional educational system of the United States, which may have gotten past the worst of schoolteacher's racial model but still presents politically motivated versions of knowledge and history while masking these representations in a rhetoric of "facts" and scientific method. Through schoolteacher Morrison demonstrates that discourse, definitions, and historical methods are neither arbitrary nor objective; they are tools in a system of power relations. When Sixo, the African slave at Sweet Home, deftly talks his way out of charges of theft, Morrison writes, "[S]choolteacher beat him anyway to show him that definitions belonged to the definers—not the defined" (190).

According to Baby Suggs's morality, good and evil are undefinable, not based on absolute knowledge; they are part of a situational ethics. "'Everything depends on knowing how much,' she said, and 'Good is knowing when to stop'" (87). Slavery exemplifies the connection between a lack of morality and a lack of limitations. Baby Suggs made this her last pronouncement before she died—"the lesson she had learned from her sixty years a slave and ten years free: that there was no bad luck in the world but white people. 'They don't know when to stop,' she said" (104). The lack of limitations of the white people is shown over and over as the destruction of the slaves. The story of Halle's going mad, Sethe's murder of her baby, Paul D's memories of Mister and the bit—all demonstrate the connection to the white slaveholding society's immorality, its lack of human limitations on its actions, that reciprocates in the minds of its victims as too much suffering to be endured. In Morrison's powerful description of double consciousness, Stamp Paid thinks, "[I]t wasn't the jungle blacks brought with them to this place from the other (livable) place. It was the jungle whitefolks planted in them" (198).

Although Baby Suggs's dying words of despair condemn white people, Morrison makes it clear that race is not an absolute division either. Clearly within the context of American slavery, racial oppression is inseparable from social domination and abuses of power. But in *Beloved* the white "slave," Amy Denver, helps Sethe to cross the river to freedom and acts as a midwife for the birth of Denver (i.e., Sethe's daughter, who is named after Amy Denver). The similarity between the two women's situations supercedes their mutual, racially based mistrust, indicating that class relations (as well as differences in inherited cultural values) are central in shaping racial differences.

Because the white people don't know "when to stop," as Baby Suggs says, slavery pushes the limits of the human capacity for suffering. The overwhelming pain of the past necessitates a closing down of memory, as it does for Sethe, who "worked hard to remember as close to nothing as was safe" (6). But traumatic repression causes neurosis, and although Sethe's suppression of memory enables her to survive and remain sane, it also leads to a stultifying and isolated life. Paul D has a concrete image of his repression:

> He would keep the rest [of his past] where it belonged: in that tobacco tin buried in his chest where a red heart used to be. Its lid rusted shut. He would not pry it loose now in front of this sweet sturdy woman, for if she got a whiff of the contents it would shame him. And it would hurt her to know that there was no red heart bright as Mister's comb beating in him. (72–73)

Paul D and Sethe have found it necessary to lock away their memories and their emotions as a means of surviving the extreme pains of their past. Baby Suggs understands the lack of moral limits of the white slaveholders and the limits of psychological endurance of the black slaves that make up the devastating dynamic of slavery. Baby Suggs is already dead when the novel begins, but her ritual in the Clearing is a model of the process of healing that Paul D and Sethe must undergo to free their hearts from the pain and shame of the past.

Beloved as the Trickster of History

Amy Denver tells Sethe that "anything dead coming back to life hurts" (35). Beloved makes this maxim literal, as the physical manifestation of suppressed memories. Beloved is both the pain and the cure. As an embodiment of the repressed past, she acts as an unconscious imp, stealing away the volition of the characters, and as a psychoanalytic urge, she pries open suppressed memories and emotions. In a sense she is like an analyst, the object of transference and cathexis that draws out the past, while at the same time she is that past. Countering traumatic repression, she makes the characters accept their past, their squelched memories, and their own hearts, as beloved.

Beloved is the incarnation of Sethe's baby girl and of her most painful memory—the murder of her daughter to protect her children from slavery. Beloved is Sethe's "ghost," the return of her repressed past, and she forces Sethe to confront the gap between her motherlove and the realities of motherhood in slavery. But Beloved is also everyone's ghost. She functions as the spur to Paul D's and Denver's repressed pasts, forcing Paul D to confront the shame and pain of the powerlessness of a man in slavery, and enabling Denver to deal with her mother's history as a slave. Beloved initiates the individual healing processes of the three characters, which subsequently stimulate the formation of a family unit of love and support, in which the family members can provide for each other in ways that slavery denied them. And Beloved is the reader's ghost, forcing us to face the historical past as a living and vindictive presence. Thus Beloved comes to represent the repressed memories of slavery, both for the characters and for the readers. Beloved catalyzes Sethe's memories as the novel *Beloved* catalyzes the reader's historical memories (and according to Sethe's idea of "rememory," personal memories come to exist independently in the world and thereby become historical memories).[8]

Beloved symbolizes the past and catalyzes the future. But Beloved cannot be reduced to a symbol as she manipulates the characters with her sweet, spiteful, and engulfing presence. The contradictions of her symbolic position, along with her enigmatic personality, her thoughts and speech filled with the fragmented and vague images of a baby as woman and the once-dead as living, make Beloved a character too complex to be cataloged and contained. Morrison succeeds in creating more in her novel than a sense of history; she makes the past haunt the present through the bewildered and bewildering character of Beloved.

Beloved also develops as a character, from a soft, voracious baby-woman to her final form as a beautiful pregnant woman. During the ritual in which she is exorcised the women see her at last:

> The devil-child was clever, they thought. And beautiful. It had taken the shape of a pregnant woman, naked and smiling in the heat of the afternoon sun. Thunderblack and glistening, she stood on long straight legs, her belly big and tight. Vines of hair twisted all over her head. Jesus. Her smile was dazzling. (261)

Beloved embodies the suffering and guilt of the past, but she also embodies the power and beauty of the past and the need to realize the past fully in order to bring forth the future, pregnant with possibilities. In her last moments, Beloved stands as a contradictory image, both as the African ancestor, the beautiful African mother, connecting the mothers and daughters of African descent to their preslavery heritage and power, and as the all-consuming devil-child. The spirit of the past has taken on a personality in this novel, and thus Morrison makes the writing of history a resurrection of ancestral spirits, the spirit of the long buried past. Morrison resurrects the devil-child, the spiteful, beautiful, painful past, so that Beloved—and the novel—will live on to haunt us.

To look further at the way the unfathomable and disruptive Beloved works in the novel, it is useful to turn now to a literary ancestor of Morrison's novel—the trickster tale. The trickster has long been a part of African and African-American storytelling. Most recently in African-American literary criticism, the trickster has been evoked as a deconstructive force in culture and in texts, as in Henry Louis Gates, Jr.'s version of the signifyin(g) monkey. Gates argues, in "The Blackness of Blackness," that the African-American rhetorical tradition has always denied the monolithic voice of the white father that while poststructuralists have only recently identified and (to varying degrees) challenged. In any case, the trickster has always been part of African-American culture, signifying on itself and on the "white masters" who "know what God knows."

One basic function of the trickster as deconstructor is to bring about role reversals in which a weaker animal or character outwits and outtalks a more powerful one—although the trickster's success is never guaranteed. In *Beloved,* Sixo, the African slave, combines this role of the trickster with the image of a heroic slave who resists slavery to his dying breath. Even his name—"Sixo"—keeps him outside the signifying system, with "a number for a name."

The trickster tales are also employed in healing processes. In his work *Black Culture and Black Consciousness,* Lawrence Levine argues that "the propensity of Africans to utilize their folklore quite consciously to gain psychological release . . . needs to be reiterated if the popularity and function of animal trickster tales is to be understood" (102). Levine goes on to quote anthropologist R. S. Rattray, who concludes, "beyond a doubt, that West Africans had discovered for themselves the truth of the psychoanalysts' theory of 'repressions,' and that in these ways they sought an outlet for what might otherwise become a dangerous complex" (102).

The trickster is also the manifestation of the irrationality of life. Levine argues that, although the antebellum trickster figure often represents the slave, as the weak outwits the strong, other tricksters are best understood to represent the masters, to expose the deceit of the powerful. The trickster defies categorization as good or evil, expressing the amorality of the world. Levine writes that trickster tales "emphasize in brutal detail the irrationality and anarchy that rules Man's universe" (117).

By placing Morrison's novel in the trickster tradition we can see how her narrative strategies derive from the multiculturalism of the American novel, as well as from the African-American storytelling tradition. Beloved represents the irrationality of the world by defying definition and categorization, while at the same time participating in the novel as sister, daughter, lover, and finally, perhaps, mother. Her relations to the characters are both "real" and symbolic; her confused words and thoughts are perplexing; even her physical form is shifting and multiple. Beloved, as a trickster figure, participates in the healing function of the novel, but by refusing to be fixed by a unitary meaning she also remains unhealed—a rift in the attempt to close meaning and thereby close off the past from the present. The character Beloved, like the novel *Beloved,* works to fight a complacency toward history by both healing and disturbing the readers.

Sethe's Healing Ritual

Sethe's healing process is the focal point of the novel, as she gradually and painfully recollects the repressed past. Like Paul D's tobacco tin, Sethe's repressed past is like a rusted box closed inside of her. When she finally realizes that Beloved is the reincarnation of her dead baby, she feels as if she's found buried treasure:

> A hobnail casket of jewels found in a tree hollow should be fondled before it is opened. Its lock may have rusted or broken away from the clasp. Still you should touch the nail heads, and test its weight. No smashing with an ax head before it is decently exhumed from the grave that has hidden it all this time. No gasp as a miracle that is truly miraculous because the magic lies in the fact that you knew it was there for you all along. (176)

Beloved's resurrection exhumes the past Sethe has buried deep inside her. The treasure chest combines images of great discovery and wealth with images of death, the casket and the grave. As Amy Denver says, "Anything dead coming back to life hurts," and Sethe's attempts to prove her love to Beloved and gain Beloved's forgiveness nearly destroy Sethe.

Beloved is the murdered child, the repressed past, Sethe's own guilt and loss, and so Beloved can never forgive Sethe. But the former slave women understand the context within which Sethe acted; they shared in many of her miseries. And so her fellow sufferers come to her aid to exorcise the ghost of her past preying on her life, because Beloved is in some sense their ghost, too. Another local woman, Ella, had also killed her child, although it was not out of love, and when she found out about Beloved's presence "there was also something very personal in her fury. Whatever Sethe had done, Ella didn't like the idea of past errors taking possession of the present" (256).[9] Ella brings the local women to Sethe's house to banish the ghost, and their chanting summons Sethe and Beloved from the house.

The power of the women's voices joined together has a creative capacity that symbolizes and ritualizes Sethe's cycle from spiritual death to rebirth. In the chapter in which Sethe kills her baby, the imagery is from the Book of Revelations, beginning with the apocalyptic image of the four horsemen and concluding with a sense of doom and judgment (148 ff.). In the exorcism ritual, near the end of the novel, the women's voices carry Sethe back to an original creative power:

> They stopped praying and took a step back to the beginning. In the beginning there were no words. In the beginning was the sound, and they all knew what that sound sounded like. (259)

The women's voices carry Sethe from the apocalyptic end to a new beginning. But in contrast to the Gospel of John, which begins, "In the beginning was the Word, and the Word was with God, and the Word was God," the women bring Sethe to a beginning of voices without words. Just as Baby Suggs rejected religious dicta, the spiritual power of the purgation ritual lies beyond the meaning of words, in sound and sensation rather than in logical meaning and the Logos.

The exorcism of Beloved is a purgation ritual, a baptismal cleansing and rebirth, and a psychological clearing:

> For Sethe it was as though the Clearing had come to her with all its heat and simmering leaves, where the voices of women searched for the right combination, the key, the code, the sound that broke the back of words. Building voice upon voice until they found it, and when they did it was a wave of sound wide enough to sound deep water and knock the pods off chestnut trees. It broke over Sethe and she trembled like the baptized in its wash. (261)

The other women's voices, sound without words, have the power of cleansing waters, bringing Sethe back to the Clearing and to Baby Suggs's rituals during Sethe's brief period—between slavery and the return of schoolteacher—of freedom (95).

The cleansing ritual also brings Sethe back to the original scene of repression and enables her to relive it with a difference. When Denver's white employer arrives in the midst of the ritual, the confused Sethe believes him to be one of the white men who has come to take her and her children back into slavery, and Denver must hold her mother back as Sethe launches a murderous attack on the white man. As a freed woman with a group of her peers surrounding her, Sethe can act on her motherlove as she would have chosen to originally. Instead of turning on her children to save them from slavery, she turns on the white man who threatens them. The reconstruction of the scene of the trauma completes the psychological cleansing of the ritual, and exorcises Beloved from Sethe's life. Sethe can finally "lay down the sword and shield" that she has needed to fend off her memories (86).

The author and reader, too, have gone through a ritual recovery *of* history and *from* history. Sethe's ritual and her memories are Morrison's story, a story that—like the voices of the women—reaches beyond meaning to the unconscious pains of the past. Morrison's story combines the creative and cleansing power of the women's voices surrounding Sethe, as well as the spiritual power of Baby Suggs and the disturbing power of Beloved, to construct the story as a ritual both healing and painful for the reader. Finally, Sethe's daughter Denver represents both the future and the past: Denver will be the new African-American woman teacher, and she is Morrison's precursor, the woman who has taken on the task of carrying the story through the generations to our storyteller.

Denver and the History of Slavery

Denver's favorite story is the story of her birth, in which Sethe bears her into a nether world between freedom and slavery. Born on the river that divides "free" and slave land in the midst of Sethe's flight from slavery, the dual inheritance of freedom and slavery tears Denver apart. When schoolteacher comes to take Sethe and her children back to Sweet Home as slaves, Denver drinks the blood of her murdered sister with her mother's milk, and she goes to jail with Sethe. A mirror image of her mother's repressed past, Denver goes deaf when she is asked about her time in prison. From then on Denver lives in seclusion, with only Sethe, Baby Suggs, and the baby ghost as companions. In her lonely withdrawal from the world, due in part to Sethe's isolation, Denver is as trapped by Sethe's past and Sethe's inability to find psychological freedom as Sethe herself is.

Sethe intentionally keeps Denver in the dark: "As for Denver, the job

Sethe had of keeping her from the past that was still waiting for her was all that mattered" (42). But the unacknowledged past keeps Denver from moving into the future. She is jealous of her mother's past, and her exclusion from the past increases her loneliness and bitterness. Beloved, on the other hand, thrives on stories of the past, on pulling from Sethe details of her past, and Denver's love for Beloved forces her to confront the past she hates.

Denver's relation to the past is primarily historic rather than personal. Denver's personal stake in retrieving the past, like the reader's, involves a familial and ancestral inheritance, and her encounter with the past is "necessarily painful," just as Arnold Rampersad suggests a black American's historical encounter must be. Without knowledge of her mother's past, Denver must remain in isolation from history and from her position in the world that can only be understood through history.

As I've argued throughout this essay, history for Morrison is not an abstract factual recital; it is a ritual engagement with the past. Denver begins to experience the past through the stories she tells Beloved. When she repeats her birth story for Beloved, "Denver was seeing it now and feeling it—through Beloved. Feeling how it must have felt to her mother. Seeing how it must have looked" (78). But Denver does not fully remember her past and her mother's past until she undergoes a "ritual of mergence" in part two of the novel.

Four chapters in the middle of part two form a ritual of mergence and possession for Sethe, Denver, and Beloved. These four chapters emerge from the minds of the three characters, who are left alone after Paul D is gone. Sethe has recognized Beloved as her baby girl and is submerged in her attempt to prove her love and atone for her murder, while Denver tries to stay inside the intense circle of possession Sethe and Beloved have created. In the first three chapters, Sethe first proclaims her possession of her daughter Beloved, then Denver of her sister Beloved, then Beloved of her mother. The fourth chapter is in the form of a poetic chant, in which the memories and minds of the three combine in a mutual song of possession—"You are mine" (217). While Denver is possessed by the past she remembers everything—her own past and her mother's past, her fear of her mother as a child murderer, and her imaginary reunions with her father. The ritual of possession breaks through her isolation and grants Denver an experience of the past that can lead her into the future.

After the winter of possession, Denver decides she must leave the house to save her mother from madness and from the ravenous Beloved. In her last moment of fear as she reaches the door, Baby Suggs speaks to her.

Baby's words conjure up the history of her family's struggle for survival and freedom as well as Baby Sugg's own defeat against the horrors of slavery. Denver silently asks Baby:

> But you said there was no defense.
> "There's ain't."
> Then what do I do?
> "Know it, and go on out the yard. Go on." (244)

Although Baby Suggs gave up struggling at the end of her life, her knowledge and spirit, and the knowledge of the past, make possible Denver's emergence into the world. With understanding comes the power to endure and to change.

Denver's position parallels the reader's in her historic relation to her mother's past. But Denver also takes on another role by the end of the novel—that of the teacher, the historian, and the author. Denver will become a schoolteacher, taking up the educational task from her teacher, Lady Jones, and Baby Suggs, and taking over the tools of literacy and education from the white schoolteacher. Paul D worries when he hears of her intentions to go to college, silently cautioning her: "Watch out. Nothing in this world more dangerous than a white schoolteacher" (266). But this is the very reason that Denver must usurp schoolteacher's position; she must take away from him the power to define African-Americans and make their history in a way that steals their past, their souls, and their humanity.

Denver is Morrison's precursor, the historian with her roots in African-American history and culture, who has a relationship with her ancestors. Sixo chooses another course, rejecting Halle's offer to be taught English, as Denver recalls:

> One of them with a number for a name said it would change his mind—
> make him forget things he shouldn't and memorize things he shouldn't
> and he didn't want his mind messed up. But my daddy said, If you can't
> count they can cheat you. If you can't read they can beat you. (208)

While Halle discovers that the white man can cheat and beat you whether or not you are literate, Sixo keeps his cultural integrity and his oral tradition intact. But Denver, as a member of a different generation, must "know it and go on." With the knowledge of this cautionary tale, Denver points the way to a recovery of literacy, one that is suspicious of white definitions and discourse, and one that uses the African oral and cultural heritage and African-American values to take over the task of African-American history-making.

Conclusion: A Haunting History

In *Beloved* Morrison brings together the African-American oral and literary tradition and the Euro-American novel tradition to create a powerful and intensely personal representation of slavery in America. In this way, Morrison indirectly critiques historical and pedagogical methods prevalent in the United States. She counters a fact-based objective system with a ritual method, based in initiatory and healing rituals, in which the acquisition of knowledge is a subjective and spiritual experience. Through the conceptualization of knowledge as culturally constructed, Morrison points the way to a reconstruction of history, both national and personal, to combat the persistent intellectual and spiritual oppression of African-Americans and other Americans and bring about a freedom of the heart and imagination, as Baby Suggs dreamed.

In the last chapter of part one of *Beloved*, Sethe tries to tell Paul D about the secret she has never spoken of before—her killing of her baby girl. Throughout this chapter, as Sethe attempts to explain her past, she is described as "spinning. Round and round the room" and "turning like a slow but steady wheel" around Paul D (159); "Circling him the way she was circling the subject" (161). Like Sethe, Morrison proceeds circuitously toward the revelation of this central secret. Morrison's circularity and indirection correspond to the process of healing undergone by Sethe, as well as to the depiction of the character of Beloved. Sethe's spinning motion around the room, around her subject, describes the necessity for approaching the unutterably painful history of slavery through oblique, fragmented, and personal glimpses of the past—that is, through means most often associated with fiction.

Beloved depicts a healing ritual, or "clearing," for Sethe, whose inability to confront her painful memories of slavery, and especially her guilt for killing her child, keeps her mentally and emotionally enslaved despite eighteen years of freedom. Morrison's fragmented revelation of Sethe's terrible act works to postpone the reader's judgment. By weaving together the complex and emotion-laden incidents and images of the past, Morrison situates Sethe's act within the historical and personal context of slavery. But Morrison's indirection also has to do with the nature of memory itself. The process of the novel corresponds to Sethe's healing ritual, in which the unspoken incident is her most repressed memory, whose recollection and recreation are essential to her recovery. The nature of repression makes this event indescribable—it is part of the inarticulate and irrational unconscious, like an inner ghost plaguing and controlling Sethe's life.

In the last chapter of part one, as Sethe moves in circles around Paul D, she comes closest to explaining the murder of her baby, but her revelation is still internal and silent. Morrison writes:

> Sethe knew that the circle she was making around the room, him, the subject, would remain one. That she could never close in, pin it down for anybody who had to ask. If they didn't get it right off—she could never explain. Because the truth was simple, not a long-drawn-out record of flowered shifts, tree cages, selfishness, ankle ropes and wells. Simple: she was squatting in the garden and when she saw them coming and recognized schoolteacher's hat, she heard wings. Little hummingbirds stuck their needle beaks right through her headcloth into her hair and beat their wings. And if she thought anything, it was No. No. Nono. Nonono. Simple. She just flew. Collected every bit of life she had made, all the parts of her that were precious and fine and beautiful, and carried, pushed, dragged them through the veil, out, away, over there where no one could hurt them. Over there. Outside this place, where they would be safe. (163)

In this passage, the simple truth is not suited to a logical, causal description. The narrator describes Sethe's reaction as an emotional and physical response. The hummingbirds suggest frenzy and confusion, as well as an unnatural event, signified by their beaks thrust into Sethe's hair. The hummingbirds also represent Sethe's physical urge for flight, and at the same time the small jewel-like birds signify Sethe's children—"all the parts of her that were precious and fine and beautiful." The repetition of the single sound—"No. No. Nono. Nonono"—contains the visceral and inarticulate reaction, the protective reaction that compels Sethe to take her children "through the veil." The veil, used by Du Bois to represent the "color-line," the division between black and white flesh and vision (16), here represents the division between life and death, as if at this moment the only escape from the threat of the white world is death.

Sethe can never explain what she did because the event is outside of the logic of words and justifications, of cause and effect. Her act was a physical and emotional reaction, the culmination of her life up to that moment. Even her circling, repeatedly, around the subject with stories and contexts can never really reconstruct the moment, the event, that is beyond explanation. Similarly, Morrison's novel reconstructs slave history in a way that history books cannot, and in a way that cannot be appropriated by objective or scientific concepts of knowledge and history. By inscribing history as a trickster spirit, Morrison has recreated our relationship to history in a process baffling and difficult but necessary. Through the character

Beloved, Morrison denies the reader analytical explanations of slavery. Instead, the reader is led through a painful, emotional healing process, leaving him or her with a haunting sense of the depth of pain and shame suffered in slavery.

Beloved is the forgotten spirit of the past that must "be loved" even if it is unlovable and elusive. As Morrison tells us in the end, "This is not a story to pass on" (275). This line recapitulates the tension between repression and rememory figured throughout the novel. In one reading, the story is not one to pass by or to pass over. At the same time, the more evident meaning is intensely ironic—"This is not a story to pass on," and yet, as the novel shows us, it must be.

Notes

1. There is now an extensive literary corpus of African-American perspectives on slavery in slave narratives, histories of slavery, and novels about slavery from the nineteenth century to the contemporary period, as well as literary criticism on these forms.

2. In *"Beloved* and the New Apocalypse," Susan Bowers also relates Morrison's revision of history to African-American and African religious and philosophical concepts. In "Toni Morrison's *Beloved:* Re-Membering the Body as Historical Text," Mae G. Henderson brings together historiography and psychoanalysis to argue that Sethe must learn to narrativize her story, and that in this process Sethe "tells" and reassembles (re-members) her own body as a text of black womanhood.

3. Rampersad's quote makes it clear that this healing process has particular applications for African-American readers, but this does not deny the importance this process may have for non-African-American readers, since we must all reckon with our historical positions regarding race, class, and gender.

4. Morrison writes, in her essay "Unspeakable Things Unspoken," that the purpose of this haunting of the reader "is to keep the reader preoccupied with the nature of the incredible spirit world while being supplied a controlled diet of the incredible political world" (32).

5. In the *Introductory Lectures,* Freud writes, "The distinction between nervous health and neurosis is thus reduced to a practical question and is decided by the outcome—by whether the subject is left with a sufficient amount of capacity for enjoyment and of efficiency" (568).

6. See Levine 7–10 and 102 for a discussion of the African tradition of oral expression for psychological healing. A variety of works have been written about the trauma and psychological recovery from situations with similarities to slavery, such as torture and concentration camps. See, for example, Frantz Fanon's *The*

Wretched of the Earth, Viktor Frankl's *Man's Search for Meaning,* and Primo Levi's *Survival in Auschwitz.* See Blassingame 20—48 and 130—37 for a discussion of the compatibility and adaptations between the African and Christian religions.

7. Many slave narratives focus on the abuse and manipulation of religious doctrine and discourse by white slaveholders who are interested in establishing "moral" arguments for the legitimacy of slavery.

8. Beloved, in her own reminiscences, represents the most repressed aspect of slave history, the Middle Passage.

9. Sethe was the only one of *her* mother's children that her mother did not kill, suggesting the historical rather than moral impetus of the act.

Works Cited

Blassingame, John W. *The Slave Community: Plantation Life in the Antebellum South,* New York: Oxford Univ. Press, 1979.

Bowers, Susan. "Beloved and the New Apocalypse." *Journal of Ethnic Studies* 18 (1990): 59—77.

Du Bois, W. E. B. *The Souls of Black Folk.* 1903. Rpt. Greenwich: Fawcett, 1967.

Freud, Sigmund. *Introductory Lectures on Psychoanalysis.* Trans. and ed. James Strachey. New York: Norton, 1966.

Gates, Henry Louis, Jr. "The Blackness of Blackness: A Critique of the Sign and the Signifying Monkey." *Black Literature and Literary Theory.* Ed. Gates. New York: Metheun, 1984, 285—321.

Henderson, Mae G. "Toni Morrison's *Beloved:* Re-Membering the Body as Historical Text." *Comparative American Identities: Race, Sex, and Nationality in the Modern Text.* Ed. Hortense J. Spillers, New York: Routledge, 1991. 62—86.

Levine, Lawrence W. *Black Culture and Black Consciousness: Afro-American Folk Thought from Slavery to Freedom.* New York: Oxford Univ. Press, 1977.

Morrison, Toni. *Beloved.* New York: Knopf, 1987.

————. "Unspeakable Things Unspoken: The Afro-American Presence in American Literature." *Michigan Quarterly Review* 33 (1989): 1—34.

Rampersad, Arnold. "Slavery and the Literary Imagination: Du Bois's *The Souls of Black Folk."* *Slavery and the Literary Imagination.* Ed. Deborah E. McDowell and Rampersad. Baltimore: Johns Hopkins Univ. Press, 1989.

Beloved

Woman, Thy Name Is Demon

TRUDIER HARRIS

◆　　◆　　◆

Ｉｆ ＷＥ ＴＨＩＮＫ ＯＦ Toni Morrison's work on a continuum from *Sula* (1974), where she begins the transformation of woman from human being to something other than human and where she experiments with sentience beyond death, through *Tar Baby* (1981), with its talking trees and butterflies, then *Beloved* (New York: Knopf, 1987), with its emphasis on the temporal transcendence of the grave, is a natural extension of those ideas. The ancient tree mothers who would claim Jadine as their sister by drowning her in tar if necessary are not so far removed from the single-mindedness of Beloved, who would kill Sethe as quickly as she would claim her as mother. In exploring the novel's basis in folk traditions, some prevailing ideas about the female body, especially those grounded in myth and fear, are especially illuminating.

Stereotypical conceptions of the female body as "Other" have pervaded oral and written literature. In contemporary times, athletes are warned against intimacy with women before important competitions, some husbands believe their wives poison food if they are allowed to cook while menstruating, and yet others believe their penises could literally be engulfed by women's vaginas. We could document a host of additional persistent and often destructive images of women; underlying these notions is a basic clash between the masculine (those who have power and voice) and the feminine (those who are acquiescent and silent but potentially destruc-tive), which is also worked out in Morrison's novel. These folk and popular stereotypes about the female body have often been bolstered by "scientific" research.

For example, in 1968 psychiatrist Wolfgang Lederer published a volume called *The Fear of Women*.[1] It is a storehouse of information on the control of female images throughout the ages, on how the female body was used to account for a plethora of problems in the world. As early as medieval times, woman stood as Frau Welt ("Mrs. World"), a deceptively beautiful damsel from the frontal view, who, upon being viewed from the rear, showed a disgusting, maggot-filled eruption crawling with snakes, frogs, and other vile creatures with whom she shared inclinations to make man's righteous path in the world difficult if not impossible. The ability to engulf and destroy, as well as to poison the air, were commonplace notions about women. Lederer documents those practices in certain cultures where menstruating women were encouraged to walk over newly plowed and planted fields in order to poison the insects and ensure the growth of the crops.

The blood that flowed every month concentrated the distinguishing differences between men and women that Lederer documents so carefully. And not only was woman the bleeder, but she was also insatiable in her de-sire for blood. Kali, the Indian goddess, is the epitome of the bloodthirsty female on the rampage against human, especially *man*-kind. Tales about her illustrate the recurring ambivalence of the traditions. On the one hand, woman is the mother/nurturer; on the other, she is the goddess/de-stroyer.

As recently as 1986, a song played repeatedly on black radio stations was the Isley Brothers' "Insatiable Woman." Its upbeat tempo, coupled with the soothing voice of the male singing the lyrics, quickly lulled one into forgetfulness against its evil intent. The female body, the singer com-plained, could never be satisfied; no matter what he gave—probably sperm donations—she wanted more. Obviously he could not keep delivering the donations at the rate at which she could receive them, so he could only verbally affirm: "Baby, I'm yours," and perhaps hope that she would let him be. The song and the verbal tradition it perpetuates of the engulfing, never-satisfied woman recalls the tale of the preacher and the pretty young woman. Preacher tales, a special subcategory of African-American folk narrative, frequently debunk the authority and prestige of ministers. Preachers are invariably painted as greedy; they especially love fried chicken, alcohol, and money. They are also impious and sexually unrestrained. As the story goes, a preacher who thought he would take advantage of her parents' absence and seduce a young woman gets the tables slightly turned on him. He sends her upstairs to the bedroom and maintains that he will be up shortly to "scare" her, his euphemism for sexual intercourse. He discovers, however, that her receptivity is longer than his stamina. After three trips upstairs and increasingly weaker, near-crawling returns, when she requests that he come upstairs and "scare" her yet another time, he responds: "Well, BOO, goddamn it!"[2]

The female body, as it has been written in the oral tradition and in sexist literature, is in part a source of fear, both an attraction and a repulsion, something that can please, but something that can destroy. The tricksters of tradition find one of their chores the task of bravely entering the vagina to break those teeth that tradition has long identified with it. Such actions are considered heroic—and at times helpful even to the woman herself, for the poor dear never realizes what difficulty she is in until some man tells her and proceeds to rescue her. And in *his* ending to the tale, she usually appreciates the rescue and indeed becomes more decorous in her sexual habits. Witchlike, Other, Strange, Fearful—that is how the female body has been characterized. In many instances the attributes center upon the demonic, as indeed many of those traditions I have described would encompass. Women could be witches or healers—depending upon point of view—only because they were in some way in league with the devil. Or indeed, just the nature of being female was considered evil, without the specific connotations of satanic contact.

The nature of evil—the demonic, the satanic—those are the features of the female body as written by Toni Morrison in *Beloved*. We can describe the title character as a witch, a ghost, a devil, or a succubus; in her manipulation of those around her, she exerts a power not of this world. In her absence of the tempering emotions that we usually identify with humankind, such as mercy, she is inhumanly vengeful in setting out to repay the one upon whom she places the blame for her too-early demise. We should note that this is not the first time that Morrison has called woman Demon.

In *Sula*, she begins the transformation of woman from human being to something other than human. The people in the Bottom make Sula into a witch whom they believe to be in league with the forces of evil if not with the devil himself. They believe that she makes Teapot fall off her steps, that she causes Mr. Finley's death when he chokes on a chicken bone, and that she is a witch who can make herself appear much younger than she is. Her suprahuman qualities lead them to ostracize her to the point of circumventing the rituals that usually apply to death and funerals in black communities. Sula's demise, however, points to another source for comparison with Beloved. Sula's sentience beyond death, presented briefly in the book, is enough to signal that Morrison has drawn no final lines between the planes of life and death. Indeed, Morrison has asserted that the call of one of the stories that inspired *Beloved* worked on her so strongly that it may have surfaced unwittingly in her earlier novels: "I had been rescuing [the dead girl] from the grave of time and inattention. Her fingernails maybe in the first book; face and legs, perhaps, the second time. Little by little bringing her back into living life."[3]

Following the African belief that the demise of the body is not the end of being, which David Bradley develops so vividly in *The Chaneysville Incident* (1981), Morrison hints with Sula what becomes her major preoccupation in *Beloved.* During her life, Sula has given some insight into the actions of those who are set apart or deemed demonic. They owe allegiance only to themselves; Sula is interested only in making herself, Beloved is interested only in claiming and punishing her mother. Their desires are foremost; the wishes of others are inconsiderable. Sula sleeps with her best friend's husband without compunction; Beloved sleeps with her mother's lover. Though one is alive and the other returned from the dead, at several points the actions of the two characters are strikingly similar in motivation and execution.

The world view in *Sula* prepares us for the seeming topsy-turviness of *Tar Baby,* with its racing blind horsemen and mythic life forms, for the otherworldliness represented by Pilate's lack of a navel in *Song of Solomon,* and for the emphasis on the temporal transcendence of the grave in *Beloved.* Remember, too, that Eva talks to Plum after his death (he comes back to tell her things) and that Valerian sees Michael's ghost in the dining room on the night that Son intrudes into the island world. Morrison has well prepared her readers, therefore, for complete suspension of disbelief in the human and natural worlds. The female body reduced to desire makes Sula kindred in spirit and objective to Beloved. Consider, too, that Ajax, Sula's lover, leaves her when he begins to fear her body as woman, when he judges that she wants to trap him into marriage, or at least domesticity.

Woman's body is a threat to men in *Beloved* as well; that is the vantage point from which we see what happens in the novel. Paul D's arrival at Sethe's house brings with it the ancient fear of women. When he enters the house haunted by Beloved's ghost, it becomes the enveloping enclosure of the vagina; the vagina dentata myth operates as Paul D *feels* the physical threat of the house. The red light of the baby's spirit drains him, makes him feel overwhelming grief, feminizes him. Sethe and Denver live in the presence of the spirit; they may be annoyed by the spirit of the "crawling-already?" baby, but they have little to fear from it as females. Indeed, there is evidence that Beloved may be nurturing them into acceptance of her later physical, human manifestation. They comment at one point that "the baby got plans" (37).

For Paul D, however, the house is immediately his enemy, a veritable threat. He perceives that it bodes no good for him, and he senses—more than he knows—that the contest is between male and female spirits. Walking through the "pulsing red light," "a wave of grief soaked him so thoroughly he wanted to cry. It seemed a long way to the normal light surrounding the table, but he made it—dry-eyed and lucky" (9). To cry is to be broken, diminished as a man. Holding himself together against such a feminine breakdown, Paul D already views the house as a threat to his masculinity. He therefore enters it like the teeth-destroying tricksters of tradition entered the vagina, in the heroic vein of conquering masculine will over female desire. The competition, as it develops, then, seems initially unfair—a grown man against a baby. The supernatural element of the baby's spirit neutralizes the inequality somewhat, but the spirit of maleness in this initial battle seems stronger even than Beloved's supernaturalism. In his confrontation with the house, Paul D *wills* Beloved's spirit away. His vocal masculine will is stronger than her silent, though sometimes noisy, desire. The power of his voice to command behavior, even that of spirits, is ultimately stronger than the spirit's desire to resist.

Or at least that is one possible reading of the confrontation. Another would be to explore it from the perspective of Beloved's demonic nature. In this seeming rite of exorcism, it is not Beloved who is removed but Paul D who is lulled into a false sense of victory. The demonic Beloved voluntarily leaves the scene in order to prepare for a greater onslaught of female energy. In seemingly forcing Beloved to leave, Paul D, like the heroes of tradition, gives to Sethe and Denver the peace that they have been unable or unwilling to give to themselves. Presumably he has made the society better. The house is quiet, he and Sethe can pretend to be lovers, and the women can contemplate such leisure activities as going to a circus.

By blending the temporal and the eternal planes of existence, however, Morrison gives Beloved the upper hand for most of the novel. As the shapeshifter who takes on flesh-and-blood human characteristics, Beloved introduces a logic and a world view into the novel that defy usual responses to such phenomena. Certainly in the black folk tradition, a ghost might occasionally appear among the living—to indicate that all is well, to teach a lesson, or to guide the living to some good fortune, including buried treasure. There are few tales, however, of revenants that actually take up residence with living relatives. One such tale, "Daid Aaron," which is from the Gullah people, centers upon the theme of revenge. Aaron refuses to go to the dwelling of the dead because his wife is already showing signs of her intention to have other suitors. But then, that is a male/female conflict as well. The widow finally gets rid of Aaron when he requests that her fiddler suitor provide dance music. Aaron dances gleefully and madly, faster and faster, until he comes apart, literally bone by bone.[4] Whether she knew of such tales or not, Morrison has asserted that she and her family members "were intimate with the supernatural" and that her parents "told thrillingly terrifying ghost stories."[5]

Beloved has a brief experience that brings to mind the possibility of disintegration comparable to Aaron's. She pulls a tooth, then speculates:

> Next would be her arm, her hand, a toe. Pieces of her would drop maybe one at a time, maybe all at once. Or on one of those mornings before Denver woke and after Sethe left she would fly apart. It is difficult keeping her head on her neck, her legs attached to her hips when she is by herself. Among the things she could not remember was when she first knew that she could wake up any day and find herself in pieces. She had two dreams: exploding, and being swallowed. When her tooth came out—an odd fragment, last in the row—she thought it was starting. (133)

But Beloved does not decay. Like a vampire feeding vicariously, she becomes plump in direct proportion to Sethe's increasing gauntness. Vengeance is not the Lord's; it is Beloved's. Her very body becomes a manifestation of her desire for vengeance and of Sethe's guilt. She repays Sethe for her death, but the punishment is not quick or neat. They attempt to choke Sethe to death in Baby Suggs's clearing and the lingering pain of that encounter is but the beginning of Beloved's taking over the women's lives. Before she can accomplish that, however, she must extricate the most formidable opposition, Paul D. In another demonic parallel in the male/female clash, she becomes the traditional succubus, the female spirit who drains the male's life force even as she drains him of his sperm. Beloved makes herself irresistible to Paul D, gradually forcing him, through each sexual encounter, to retreat farther and farther from the territory she has claimed as her own. Her "shining" or sexual latching on to him causes him initially to sleep in a rocking chair in the kitchen, then in Baby Suggs's keeping room behind the kitchen, then in the storeroom, and finally in the "cold house" outside the main house. *"She moved him,"* and Paul D "didn't know how to stop it because it looked like he was moving himself" (114, emphasis added). Their three weeks of sexual encounters in the cold house result in a guilty Paul D trying to confront Sethe with the news only to find that he cannot; Beloved's control over him, together with his discovery of Sethe's killing of her baby, force him off the premises altogether. After all, what option does he have? To stay is to contemplate the violations he has committed—sleeping with a woman who has been much abused and abusing her further by sleeping with her daughter/ghost. To go or to stay is to contemplate a possible further evil—having slept with the devil—either in the form of the mother or the daughter.

Paul D's departure makes clear that Beloved has used her body to drain him not only physically but spiritually as well. He becomes a tramp of sorts, sleeping where he can, drinking excessively, literally a shadow of his former self. From the man who was strong enough to exorcise a spirit, Paul D reverts to his wandering, unsure of his residence from day to day and unclear about what kind of future, if any, he has. The picture of him sitting on the church steps, liquor bottle in hand, stripped of the very maleness that enables him to caress and love the wounded Sethe, is one that shows Beloved's power. There is no need for her to kill Paul D; she simply drains him sufficiently to make him one of the living dead, in a limbolike state from which he cannot extricate himself as long as Beloved reigns at 124 Bluestone Road. For this male warrior, therefore, the demonic female has won over him in the very realm he has used to define himself; his sexual fear of woman is justified.

But the parasitic Beloved is not content to destroy maleness; she also attacks femaleness. Or, I should say it is perhaps less femaleness that she attacks in Sethe than motherhood, another symbol of authority almost masculine in its absoluteness. We could say, then, that as far as Beloved is concerned, Paul D and Sethe are in some ways shaped from the same mold—those who have the power to command, those who have power over life and death. In her resolve to escape from slavery, Sethe, like Jean Toomer's Carma, is "strong as any man."[6] In the resolve that keeps her going during the ordeal of Denver's birth she is again, stereotypically, strong as any man. In her determination to kill her children to keep them from being remanded to slavery, she is again as strong as any man. Beloved's anger with Sethe for having killed her may be centered in mother love, but it is also centered in the patriarchal authority that Sethe assumed unto herself in killing Beloved, in becoming the destructive, authoritative mother/goddess. Beloved's war against Sethe, then, can be read from one perspective as a further attack against masculine privilege, against the power over life and death that is stereotypically identified with males or with those masculine mother/goddesses.

Think, too, about how Sethe is viewed in the community. Comparable to Sula, she is too proud, too self-sufficient, too independent, generally too much on her own for the neighbors. Her rugged individualism is more characteristic of males than females of the time. The more feminine thing would be for her to need help from the community. She neither seeks nor accepts any before Beloved arrives; later, she is too transformed to care.

Perhaps we are sufficiently encouraged, then, to see Sethe as a masculine presence that the female demon seeks to exorcise. Beloved symbolically begins feeding upon Sethe as the succubus feeds upon males; she takes food from her mouth, eats whatever there is to eat, and inspires Sethe to leave her job, thereby relinquishing her ability to feed herself, and causing her to shrink, to become diminished in stature as well as in self-possession. By denying to Sethe the power to support herself, Beloved initially attacks Sethe's spirit of independence. She sends her into a stupor comparable to that of Paul D. But Beloved is not content to stupefy Sethe; she is after her life force. She drains her by slowly starving her and, as the neighbors believe, beating her (255). The apparently pregnant Beloved blossoms, glows, and continues to get plump as the shrinking Sethe literally becomes a skeleton of her former self. Like Paul D, Sethe loses willpower, thereby losing the ability to control her own body or her own destiny. She and Paul D are assuredly slaves to Beloved's desire as Sethe and the Pauls were literally slaves earlier. Beloved becomes the arbiter of life and death, so playfully so that Sethe acquiesces in her own decline.

It is in part the playfulness of the situation that tones down its potentially destructive side. With Beloved, Sethe has the opportunity to live out two fantasies. First of all, she can be mother to the daughter she has never known. Giving all her time and attention to Beloved makes it easy for the demon to execute her desire. On the other hand, by giving all to Beloved, Sethe becomes childlike, pleading for acceptance by a harsh "parent" who is more intent upon cruel punishment than understanding forgiveness. By relinquishing her will to survive, Sethe again becomes Beloved's willing victim.

Their relationship raises questions about Morrison's intentions in the novel. Is guilt the central theme, thereby making it understandable how Sethe acquiesces in her own slow destruction? Does the guilt deserve the punishment of the demonic? Is infanticide so huge a crime that only other-worldly punishment is appropriate for it? If, on the other hand, we understand, accept, and perhaps even approve of the dynamic that allowed a slave mother to kill rather than have her children remanded to slavery, would not the dominant theme be love? After all, Sethe has precedence in her action; her own mother killed some of her children rather than allow them to be slaves, or to recognize her own forced depravity in having given birth to them (62). If the theme is love, what warrants allowing Sethe to be so violated for her love of Beloved?

As the novel develops, it would seem that Beloved's *desires,* irrational as they are, are the acceptable force driving the story. I emphasize desire as opposed to will simply because Beloved is not to be denied in what she wants. Her desire is for a mother, and she will have that mother even if it means killing her in the process of claiming her. She desires Paul D and takes him in spite of her mother's involvement with him. As it manifests itself in the novel, desire is unbridled id, self-centered and not to be easily denied.[7] Will, on the other hand, can be altruistic; Paul D wills Beloved out of 124, it can be argued, in part to bring a measure of peace to Sethe and Denver. The destructive, irrational force is pure desire, which in turn is perhaps the most otherworldly. It is out of desire for something that spirits are able to make the journey between the two worlds. Beloved, the personification of desire, thus epitomizes the demonic.[8] Her lack of caring is spiteful retaliation for not being allowed to live; she is the unleashed force of the childish mentality at which her life ended. Twenty years in body but eighteen months in mind, she is the objective, physical distillation of desire.

Beloved's characterization ultimately makes her "Thing," unhuman, unfeeling, uncaring except in the perpetuation of what she wants. Like Frau Welt, she cannot live up to the promise of herself; to become involved with her is to be destroyed. As Thing, Beloved has no consistently seen reflective trait; the point of view of the narrative encourages us to see her as the traditional vampire. We see her inner thoughts for only brief moments, which do not evoke undue sympathy for her. We are left to judge her objectively, to infer motive from a distance, and thereby to solidify our evaluation of her as demonic. Her actions suggest that she has ultimate power of judgment, that vengeance is indeed hers, that her brand of justice has no guiding morality to temper it with mercy.[9]

In her amorality, Beloved shares kinship with some of the tricksters of tradition—ever guided by personal desires and frequently identified as masculine. Such figures are recognizable by the power they wield, without consideration for those being affected by that power. Brer Rabbit kills the elephant simply to escape detection for a crime he has committed, or he avenges himself on the entire alligator family because of an insult by Brer

Alligator. Unleashed and unrestrained, Brer Rabbit is limited only by the power of imagination that conceived the cycle of tales in which he stars. With her supernatural dimension, Beloved has no obvious limits. Nonetheless, she ultimately seems subject to a force greater than herself.

A potentially troublesome part of the novel is how Beloved is exorcised from 124. Paul D's initial driving of her spirit from the premises is merely temporary. She is finally exorcised not by individuals working in isolation but by a community of effort directed against her presence. And that community of effort comes from a group of women, women who call upon ancient and contemporary messages, murmuring incantations and singing songs, to control Beloved. Is Morrison suggesting finally that women, who may themselves be demonic—or *because* they are demonic—are the only force with sufficient power to control that evil? Is it a question of good versus evil? Are the women who send Beloved away in any way identified with the forces of good? Most of them are certainly not the image of stereotypically traditional churchgoing black women. Nor do they pursue the exorcism from altruistic motivations. Rather, like Richard Wright's District Attorney Ely Houston pursuing the murderous Cross Damon in *The Outsider* (1953), they are simultaneously attracted to and repulsed by the evil in their midst. They see in it tiny mirrors of the selves they have suppressed, and they want it extracted before it touches them too greatly or even has the potential to reclaim them. And they are offended. They "didn't mind a little communication between the two worlds, but this was an invasion" (257).

In other words, Beloved is a threat to them in the psychological sphere as effectively as Sula is a threat to the women in the Bottom in the sexual sphere. Extending the philosophy from that novel, where the community is content to recognize evil and let it run its course, the women in *Beloved* cannot afford that detachment. Letting Beloved run her course may mean the destruction of them all. They must exorcise that part of themselves, therefore, that is a threat to them. If thy right eye offend thee, pluck it out. This is not a far-fetched philosophy when we consider that throughout history it is a frequently women who cast sanctions most vehemently upon other women.

Exorcising the demonic part of the self so that all women are not judged to be demons—that is what the women are about in getting Beloved to leave 124. And how do they accomplish this? With a combination of pagan and religious rituals. They initially find power in numbers as they gather in a group of thirty to move toward 124. They raise their voices in singing and in religious murmurs as they march along the road. The comparative images that come to mind are straight out of *The Golden Bough*. The voices raised serve the same function as the sticks and pans villagers of pretechnological cultures might have used to drive evil spirits from their midsts. The act of singing itself serves as a chant, perhaps as the proverbial "witch doctor" of ancient times might have used to implore or command that some living/hearing evil take its leave from the environs of the innocent and the helpless.

What the pregnant Beloved sees then, as she comes to the front door of 124, is that those with whom she identifies as well as despises are organized against her. The mothers are multiplied many times over, as are the breasts of the women in Eloe, Florida, whom Jadine confronts in *Tar Baby;* against the demands of that immutable force of potential mother/goddesses, who seem to represent justice without mercy, Beloved can only retreat. The vengeance of parents punishing recalcitrant children is ultimately stronger than will or desire.

But Beloved's retreat may in reality be a departure from a battlefield where she has won, accomplished what she set out to do. Consider what happens as the white Mr. Bodwin drives up. In the near-reenactment of what happened at Beloved's death, it becomes clear that Sethe is nearly deranged. She is decidedly no longer the figure of authority and independence that she has been before Beloved's arrival. When she takes the ice pick in hand to save Beloved once again, the same set of imperatives does not apply. Slavery has ended; the man approaching is a rescuer rather than an enslaver; Sethe needs rescue *from* Beloved rather than rescuing her from someone else. Reduced to irrationality engendered by the wiping out of eighteen years of her life, Sethe is now the recalcitrant child, in need of correcting and nurturing (252). In this reading of the scene, Beloved can leave instead of being sent away because she has accomplished two things. First, she has caused Sethe to become temporarily deranged. Second, the result of that derangement is that Sethe acts without thought, instinctively, to save Beloved. What Beloved could not see as a "crawling-already?" baby, she is now able to see as an adult: that her mother's action, many years before and in its current duplicate, was indeed one of love. This reading does not mean that the demon changes her nature, but that she achieves her desire: tangible evidence that her mother loved her best of all. Ironically, to achieve that goal is simultaneously to risk eventual destruction of the individual of whom the evidence was required.[10]

Again, Beloved either leaves voluntarily or is driven out. Whatever interpretation we accept, one thing is clear: Sethe and Beloved cannot exist on the same plane. If Sethe is to live, Beloved must depart. If Beloved stays,

Sethe can only die. The trip from beyond, though, is apparently a one-time thing. Once removed from 124, the undelivered, restless Beloved roams the neighboring territory, her footprints a reminder that she is there but her desire fulfilled sufficiently so that she cannot return all the way to 124. Her inability to return is attested to in the return of Here Boy, the dog, to 124 and in the return of Paul D, the masculine presence. Of the animals traditionally believed to sense ghosts and evil spirits, dogs are perhaps first on the list.[11] When Here Boy takes up residence again, that is the folkloristic signal that Beloved will not be returning. When Paul D finds the energy to pursue Sethe again, to experience the returning of sexual desire as well as general concern for another human being, that is also a signal that Beloved will not be returning. Paul D's presence means health for Sethe, the opposite of what Beloved's presence meant. With the novel ending on a sign of health, there will at least be calm at 124.

And what of Beloved? The demon comes and goes. Humans interact with it, but it ultimately transcends them, returns to another realm of existence controlled only by human imagination. Morrison lifts Beloved from a void and returns her there. Her footprints relegate her to kinship with Big Foot and other legendary if not mythical creatures. Beloved goes from imagination to humanoid to legend, basically unchanged in her category as demon, the designation of Other that makes it impossible for her to be anything but eternally alone.

Shaping the Tales in the Tale

In *Beloved,* Toni Morrison concocts a sequence of events in which she shares with her characters the creation of her novel. In the tradition of storytelling and composition, they are as much artists as she. In fact, it could be argued that there is a single master mind and that parts of that entity tell various parts of the tale. The story of Denver's birth provides the prime example of this multiple composition. Denver relates a part of the story (29–30, and especially 77–78). Sethe recounts another portion (31–32). And the omniscient narrator provides more (32–35, 78–85). Each teller carries the burden for her particular portion, which is frequently shaped by the audience before whom it is created. Consider the power of audience in the instance in which Denver feeds on Beloved's reaction to her story of the pregnant Sethe roaming through dog- and patteroller-infested woods. Inspired by her audience of one, Denver allows her creative imagination to leap far beyond the mere fact of her mother's experience:

Denver was seeing it now and feeling it—through Beloved. Feeling how it must have felt to her mother. Seeing how it must have looked. And the more fine points she made, the more detail she provided, the more Beloved liked it. So she anticipated the questions by giving blood to the scraps her mother and grandmother had told her—and a heartbeat. The monologue became, in fact, a duet as they lay down together, Denver nursing Beloved's interest like a lover whose pleasure was to overfeed the loved. (78)

Denver may know part of what Sethe relates, but she does not usurp Sethe's authorship by recounting in any great detail the part of the story that Sethe relates in detail. And Sethe takes up her portion of narration where Denver leaves off. They know, or seem to know instinctively, what is needed to complete the story; therefore, Morrison imbues them with a portion of her omniscience, a trait that makes them somewhat other-worldly and intuitive, or at least a trait that suggests the interconnected-ness of the lives, minds, and hearts of the three women. The single control-ling narration gives Morrison at some level the same relation to her story as her characters, while at another it is obvious that Morrison as author of the text ultimately controls the story. When she does share narration with her characters, Morrison shows an intuitive respect for their collective ex-perience, one that binds them as strongly to each other as they are bound to her as their creator.

The story of Denver's birth is as much rumor and conjecture as it is fact, or so the townspeople believe. It is too fantastic to be taken at face value and thus borders on folktale. As she was trying to escape from slavery, so the story goes, Sethe, then six months pregnant, met the white girl Amy Denver, who not only laid healing hands upon her lashed back and swollen feet, but also attended at Denver's birth. These basic details get embellished depending upon who is relating the story to whom. In a time when patterollers were rampant and white people were believed to be instinctively hostile toward blacks, Sethe's story violates the rules of interracial interaction with which her fellow blacks are familiar. The more logical expectation would have been for Amy to turn Sethe in. This seeming discrepancy, combined with Sethe actually escap-ing in her condition, leads some of the locals to speculate that there is something unnatural about her even before she kills Beloved and pridefully shuns them all. The tale, then, already has components of legend, myth, and outright lying before it begins to get reshaped in the minds and memories of Sethe, Denver, and their neighbors. When the other events ensue, the townspeople reject Sethe not only because of her pride, but perhaps because she is too witchlike or too otherworldly for them.

As they tell this and other stories to each other, therefore, Sethe, Denver, and Beloved form a small folk community in which they all have distinct roles to play. Sethe discovers as quickly as Denver does how much Beloved appreciates stories: "It became a way to feed her. Just as Denver discovered and relied on the delightful effect sweet things had on Beloved, Sethe learned the profound satisfaction Beloved got from storytelling" (58), so she tells Beloved about her "diamonds." Oral history joins hands with fiction and rumor in basing the stories in a germ of truth; that germ is quickly reduced—or elevated—to motif as, through repeated tellings, the stories are modified and reshaped to suit the imagination and needs of the teller and her audience. The women are inseparable in their bid to create the stories and in their need to perpetuate the lore about their existence. Their family folklore binds them to a bone-chilling, destructive interaction that may have historical parallels at its most basic level but soon transcends the traditional.

The *process* of storytelling as presented in the works of such folklorists as Zora Neale Hurston is a pleasant communal affair. In their roles as tradition bearers, narrators can weave a tale individually or with participation and encouragement from their communities. Even when the community does not actively contribute to the telling of the tale, it nevertheless contributes actively by listening to the tale, for there can be no storytellers without audiences. The community of three women that Morrison creates in *Beloved,* therefore, is a dynamic storytelling one in which the tellers and their tales have a direct impact upon the lives of those around them. Denver estimates her value in direct proportion to the way in which the stories Sethe relates focus on her birth. Other stories about Sweet Home send her into periods of depression and loneliness that drive her to her secret place in the boxwood trees. Beloved's well-being, if we can call it such, exists in direct proportion to the stories that Sethe relates, no matter the topic; the *act* of storytelling itself is what pacifies Beloved and emphasizes the childish part of her being.

For Beloved, Sethe's willingness to tell stories is a measure of Beloved's obsession for and desire to possess Sethe, an indication of her unbridled id at work. The ownership component of their relationship, which becomes so apparent later, is presaged in Beloved's attempt to control Sethe's creative imagination. From the control she exerts in this arena, it is easy for her to make the transition to control of Sethe's body. Storytelling in this context, therefore, is about power, one sometimes sinister in its manifestations. Sethe weaves a story, but Beloved weaves a web of tangled parental responsibility and morality from which Sethe is barely able to escape.

Sethe is willing to satisfy Denver's desire for information about herself, but she stops when the stories make the past live again much too vividly for her. Her whole life is about "beating back the past" (73). That past can be kept at bay if the stories are untold, the memories sheathed. The paradox of Sethe's position is that both of her daughters desire the stories but for compellingly different reasons. And they each have different powers to exert in urging her to tell the tales. Beloved relies upon Sethe's less blemished memories of Sweet Home and, later, upon the guilt Sethe feels for having killed her. Denver also appeals to Sethe's more pleasant memories of Sweet Home as well as to Sethe's sense of guilt for excluding Denver from a history in which she clearly had a vital role. Thus for Sethe, Denver, and Beloved, storytelling is an active rather than a passive art, for it has the power literally to heal or kill.

To give such power to stories is one of Morrison's extensions of the function of folklore. She elevates the narratives beyond the entertaining, psychological, and educational functions they usually serve. Beloved may be entertained by the stories, and she certainly learns a lot about her family history, but she is also drawing her very lifeblood from them; they are creating a memory for her, filling in the gaps in her life that she cannot remember. For Denver, the stories enable her to fill in a history from which she had been excluded by virtue of her youth and forbidden from entering later by virtue of Sethe's vow to continue "keeping the past at bay" (42) and "beating back the past" (73). The stories provide self-definition in the way that legends, anecdotes, and personal experience narratives define their subjects.

Denver's geographical location at the point of storytelling makes this idea clearer. She lives at 124 Bluestone Road in Cincinnati, Ohio, in a house whose porch provides the boundary for the "edge of the world." As a secluded, psychologically immature, and functionally illiterate person, she is as much heir to the horrors of falling off the edge of the world as those early explorers who believed that the world was flat. Left with an imagination uninformed by the reality beyond her porch, she can create whatever monsters she wishes. An early participant in her history but without the maturity to register it, Denver has to find means to place herself within her own life, within her own family; she must flesh out her life from one dimension to multiple dimensions, from isolation to involvement, from a house to the world. Storytelling is her continual birth process, her continual bid to find herself in the family portrait and to find value within the family. Consider how she imaginatively concocts stories about an absent father who will one day rescue her from the difficult situation she sometimes believes she is in with Sethe; evocations of fairy tales, with the passive princess waiting to be rescued, immediately come to mind. Denver's fantasy, like those of many children, locates her squarely at the center of value in her family portrait.

Her contacts with people during Baby Suggs's lifetime were not sustained enough for her to develop a sense of what is normal. She may well have grown up thinking that spending time in jail with her mother was not unusual if Nelson Lord had not asked the question that brought on her deafness. Certainly her becoming deaf is an indication that she believes she is somehow stigmatized, but she is able to judge that only in relation to her rejection by the other children. She has not previously thought that her situation was somehow wrong, that her mother's act was an unlawful, immoral, isolating one.

Denver is a tablet upon which her own life can be written. The stories of her birth are the chalk for that creation. Stories, for Morrison, then, are much more vibrant and viable forces in the lives of her characters than they are in historic folk communities. They are not just effects; they are effects with consequences. The consequence of Denver learning about herself is that she can begin to form the basis upon which to grow into an adult human being. The consequence of Beloved learning about herself is much more destructive; it enables her to exert more control over the lives of those around her, and indeed the knowledge she gains through the information provided by storytelling could enable her to become a murderer. Morrison therefore strips the word down to its original, creative essence; it can be made flesh, or it can destroy.

It is no wonder, then, that Morrison describes Denver's telling of her birth story to Beloved as a creative act of godly proportion. Denver gives "blood," a life force, to the "scraps" of stories she has gotten from her mother and grandmother. Her infusion of blood thereby grants a "heartbeat" (78) to what she relates. We are immediately reminded of Ezekiel and the dry bones, with God asking, "Son of man, can these bones live?" (Ezekiel 37:3). Through imagination (faith), the power to create what did not exist before—or existed only in a half-formed state—Denver and the other women reiterate the power of words.

Morrison thus draws upon biblical implications of the word as well as upon those connotations of creation that pervade the African-American folk bible. From Genesis comes "And God *said*, 'Let there be light" (Genesis 1:3), "And God *said*, 'Let us make man in our image'" (Genesis 1:26), but from the pages of James Weldon Johnson's *God's Trombones* we get the specific folk impetus for what God said. The world is here *because* God *said*, "I'm lonely—I'll make me a world," and with each creation, he proclaims, "That's good." The anthropomorphic God who responds to the wishes of his people, as in the tale of the black Adam and Eve climbing up to heaven to ask God to reconcile the discrepancies in male and female power,[12] connects the human and extranatural realms in ways comparable to those Morrison devises. The invitation to appear at 124, combined with Paul D's voice, are the words that name the flesh that Beloved becomes, just as the supernatural Jesus is made flesh. "In the beginning was the Word, and the Word was with God, and the Word was God" (John 1:1). Just as the word can bring forces not of this world to life, *sound,* the pre-word condition we might say, can have equally effective consequences. It is sound that eventually drives Beloved out of 124 just as it has been the word that has made her flesh. Words, then, are an active force in the novel (and they have just as much shaping force as hands).

These single entities become even more potent when they are shaped into the larger units called stories. Consider the story—as told by whites and printed in the newspaper—of Sethe's killing of Beloved; it is almost as destructive to Paul D as stories other than those of her birth are to Denver—they diminish her. In the minds of the whites who arrest and try Sethe, and those who record her story, she is a horrible statistic, an indication of the inhuman acts of which blacks are presumably capable. Their power of the press, along with the horror it relates, diminishes her in the eyes of the black community as well as in Paul D's eyes. They use a narrative to shape a life.

The operative dynamic between Denver, Sethe, and Beloved is one in which they have the power to replenish or diminish each other by the sheer sound of their voices (remember Janie Crawford discussing the potency of lying thoughts in *Their Eyes Were Watching God*). This power is comparable to that we see in some folktales in which there is a magical component to the spoken word. Consider, for example, the ability of various conjurers to command inanimate objects to come to life (to speak, dance, or perform some other action). I think especially of the tale in which crafty John the slave has a short stint as a fortune-teller by commanding a cowhide to come to life and do his bidding.[13]

The emphasis upon the power of words becomes another way for Morrison to break down the barrier between planes of existence in the novel, to show once again that powers assigned to one realm or the other may or may not adhere to their assignments. It also stresses the blurring of lines between human and supernatural acts, which is a corollary to the breaking down of planes of existence. We might expect Beloved to act (and she does) in many ways like a demon—or a goddess—but Morrison makes it clear that Sethe's and Denver's intuitive powers, as well as the power of their voices, may also cross over the human/divine marker and become extranatural in what they can accomplish. This is also obviously the case with the women who drive Beloved out of 124; their voices combine in their power to fight the demon/devil, and who can wage such a battle successfully if not a divine/creative force? Not only do the women call upon God, but they also assume the power of godhead. Ella has made the decision about the limits of activities for spirits (that they may have legitimate reasons for returning but they do not have the right to punish the living), which is a divine decision, and she follows through on it in her control of the extranatural force (Beloved) that has made the decision necessary.

Thus Morrison adapts the dynamic of storytelling and the power of the word to create, alter, and destroy personalities. Hers is a world of friendly competition, polite verbal contests, turned dangerous. Getting the best of an opponent is apparent in storytelling sessions where teller and audience interact without restraint, but other considerations come into play with the novel.

As many scholars have recognized, the transition from oral to written necessarily distances the author/teller of a tale from the reader/listener. They maintain that the written form loses the immediacy that registers audience response to teller;[14] it also eliminates the corrective, participatory option for audiences. I would contend that Morrison succeeds in closing that gap by creating a story that insists upon response from readers. She does that by politely assaulting our acceptance of certain cultural assumptions. Initially, she challenges beliefs about morality, about the absoluteness of good and evil; she has done so in all of her books, but the challenge is more intense in *Beloved*. Killing a child is certainly antithetical to the basic roots of our society, but Morrison forces us to ask again and again what we might have done under the circumstances. And she succeeds in making Sethe so simply human and American (the God-given right to motherhood, love of one's children, desire of a better life for them, love for freedom, nonconformity) that we cannot easily condemn her act even when we clearly do not condone it. The moral issues, therefore, lock us into participation in the novel. We are constantly encouraged to ask questions: "Is Sethe right to kill Beloved? What would I have done under the same circumstances? Are some conditions of life worse than death?"

Morrison also draws us into active intellectual participation in the novel by challenging our beliefs about ghosts. In western societies, where we are taught that the demise of the body is the end of being in this realm, it is difficult to conceive of a ghost taking up residence in someone's home for more than a year. Yet Morrison treats that as a probable occurrence and invites us to suspend disbelief long enough to see where she takes up with the possibility.

We are also drawn into the active suspense of the tale. We know very early on *what* happened, but we don't know *why* or *how*. We read on to learn the answers to those questions. I suspect that there is also a kind of voyeuristic enterprise at work; we read on to see if Morrison's imagination will overstep the bounds of good taste and provide us with some of the specifics of the atrocities of whites' inhumanity to blacks during slavery. The titillation in suspense is thus centered not only upon plot but also upon the very nature of what it means to be human, how slavery alters that status, and how characters—black and white—respond to that alteration.

Reading the novel is more than an intellectual experience; it is a physical one. This is especially true with many mothers of young children. They bring to bear their identification with Sethe, their hope that mother and child can somehow be saved even when they know that Morrison will not allow them that possibility. What they feel as mothers is wrapped up in their superficial bonding with Sethe as well as in their love for their own children. Reading the novel is also a physical experience for those who are naturally squeamish about violence and brutality and who suffer some physical discomfort as a result of reading about them.

The author/reader interaction for this text may be delayed, therefore, but it is only minimally less powerful than if Morrison were sitting in our living rooms telling us the story of Margaret Garner and the research she did to create Sethe's story. The emotions and reactions Morrison is able to evoke in us as she tells her tale place her in the best tradition of oral performers who weave magical and unusual worlds for us to contemplate, applaud, evaluate, condemn, or stare at in wonder. As Morrison herself has asserted, she wants her readers actively involved in her narratives. In order "faithfully to reflect the aesthetic tradition of Afro-American culture," she observes that group involvement is essential; "the text, if it is to take improvisation and audience participation into account, cannot be the authority—it should be the map. It should make a way for the reader (audience) to participate in the tale."15

For Morrison, then, storytelling is the form as well as the substance of her creation of *Beloved*. By developing her novel associatively, that is, by narratively duplicating the patterns of the mind, the way it gathers tidbits of experiences in *seemingly* random fashion, she achieves a structural effect that evokes the process of oral narration.[16] She thereby weds folklore to literature with a finesse uncharacteristic of most writers seeking such a blend. On close examination, it becomes clear that her novel is as much folklore as fiction, as much oral history as legend. In drawing upon folk forms, characters, styles, and ideas, Morrison provides an arena for scholars to work out some of the intricacies of the ties between folklore and literature.

When the Called Rescinds Her Calling

The power of words is manifested not only in storytelling events in *Beloved* but also in the specific textual verbal art of preaching—or, I should say, of calling people together for preachinglike sessions. As the convener of the sessions and the person anointed in such traditions, Baby Suggs is the closest the novel comes to a traditional Christian world view, and she does not allow it to come very close.

In African-American folk religion, preachers are "called" to their profession, that is, they get some sign from God that He needs their energies; accordingly, they become workers in His vineyard. While Baby Suggs is certainly in the tradition of being called, she points more to the folk imagination in her anointing than to biblical traditions. With the blessings of her community, she anoints herself out of her own experiences of suffering and shame, as well as out of appreciation for the fact that she can now call her body her own. She becomes "Baby Suggs, holy." Yet in another of Morrison's intertwinings of the secular and sacred traditions in African-American culture, Baby Suggs uses the *form* of religious rituals to impart secular advice.

Baby Suggs is a "woman of words," which puts her on par with the godly, creative power of words noted earlier. From the preaching tradition documented by James Weldon Johnson in *God's Trombones,* to the toast tradition depicting characters like Shine ("The Titanic"), to Muhammed Ali's diatribes against his opponents, to contemporary rap music, the man or woman of words has held a place of respect in African-American communities. Verbal artistry is an enviable, much-admired trait. The respect given Baby Suggs is attested to not only in the crowds that gather at the Clearing, but also in her house being a way station on the underground railroad and a general community center. The fact that her neighbors become angry with her later does not erase the significance of the position she has historically held among them.

In her interactions with the crowds that gather in the Clearing (on *Saturday* afternoons, not Sunday mornings), Baby Suggs draws upon the call-and-response tradition informing almost all of African-American folklore. And the responses to her invocations are so intense that they give substance to what in many instances has degenerated into polite reactions. Unlike an audience whooping politely in response to a blues singer, the blacks in the Clearing expend heartfelt emotions at Baby Sugg's direction. They cry, dance, and laugh in celebration of the humanity they have bestowed upon themselves (87–89). In telling them that "the only grace they could have was the grace they could imagine" (88), Baby Suggs solidifies the notion that their fate is in their own hands. Like their slave ancestors who took to their feet and the woods, they must carve out for themselves a space and a place to be. In the traditional inspirational guise of the master wordsmith, Baby Suggs blends the best of the sacred and the secular worlds. Two comments from Morrison seem especially relevant here: "It's always seemed to me that black people's grace has been with what they do with language."[17] Once asked what she considered distinctive or good about her fiction, Morrison replied: "The language. . . . It is the thing that black people love so much—the saying of words, holding them on the tongue, experimenting with them, playing with them. It's a love, a passion. Its function is like a preacher's: to make you stand up out of your seat, make you lose yourself and hear yourself."[18] With a few words, selectively chosen, Baby Suggs is able to offer a transcendent experience for those who believe in her voice.

Baby Suggs becomes a communal poet/artist, the gatherer of pieces of her neighbors' experiences and the shaper of those experiences into a communal statement. Her role is in many ways like that of a ritual priestess.[19] At appointed times, she summons the group, motivates it to action, and presides over its rites of exorcism; the pain and grief of slavery are temporarily removed in a communal catharsis. Having given up seven of her eight children to slavery, Baby Suggs knows what it means to have to put the heart back together after it has been torn apart valve by valve. As a medium who gives voice to unvoiced sentiments, Baby Suggs, like Claudia MacTeer, articulates what many of her people cannot. She is therefore participant and observer, the subject and the object of creativity. Transplanted to the soil of Cincinnati, Ohio, in the northward progression typical of blacks, Baby Suggs is the archetype for leadership among those sometimes drifting masses.

Her role in the community, therefore, makes her larger than life. She becomes hope-bringer and visionary, suggesting to her neighbors that the possibilities on the northern side of the Ohio River may indeed be realized. As a holy woman, a sane and articulate Shadrack, an unselfish Eva, Baby Suggs uses her heart to become the heart of the community. People expect her to be superior to them, yet they find it hard to forgive the "excess" of the feast she gives upon Sethe's arrival on Bluestone Road. They want their goddess to keep her feet of clay visible, so they wrongly interpret the feast event. It is a ritual of possibility, a rite of incorporation for Sethe, not a slap at their poverty.[20] It is a larger version of the Saturday afternoons, of what freedom can mean. Unfortunately, Baby Suggs's neighbors can acquiesce in the routine transcendent rites, but not in the elaborate one.

By denouncing her calling, Baby Suggs rejects the power of folk imagination, which has clearly served a constructive purpose for her and the entire community along Bluestone Road. Giving up means she denies the possibility for transcendence that is inherent in folk religion as well as in the blues. She therefore finally short-circuits tradition by lifting herself away from the bonds of caring; whereas Pecola was forced out, Baby Suggs leaves voluntarily, a choice that seems to undercut her role as an ancestor figure.[21] To give up voice for silence returns Baby Suggs to the passive, acquiescent role that defined her character during slavery and indeed makes her a slave to life rather than a master of it. Instead of remaining one of the shapers of the tales in the novel, of the destinies of its people, she chooses instead to become an object for contemplation by her neighbors and the readers. By abdicating her creative role, Baby Suggs descends from the legendary status that has defined her to become just another victim of slavery, a victimization all the more tragic because she clearly had the power not to adhere to such a fate.

The Myth of Sweet Home

In Paul Laurence Dunbar's "The Party" and in the popular folktale "Master's Gone to Philly Me York," the image of slavery is unlike that in most revisionist history books. Dunbar depicts black people as having a delightful ball to which four plantations of slaves have been invited. They have plenteous quantities of mouth-watering food, leisure time for games and dances, and the unmatched good humor to appreciate the wonderful lives they lead. "Master's Gone to Philly Me York" is a tale of classic slave wish fulfillment. The master goes away for a few days and leaves a faithful slave in charge with the expectation that the plantation business will be run as usual. Seizing his opportunity, the slave slaughters a number of the master's livestock, invites slaves from surrounding plantations for a barbecue, and assumes the throne of power the master previously held.[22]

The worlds depicted contrast strikingly to the beatings, separation of families, inadequate diet, and other atrocities that characterized slavery, yet in concept they bear striking similarity to the world created on the Garner plantation in *Beloved;* there are no beatings, food is plentiful, and freedom of judgment and action are not only allowed but encouraged. Sweet Home—before the arrival of schoolteacher—is every slave's dream of how that intolerable condition can be made tolerable. Women are not raped; men are not beaten like mules; and Garner is willing to allow slaves to hire their time and purchase their families and themselves.

From a relative perspective, the place is as sweet as its name. In remembering what it was before schoolteacher arrived, Sethe and other of its inhabitants imbue it with an aura of myth, of folktale larger than life, and the persons who inhabit it in turn become larger than life.[23] Schoolteacher's appearance is significant in contributing to this image, for as he destroys what once was, that former state is highlighted even more in the memories of those who knew it earlier. The mythical Sweet Home, then, assumes such proportions in direct relation to the memories of atrocities that spoiled its paradisiacal state. And these memories in turn shape the narrative structure of the novel. Defying linearity, memory and imagination combine to give an oral quality to the telling of the tale, just as they give a folkloristic bent to the perception of characters and the territory on which they reside.

Garner has been very much god in that paradise of Sweet Home. Like Eva Peace, he appropriates to himself the power of naming as the tangible symbol of his godhead; he goes further than Eva, however, for where she was content to name individuals, he names a species. He can call slaves men in the world that he has created, in his plantation paradise, just as Valerian Street can invite Son to dinner in the world in *Tar Baby* where he plays with shaping everyone's life. Before the satanic schoolteacher arrives, Garner has clearly given unprecedented license to the slaves and has won the enmity of his neighbors. In designating his slaves men, he has violated the boundaries of master/slave interaction (most of his fellow slaveholders consider their charges less than human), and he has set himself apart in a world where the maintenance of the system depends upon conformity from slaves as well as from masters.

Garner's unorthodox position, though, elevates him to legendary status with his neighbors as well as with his slaves. His forced physical contests with other white men are a constant reminder to them that he is different and a constant challenge to himself to live up to the physical prowess implied in that difference. As the following exchange illustrates, Garner seeks challenges from his neighbors:

> "Y'all got boys," [Garner] told them. "Young boys, old boys, picky boys, stroppin boys. Now at Sweet Home, my niggers is men every one of em. Bough em thataway, raised em thataway. Men every one."
>
> "Beg to differ, Garner. Ain't no nigger men."
>
> "Not if you scared, they ain't." Garner's smile was wide. "But if you a man yourself, you'll want your niggers to be men too."
>
> "I wouldn't have no nigger men round my wife."
>
> It was the reaction Garner loved and waited for. "Neither would I," he said. "Neither would I," and there was always a pause before the neighbor, or stranger, or peddler, or brother-in-law or whoever it was got the meaning. Then a fierce argument, sometimes a fight, and Garner came home bruised and pleased, having demonstrated one more time what a real Kentuckian was: one tough enough and smart enough to make and call his own niggers men. (10–11)

By implying that slaves designated as men are capable of violating the sexual taboo between the races, perhaps with the consent or invitation of the white woman, Garner marginalizes himself from white society, then reclaims his place in it by showing what a *man* he is—rugged, individualistic, capable of insult, and capable of defending himself physically against the implications of his insult.

The man who makes a name for himself among his neighbors, therefore, is as much legendary to them for his physical prowess as for what they avow as his stupidity in not treating his slaves as they treat theirs. A man capable of broad gestures, such as escorting Baby Suggs across the river to Ohio when Halle's purchase of her is complete, Garner is a dangerous enigma to his neighbors. In the tradition of legendary perpetuation, they elevate and/or kill that which they do not understand.[24]

Garner is not the only larger-than-life personality at Sweet Home. The slaves and their interactions with Garner as well as with each other are equally legendary. Sethe, for example, is able to experience a period of sexual abstinence and courtship undocumented in the annals of slave history. In leaving the young virgin to herself, the Sweet Home men exhibit almost superhuman control. Other than Sixo, they have no human sexual outlet. For them to allow Sethe the year it takes for her to choose one of them is perhaps reflective of a larger definition of manhood than that Garner has assigned to them. They elect to be human in a world that usually gives them permission to act like dogs.

The respect Paul A, Paul F, Paul D, Sixo, and Halle show to Sethe and what that means within self-imposed definitions of manhood is comparable to how Sethe later responds to being a mother. In spite of that larger world around her that has attempted to usurp her status as mother, she vows to remain one. In her actions, and in those of the men toward her, slaves show that masters cannot ultimately control the values of interaction among and between them.

These dual definitions of manhood (Garner's and the black men's themselves) enhance their legendary status, as do their individual actions. Sixo, for example, borders on folk characterization in several ways. His name sets him apart just as the repetition of names singles out the Pauls. But Sixo has an aura of mystery surrounding him comparable to many heroes of legend. He has mysterious origins; indeed, others refer to him as "the wild man" (11). He engages in solitary rituals that partly explain his unusual behavior: "Sixo went among trees at night. For dancing, he said, to keep his bloodlines open, he said. Privately, alone, he did it. None of the rest of them had seen him at it, but they could imagine it, and the picture they pictured made them eager to laugh at him—in daylight, that is, when it was safe" (25). His "flame-red tongue" and "indigo" (21) face mark him in the way that conjurers of tradition have had some distinguishing feature. He exhibits a kinship to the natural world and respects the spirits of the dead, especially those of Native Americans, whose permission he requests for use of a deserted lodge for a rendezvous (24). He chooses silence over language and gifts of interaction (baking sweet potatoes for the Pauls and Halle) over physical expressions. He executes single-minded devotion to nearly superhuman feats, such as walking thirty miles in between his field obligations to see Patsy, who becomes known as the Thirty-Mile Woman.

Sixo's solitude, occasional preference for nature over human beings, unusual behavior, and aura of derring-do bring to mind such folk figures as Big Sixteen and Stagolee. His spirit cannot be conquered even if his body is destroyed. He is the ultimate man, as illustrated in his laughing during the burning death perpetrated against him by schoolteacher and his nephews. Schoolteacher may whip him, may burn him, may kill him, but Sixo still triumphs. He triumphs physically in laughing rather than howling in pain when he is lynched, and he triumphs spiritually in knowing that Patsy is pregnant with his child. His yell of "Seven-O" (226) as he is dying makes clear that this breed of man, Garner or no Garner, cannot be contained by a system called slavery.

And his howling laughter—as if he is on his way to better things than the demise of his body—links him to the themes that Morrison develops with Beloved. This plane of reality may be intolerable, and others may be equally intolerable, but perhaps there is one (where the blind horsemen of Isle des Chevaliers reside?) where Sixo can fully exploit those parts of his personality that we see only in glimpses.

Patsy's nickname, like Sixo's, makes her equally larger than life. By her designation as the "Thirty-Mile Woman," her indication of value becomes greater than that assessed by the slave system under which she lives. She is the possibility for family ("Sixo was hell-bent to make [a family] with the Thirty-Mile Woman" [219]) and freedom, concepts antithetical to slavery but clearly the guiding forces in the lives of those enslaved. With this value attached to her, it is somewhat surprising to learn that the Thirty-Mile Woman is a girl of fourteen—a prize, certainly, during slavery, but the elevation of her before we know her age leads us to anticipate something more, perhaps that she is a wise older woman, capable of extraordinary feats. Her ordinariness highlights the process of transformation into legend that takes place in the novel.

Sethe also assumes her share of the legendary status of Sweet Home residents. It is difficult for most people to understand how she managed to escape from the Garner plantation without provisions and six months pregnant. There must have been something superhuman, if not otherworldly, in her determination. That quality is reflected in her eyes, which are frequently depicted as being totally black to indicate how absorbed Sethe can become in the tasks or memories at hand. It is a quality that Sethe exhibits in her insistence that she is a mother in a world that would declare otherwise. She lives that determination, thereby giving Denver a chance to see her legendary attributes in the next generation. Denver's image of Sethe is that of a "queenly woman" who controls herself, responds calmly to emergencies, and stares everything, including death, in the face:

> The one who never looked away, who when a man got stomped to death by a mare right in front of Sawyer's restaurant did not look away; and when a sow began eating her own litter did not look away then either. And when the baby's spirit picked up Here Boy and slammed him into the wall hard enough to break two of his legs and dislocated his eye, so hard he went into convulsions and chewed up his tongue, still her mother had not

looked away. She had taken a hammer, knocked the dog unconscious, wiped away the blood and saliva, pushed his eye back in his head and set his leg bones. (12)

Legendary status becomes, to some extent, the nature of survival for slaves and newly freed blacks. To desire to live as a free person was in itself something extraordinary, and to reach that objective—through one's own initiative—was beyond the imaginations of most slaves; those who did so could only be viewed as larger than life.

Not only are people from Sweet Home made into legends, but inanimate things and animals are as well. Just as Sweet Home is almost a tangible memory to Sethe, so are specific places and trees on the plantation; the very air is special, almost bewitched.

> [T]here was Sweet Home rolling, rolling, rolling out before her eyes, and although there was not a leaf on that farm that did not make her want to scream, it rolled itself out before her in shameless beauty. It never looked as terrible as it was and it made her wonder if hell was a pretty place too. Fire and brimstone all right, but hidden in lacy groves. Boys hanging from the most beautiful sycamores in the world. It shamed her—remembering the wonderful soughing trees rather than the boys. Try as she might to make it otherwise, the sycamores beat out the children every time and she could not forgive her memory for that. (6)

Brother, one of the trees, not only provided shade (21, 224) for the Pauls, Halle, and Sixo, but it was anthropomorphized into one of them. The tree became a brother, fit partner in conversation as Miss Jane Pittman talked to trees in Ernest Gaines's *The Autobiography of Miss Jane Pittman* (1974). When Paul D is taken away to prison, his last look is toward Brother (106); in prison, he cultivates another tree, a small sapling, unlike the "old, wide and beckoning" (221) Brother, but serving a purpose nonetheless. Brother is the objectification of love, a tangible substitute for the absence of women at Sweet Home, as well as a method of communing with forces larger than Paul D. The sapling in Alfred, Georgia, is a way for Paul D to focus on something to love just a little bit in order to retain some semblance of his humanity. The value Paul D places on trees is clear in this elevating conclusion he draws about Brother and Sixo at one point: "Now *there* was a man, and *that* was a tree" (22).

Mister, the rooster at Sweet Home, is an objectification of freedom and a metaphor for manhood. As the rooster swaggers around the barnyard, strutting for the hens present, he has more freedom and control over his

existence than Paul D. As that freedom and sexual interplay get inter-
preted, Mister is also more "man" than Paul D, more human—in the sense
of having a separate, individual identity—than human beings who are
slaves. In popular definitions of maleness, Mister is ultimately the "cock"
that Paul D can never become. It is that irony that makes the sight of Mister so painful for Paul D when he is wearing the iron bit in his mouth.
Memory for Paul D is the image of a rooster who is freer than he has been,
a rooster who has been helped out of his shell because he had been abandoned by his mother. That failing notwithstanding, Mister had reached—
and perhaps extended—his full potential as a male member of his species,
something that has been unavailable to Paul D. Mister established his place
in the barnyard lore by whipping "everything in the yard" (72).

The particularly poignant scene of Mister sitting on a tub and gazing at
Paul D when he is wearing the bit is an occasion when inequality is made
tangible and when spatial positioning signals to Paul D how incredibly devalued he is.

> "Mister, he looked so . . . free. Better than me. Stronger, tougher.
> Son a bitch couldn't even get out the shell by hisself but he was still king
> and I was . . ." Paul D stopped and squeezed his left hand with his right.
> He held it that way long enough for it and the world to quiet down and let
> him go on.
>
> "Mister was allowed to be and stay what he was. But I wasn't allowed to
> be and stay what I was. Even if you cooked him you'd be cooking a rooster
> named Mister. But wasn't no way I'd ever be Paul D again, living or dead.
> Schoolteacher changed me. I was something else and that something was
> less than a chicken sitting in the sun on a tub." (72)

As he relates his memories of Sweet Home to Sethe, Paul D is remembering Mister's metaphysical position in that world as much as he is remembering a neglected chicken carving out a space for himself. Mister had been
able to compete on an equal level with the other roosters in the barnyard;
Paul D is forced outside the arena of competition, without the ability even
to respond to those who are manipulating him.

Mister, like Brother, acquires a quasi-human status for Paul D when he
describes the world that has had such an impact upon his life. As memory
gets meshed with imagination, it perhaps looms larger than fact, and it
leads more naturally to the shaping of legends. Imagination also serves to
explain the demise of Sweet Home. Others may claim that Garner had a
heart attack or a stroke and was brought home dead on his horse. Sixo
maintains that he was killed ("Sixo had a knowing tale about everything.

Including Mr. Garner's stroke, which he said was a shot in his ear put there by a jealous neighbor" [219]), precisely for those traits that identified him as being special. No longer able to tolerate his nonconformity, one of his neighbors had simply shot him in a ritualized restoration of the status quo. Ironically, the shooting reduces Garner to the status of a slave in that his life becomes just as devalued. In suggesting that Sixo's explanation for Garner's death is the preferred one, Morrison consigns Sweet Home and its people to a land where reality is indeed large enough to contain myth and legend.

Notes

1. The volume depends upon stereotypical conceptions of women, but it is nonetheless an interesting historical recapitulation of traditional perceptions of femaleness; Wolfgang Lederer, *The Fear of Women* (New York: Harcourt, Brace, Jovanovich, 1968).

2. Daryl C. Dance, *Shuckin' and Jivin': Folklore from Contemporary Black Americans* (Bloomington: Indiana University Press, 1978), 56–57.

3. Gloria Naylor and Toni Morrison, "A Conversation," *Southern Review* 21 (July 1985): 593. While this comment could apply to the writing practice Morrison gained in her previous novels in preparation for writing the difficult tale of a mother killing her child, it could also apply to touching briefly on the unorthodox ideas that would inform the substance of *Beloved.* See pp. 583–84 of the above interview for Morrison's discussion of the two incidents that shaped the idea for *Beloved:* that of Margaret Garner, the slave woman who preferred death rather than slavery for her children, and that of an eighteen-year-old dead girl photographed in Harlem by James Van der Zee; the girl had sacrificed her own life in order to allow the jealous lover who had shot her sufficient time to escape the scene of the crime.

4. See "Daid Aaron," in Langston Hughes and Arna Bontemps, eds., *The Book of Negro Folklore* (New York: Dodd, Mead and Co., 1958), 175–78.

5. Jean Strouse, "Toni Morrison's Magic," *Newsweek* (30 March 1981): 54.

6. Jean Toomer, *Cane* (New York: Boni and Liveright, 1923), 16.

7. Indeed, some of the comments that Charles Scruggs makes about desire in *Song of Solomon* could also apply to *Beloved.* See "The Nature of Desire in Toni Morrison's *Song of Solomon,*" *Arizona Quarterly* 38 (Winter 1982): 311–35.

8. While Terry Otten also recognizes Beloved's demonic nature and the fact that she is "an evil thing," he asserts that she may be "a Christ figure come to save," "the 'beloved' one come to reclaim Sethe and from whom Sethe seeks forgiveness." See Otten, *The Crime of Innocence in the Fiction of Toni Morrison* (Columbia: Univ. of Missouri Press, 1989), 84, 85. In *Toni Morrison* (Boston: Twayne Publishers, 1990) Wilfred D.

Samuels and Clenora Hudson-Weems, assert that Paul D is a Christ figure (134). Instead of this designation, with its attendant connotation of absolute goodness, perhaps it would be more productive to view Paul D in the ambivalent mode of some of Morrison's earlier heroes, such as Milkman and Son.

9. For a discussion of the multiple voices and characters Beloved represents in the novel, see Deborah Horvitz, "Nameless Ghosts: Possession and Dispossession in *Beloved,*" *Studies in American Fiction* 17 (Autumn 1989): 157–67. On the other hand, Elizabeth B. House, in "Toni Morrison's Ghost: The Beloved Who Is Not Beloved," *Studies in American Fiction* 18 (Spring 1990): 17–26, argues that Beloved is not a ghost but merely a runaway who has suffered the blights of slavery. These in turn intersect coincidentally with Sethe's relationship to her deceased daughter.

10. Otten comments that "in attacking [Bodwin], Sethe achieves an exorcism; in saving Beloved by offering herself, she at last frees herself from the demonic presence that will not release her from the past. Once Sethe acts to save Beloved, retestifying to her love, the ghost disappears"; *The Crime of Innocence,* 94.

11. See Wayland D. Hand, ed., *The Frank C. Brown Collection of North Carolina Folklore,* vol. 7 (Durham: Duke University Press, 1964), 144, 145, 147. Dog ghosts are also painted in the lore as being some of the most benign spirits humans can encounter. See J. Mason Brewer, *Dog Ghosts and Other Texas Negro Folk Tales* (Austin: Univ. of Texas Press, 1958).

12. See Hughes and Bontemps, "De Ways of De Wimmens," in *The Book of Negro Folklore,* 130–35, and Hurston, "Why Women Always Take Advantage of Men," in Zora Neale Hurston, *Mules and Men* (Bloomington: Indiana University Press, 1935/1978), 33–38.

13. See Hughes and Bontemps, eds. *The Book of Negro Folklore.*

14. See David A. Stanley, "The Personal Narrative and the Personal Novel: Folklore as Frame and Structure for Literature," *Southern Folklore Quarterly* 43 (1979): 39–62.

15. Toni Morrison, "Memory, Creation, and Writing," *Thought* 59 (Dec. 1984): 388–89.

16. Earlier in her career, Morrison commented that she worked to achieve that effect in her work: "To make the story appear oral, meandering, effortless, spoken . . . is what's important"; see her "Rootedness: The Ancestor as Foundation," in *Black Women Writers (1950–1980): A Critical Edition,* ed. Mari Evans, 341.

17. Mel Watkins, "Talk with Toni Morrison," *New York Times Book Review,* Sept. 11, 1977, 48.

18. Thomas LeClair, "'The Language Must Not Sweat': A Conversation with Toni Morrison," *The New Republic* 184 (March 21, 1981): 27.

19. Samuels and Hudson-Weems also refer to Baby Suggs as a "ritual priestess," which also brings to mind secular rather than Christian connotations; *Toni Morrison,* 117.

20. For a discussion of the importance of such rites, see Arnold van Gennep, *The Rites of Passage* (1908; rpt., Chicago: Univ. of Chicago Press, 1960).

21. Of course it could be argued that Baby Suggs retains a somewhat legendary, positive effect upon Denver, who uses memories of her as a touchstone of sanity when she contemplates the circumstances at 124 Bluestone Road.

22. "Master's Gone to Philly-Me-York," in Richard M. Dorson, *American Negro Folktales* (Greenwich, CT: Fawcett, 1967), 151–52, and Hurston, *Mules and Men*, 88–89. Paul Laurence Dunbar, "The Party," in *The Collected Poems of Paul Laurence Dunbar* (New York: Dodd, Mead, 1967), 134–38.

23. Morrison has defended this tendency by commenting: "Sometimes I have been accused—or complimented, I'm not sure—of writing about people who are bigger than life. I was always befuddled by that observation, and I still am a little bit. But I felt that I was writing about people who were as big as life, not bigger than. Life is very big. There are people who try to make it small, safe, unexamined. If some of my characters are as big as the life they have, they may seem enormous exaggerations, but [only to] a reader whose sense of life is more diminished than mine"; in Amanda Smith's interview, "Toni Morrison," *Publishers Weekly*, Aug. 21, 1987, 51.

24. Terry Otten adopts Hannah Arendt's term in calling the Garners "nice Nazis": "The Garners were kindhearted people but also participants in the system—nice Nazis, but Nazis nonetheless. By their accommodation of slavery, they made possible the prototypal evil of schoolteacher"; *The Crime of Innocence*, 86.

Remodeling the Model Home in
Uncle Tom's Cabin and *Beloved*

LORI ASKELAND

◆　　◆　　◆

> One hundred years later, the Negro is still lan-
> guishing in the corners of American society and
> finds himself an exile in his own land.
> —Martin Luther King, Jr.,
> "I Have a Dream"

WITHIN THE LABELS "structuralism" and "poststructuralism" resides an architectural view of language and meaning. Even when such views are deconstructive ones, building and dwelling metaphors inevitably inhabit these critical discourses—as it simultaneously becomes more difficult to establish clear boundaries and build firm walls. Thus, not surprisingly, the critical theories being debated and reworked in English departments also wormed their ways into the walls and offices of architecture departments. Amos Rapoport, for example, became one of the founders of environment-behavior studies during the 1960s and 1970s, helping to broaden the study of architecture to include "vernacular" (or "folk") architecture as well as the canon of buildings designed and conceived by professional architects. Rapoport finds that as social and cultural institutions buildings are related to language because "both express the cognitive process of making distinctions, reflecting the tendency of the human mind to impose an order on the world through schemata and naming." He insists that "[o]ne can, therefore, look at built environments as physical expressions of schemata and cognitive domains: *environments are thought before they are built.*"[1]

As proponents of the "Cult of Domesticity" during the mid-nineteenth century, Harriet Beecher Stowe and Catharine Beecher were clearly aware of the power of ordering that comes from the creation of a model home.

Hence, in their "textbook" for young homemakers, *The American Woman's Home,* the sisters argue that the "employments" of housewives not only are difficult and deserving of "honor and remuneration" but also compose the "sacred duties of the family state."[2] As females, however, they were conscious of the vulnerability of Victorian women, whose employments were usually uncompensated and whose domains were always conceived, designed, and owned by males. This double awareness fits with Arthur C. Danto's recent reflection on the linguistic roots of the words we use to describe our dwelling places. He notes that the word "domain" shares a root with a family of English terms that refer back to the Latin *domus* and asserts that through these words "the house speaks to us precisely as the symbol of rulership, ownership, mastery, power." Rapoport's "cognitive domain," then, views the built environment only as an expression of human domination, looking beyond the all too human need for shelter, which Danto relates to the Old English root of the word "house." This root, *hus,* was "cognate with *huden*—to hide, shelter, conceal, cover"—which shows us "the fragile, threatened, exposed side of our self-image as dwellers: beings that need protection, a place to crawl into . . . and our walls announce our vulnerability."[3] Thus, by conceiving of a location as being "ours," we cognitively create a domain, an area of power, while in the back of our minds we may have "housed" the knowledge of how arbitrary and fragile that power always is. For the Victorian woman, this fragility was emphasized by the fact that she did not even own the walls she needed for shelter, let alone power.

By using what power women did have, Stowe and Beecher desired to increase the individual power and status of women, mothers in particular, and thereby to increase the strength of the family by creating a "family state," that is, a domain as big as the country. Numerous critics have discussed the influence of the ideology of domesticity on *Uncle Tom's Cabin,* with most viewing it as a method of female empowerment. As Elizabeth Ammons puts it, Stowe's radical version of the domestic ideal converts "essentially repressive concepts of femininity into a positive (and activist) alternative system of values in which woman figures not merely as the moral superior of man, his inspirer, but as a model for him," while she remains in a separate domestic sphere.[4] The vulnerability of this domain, however, must not be overlooked; the house remains a sheltered "feminine" space, that is, a *hus* for true spiritual growth, which by virtue of its enclosure in the "masculine" domain of materialism and commercialism, always remains in danger of being invaded and corrupted by it.

Beginning in the Beecher sisters' era, Gwendolyn Wright's *Moralism and the Model Home: Domestic Architecture and Cultural Conflict in Chicago, 1873–1913* traces housing reform movements across the country and explains the importance of "schemata and cognitive structures" for the Victorian American culture she is confronting. She notes that "the word 'model' evokes an abstract, artificial construction, following ideal laws, against which ambiguous and complex social situations are judged," yet argues that Victorian reformers "envisioned their model homes as one means for bringing order and control to what seemed dangerously volatile social conditions."[5] Implicitly, then, the "model home" represented both shelter from and dominance over the chaos of the world. As several scholars have noted, the kitchen was one place where Stowe and Beecher in particular believed that order and control could be brought to bear on society's problems.[6] Wright, in fact, calls *The American Woman's Home* "[t]he most important book" for rationalizing kitchen work-space and praises it for featuring "revolutionary approaches to housework and layout." Yet, despite the widespread popularity of the book and attempts by middle-class housewives to achieve the sisters' ideal of the "selfless, self-sufficient housewife," Wright notes that "builders did not follow through on the innovative proposals of the two authors."[7] Thus, because their domain was always undermined by their need for shelter in the larger masculine domain, Victorian women were often forced to enact the reverse of Rapoport's dictum: to "think" their domain, create a mental ideal of it, after it had already been built, and thereby remodel as best they could.

It is my contention that Toni Morrison's *Beloved* sets itself up as a remodeling of *Uncle Tom's Cabin* that examines this ideology and revises it in a way that avoids reification of a patriarchal power structure. The parallels in the texts are numerous. *Beloved* is set in part in the same place and during the same period as *Uncle Tom's Cabin:* Sweet Home's northern Kentucky must be near the location of the Shelby plantation, and both novels' initial action represents a response to the Fugitive Slave Act. Moreover, *Beloved's* main action takes place near Cincinnati in 1873, which was the Beechers' home from 1832 to 1849—a significant factor in Stowe's writing of *Uncle Tom's Cabin,* since it was there that she gained firsthand experience of recently "freed" slaves. The mid-1870s also saw both the waning of the housing reform movements in the North as houses served more and more materialistic goals and the "reconstruction" of the patriarchal structure of the South. Finally, both novelists use and remodel traces of slave history to create narratives that will also remodel the ideologies that dominate the country's power structure. Yet both novels remain haunted by the figures that represent that power.

The epigraph to chapter 32 of *Uncle Tom's Cabin* provides what is to be our introduction to Simon Legree's house: "The dark places of the earth are full of the habitations of cruelty."[8] As Theodore Hovet has noted, the fall from spirituality to materialism could not be better symbolized in *Uncle Tom's Cabin* than by Simon Legree's significantly kitchenless, utterly materialistic "anti-home."[9] Moreover, the enigmatic, ghostly character of Cassy as the haunter of this house has also recently received careful treatment from a number of readers. In her study "The Haunted Houses of Lyman Beecher, Henry Ward Beecher, and Harriet Beecher Stowe," Karen Halttunen suggests that Stowe's application remodels her father's and brother's ghostly metaphors by focusing on the psychological haunting suffered by evildoers like Legree, while incorporating her ideal of domestic social reform.[10] Halttunen's reading builds on Gilbert and Gubar's paradigm of the "madwoman in the attic" and suggests that Cassy both reforms and is reformed by her environment—which is exactly the dream of the housing reform movement. In the language of my paradigm, then, because Cassy exploits the madwoman in the attic story to suit her needs, she is empowered to remodel the attic into a "model home," centered on a motherly love for Emmeline. We see her transformed from a madwoman capable of murdering her children into a woman who can transform a *hus,* her temporary shelter from the wrath of Legree, into a matriarchal *domus*—complete with makeshift kitchen, sitting room, and bed—by which she gains power over her utterly masculine, materialistic "master."

Regardless of this power, however, Cassy's domain remains in the corner of a house owned by white men and in a religion controlled by white men.[11] Just as "a vestige of the rough logs" of Uncle Tom's cabin can always be seen beneath its beflowered exterior, so a vestige of slavery and male-dominated culture can be seen beneath even the most idyllic utopias in the book. Stowe dreams of reforming society, and even the world via George Harris's African mission, on the basis of Rachel Halliday's model home—the center of a utopian Quaker community where men are peripheral figures who are at their best when off "in the corner, engaged in the antipatriarchal operation of shaving" (146). Yet this ideal community is only a very small corner of the slaveholding union; like Cassy's attic in Simon Legree's house, this community represents for the slaves a safe but only temporary shelter from the domain of the larger community. It houses an idealized matriarchal domain, but a domain that has its boundaries drawn for it by the larger culture—boundaries it admittedly haunts and subverts by its presence. Further, although Rachel's "Hadn't thee better?" is obeyed as a command, one wonders if the domain that she has created is tied up in her existence as primary power in the home. That is, if "everything rests on her presence," as it does on Mr. Garner's in *Beloved's* Sweet Home, is a matriarchy all that different from a patriarchy?

Likewise, although George Harris is supposed to employ Stowe's ideas on a global level to lift Africa out of the corners and into the living room of the house that is humanity, one cannot help wondering if Africa is but another, more faraway corner of this male-dominated society and Stowe's matriarchal world, a corner that does not reform the house because, as William L. Andrews asserts, it "reconcile[s] black progress with black alienation without threatening the white status quo."[12] Instead, it becomes a place to send a strong, fighting black man who does not fit with Stowe's "romantic racialism," a perspective that makes Africans, by virtue of race, "affectionate, magnanimous, and forgiving" (446)—just as women are, by virtue of gender.[13] One must not ignore the importance of Stowe's feminized remodeling of Christianity, as Elizabeth Ammons's recognition and appreciation of the ideal of the feminized Christ in Tom and Eva has demonstrated. Nevertheless, a trace of the Christian father-God pervades the Quaker community, George's plans for Africa, and the language of the entire book and continues to evoke the patriarchal ideal of church as bride to the masculine God. George, and even Africa itself, require an "essentially Christian" development; his self-sufficient, inventive, and rebellious "Anglo" self must be claimed by God and subjected to his magnanimous "African" self.

The progressive transformations of Cassy's threatening power and pride further demonstrate the delimiting power of this trace of patriarchal Christianity on the characters of Africans and women. First, to make a woman who has murdered her children "safe" for this Christian and domestic perspective, she must be portrayed as slightly mad. Hence, although she has the power and strength of a male field hand, that power is ascribed to "the debil and all his angels," as Sambo and Quimbo put it (363). She must operate "by magic," and her eyes must be "wildly," as well as "mournfully," despairing (360). Then, in the chapter entitled "The Quadroon's Story," Cassy plays a combination Good Samaritan and Mary Magdalene to Tom's Jesus—he, wounded, accepts her ointments gratefully and listens to her tale of woe without casting any stones. In this role, Cassy, like the biblical prostitute, considers herself a "lower" slave than Tom can ever be, because of the sexual and maternal fall that she describes in her subsequent slave narrative.[14] In that story, even to justify her very motherly violence against the men taking away her son, she must say that "something in [her] head snapped" (374). When she concludes her story with the murder of her own son, her voice is full of a "beguiling" force that affects even the pure, wounded Tom—and an "insane light glance[s] in her heavy black eyes" as she plots the murder of Legree (376). Just as George's natural "African" qualities have been possessed by the aggressive "Anglo" ones, making him too dangerous for Stowe's vision, so Cassy's natural, domestic female self has been "possessed" by slavery and made strong and mad.

But this possession does not end with slavery. When Cassy is united with and enabled to "sink into the bosom of the family," Eliza's "steady, consistent piety" must transform even the strong maternal force that Cassy redeveloped in the attic with Emmeline into the "gentle, trusting" love of a grandmother. Her maternal love might still be judged too powerful, or "too thick," as Paul D will put it to Sethe in *Beloved*. After all, like Sethe's, Cassy's motherlove has led to the attempted murder of a white man and to the murder of her own child. Thus, her "shattered and weary mind" must be so weakened by Eliza's mothering that Cassy is able to "[yield] at once, and with her whole soul, to every good influence, and bec[o]me a devout and tender Christian" (443). This Christianity, however, has a masculine force reminiscent of Cassy's old masters who "can do anything with a woman when [they've] got her children" (374). Her claim to herself has been taken once again by a God whose benevolent force haunts *Uncle Tom's Cabin* like the ghost of Simon Legree.

The trace of God's patriarchal power is made most overt at Tom's death. Although George has "come to buy" Tom and "take him home," God is, at least in part, the traditional big slaveholder in the sky, who, Tom says, " 's bought me and is going to take me home,—and I long to go. Heaven is better than Kintuck" (429). Heaven is here another, if better, slaveholding state than Kentucky, presided over by a more benevolent and more permanent master than George or Arthur Shelby. At the end of the novel, George Shelby remains a lesser version of God as "The Liberator," even though he operates in the domestic, feminine scheme of his mother's moral, familial suasion. He now will teach his newly freed slaves what it means to be free, and he reappropriates Uncle Tom's cabin as a symbolic reminder for the slaves of what it means to be a good Christian servant (451). A double realm of masculine domination surrounds Stowe's brave movement toward the increased "global" power of domesticity: the ever-present power of the masculine state that has infiltrated even some of her ideal matriarchies, with which the even more overarching power of God's slave-owning kingdom operates in complicity.

Although parts have been remodeled, the house is ultimately owned and haunted by a patriarchal figure who cannot be easily overcome, even while He, like Simon Legree, is invaded, subverted, and haunted by memories of a feminine, domestic ideal of motherhood and spirituality. Stowe's scheme still depends on racial and gender distinctions that cannot stand up to the strength of a character like George, who must be shipped off to an African corner, or Cassy, whose character (like George's) must be quickly subverted and made into the docile domain of a patriarchal God whose claim problematizes the philosophy upon which *Uncle Tom's Cabin* is founded. Ultimately, because it still maintains the metaphor of being "bought," privileges white slaveowners as a class over their slaves, and exalts the duty of self-sacrifice, Stowe's Christianity, in the words of Harriet A. Jacobs, will be "too much like slavery" for *Beloved*'s Baby Suggs. It cries out for her further remodeling.

Beloved offers an exemplary Victorian model home, Sweet Home, as a critique of a system covered with the "bignonias" of the domestic ideal but built of the "rough logs" of slavery. Mrs. Garner is presented as a self-sacrificing, motherly woman. She works hard, humming alongside the quiet Baby Suggs without complaint. Admittedly, the crippled, elderly Baby Suggs, having already seen the worst of slavery, still recognizes it as "a special kind of slavery," but slavery just the same: "It's better here, but I'm not."[15] Sethe, however, was young and motherless when she arrived. She loves Mrs. Garner like a mother, so that even after eighteen years of "freedom" she can insist: "I tended her like I would have tended my own mother if she needed me . . . I couldn't have done more for that woman than I could my own ma'am . . . and I'd have stayed with her until she got well or died" (200).[16] The limits of the True Woman's domain, however, become clear upon Mr. Garner's death: a "decent" white woman cannot live alone on a farm with no one but slaves. Worse still, her loving, Rachel-Halliday-like intercession on behalf of the sexually abused Sethe results in the severe beating that puts the tree on Sethe's back. The familial unity and love she shared with Sethe, like that advocated by the Beecher sisters, has difficult impediments to surmount because everything still rests on the male head of the household.

After all, like Arthur Shelby, Mr. Garner is a "man of humanity" who allows his slaves to be "men": to make decisions, to use guns, and, in Halle's case, to buy his mother's freedom. His death, however, reveals the fragility of the male slaves' "domain" on Sweet Home, and indeed that of all such domains—especially those dependent upon the benevolence of a master. Paul D wonders "how much difference there really was between before schoolteacher and after," noting that "Garner called and announced them as men—but only on Sweet Home, and by his leave. Was he naming what he saw or creating what he did not?" (220). The limits of their domain and the degree to which they had been isolated in Mr. Garner's "wonderful lie" become clear in Paul D's question. They were, under Mr. Garner as under schoolteacher, simply "the defined" as men, and never the definers of themselves.

Moreover, despite its northern locale, 124 Bluestone is haunted as much by the "patriarchal institution" of slavery as by the ghost named Beloved, who is seemingly Sethe's murdered baby.[17] When we first encounter 124 Bluestone it is "spiteful," and Sethe and Denver are the only ones able to carry on life there.[18] But as with Cassy's haunting of Simon Legree, the overt haunting—the tables that move, the sound of a baby crawling up the stairs, and the fight with the house that Paul D seems to win upon his arrival—overshadows the presence of the benevolent, but nonetheless white, male owner of the space, Edward Bodwin, whose presence is for the most part covert.

But near the end of the novel we enter Bodwin's mind as he drives his carriage toward 124. He has not been to the house since he was three years old, but he remembers a few things—"that the cooking was done behind the house, the well was forbidden to play near, and that women died there: his mother, grandmother, an aunt and an older sister before he was born" (259). These women, who probably gave him such rules about where to play and did at least part of the cooking, and who were probably strong, domestic women who had a certain amount of rule in the home and the kitchen in the back, all died, inexplicably, in this strange house. Morrison leaves this enigmatic fact unexplained and undeveloped. Was it their deaths that forced the men to move away while one young daughter, herself eventually a spinster, was left? Is that why they now rent it out to "negroes"? Why does this haunted house use up women like Simon Legree uses up and throws away slaves?

More substantial than these questions, however, is Bodwin's seeming indifference to their deaths. They cling to his re-memory, but, despite the disturbing nature of this loss—the dissolution of the female core of the family—he still feels something "deeper and sweeter" about the house than about the surrounding farmland. His main concern is now remembering where he once buried things there: "Precious things he wanted to protect. As a child every item he owned was available and accountable to his family. Privacy was an adult indulgence, but when he got to be one, he seemed not to need it" (259). Bodwin developed this love for the place not through his mother's love and sacrifice but by appropriating certain long-forgotten spaces. The housing reformers believed it important that children develop such a sense of "home-feeling." Historian Clifford E. Clark, for example, quotes one reformer supporting an argument for separate rooms: "satisfying this home-feeling will also contribute immensely to [the children's] love of the homestead. Without it, it is only their *father's* home, not theirs. . . . But by giving them their own apartment, they themselves become personally identified with it."[19] As a result of his burying the toys, 124 was no longer just Bodwin's father's house, as it could easily have been to a motherless child who moved away at age three. It was, and is, his—cognitively and literally.

This ownership subverts, however, Bodwin's claim that he no longer needs privacy. Ever since that childhood dependency, his privacy has been continually guaranteed. As a white male landowner he has never had Baby Suggs's experience of having "them" come in his yard—that is, those who, like schoolteacher and Bodwin himself, already have power and privacy, for whom the entire world seems part of their domain. In fact, the glimpses we get of his yard and home are in keeping with the domestic ideal as it allied itself with the nineteenth-century beginnings of the movement toward suburbia. Clark describes this movement by quoting landscape architect Frederick Law Olmsted, who argued that, much like a kitchen, the "essential quality of suburbia is domesticity," whereas in the inner city there can be "no feeling of privacy, no security from intrusion."[20] Bodwin's is just such a suburban home, "right in the center of a street full of houses and trees," a quiet, white neighborhood that protects his home from all invasion and separates it from the rapidly developing industrial city (143). The black people who come for his benevolence enter his back door and sit in the kitchen   hidden also, in keeping with the domestic ideal, at the back of the house. Meanwhile he entertains white slave owners (whom he does not "hold with—even Garner's kind") in the front (145). It is unlikely that he does not "need" privacy, any sort of a *hus;* rather, he does not see that in his domain, privacy and shelter are a given. His vulnerability is so imperceptible that he does not even realize it exists, so he has never lost faith in the philosophy that Baby Suggs shared with him and his father until the Misery: "human life is holy, all of it" (260).

Before the Misery, Baby Suggs had literally remodeled the cast-aside house that Bodwin had "given" her as a place to live. In so doing, she remodeled the ideal of the model home. Denver mentions the literal remodeling in her narrative to Beloved:

> The room we sleep in upstairs used to be where the help slept when white-people lived here. They had a kitchen outside, too. But Grandma Baby

turned it into a woodshed and toolroom when she moved in. And she
boarded up the back door that led to it because she said she didn't want to
make that journey no more. She built around it to make a storeroom, so if
you want to get in 124 you have to come by her. (207)

Clearly, Baby Suggs associates servanthood with a back door and a corner
bedroom, and this is all tied to the placement of the kitchen. Although by
the 1870s the domestic norm stipulated a kitchen inside—but at the back
of the house—both Gwendolyn Wright and Clifford Clark comment on
the reason for this suggestive placement. The front rooms of the house
were, in the ideal, reserved for family gatherings in keeping with the ideal
of creating and protecting the unified family. Not surprisingly, however,
these front rooms usually became excuses for "lavish and prominent display" of the (male) owner's wealth as the materialistic realm asserted its
power over the "female" spiritual domain.[21] Rather than the spiritual
gathering places the idealists dreamed of, these front rooms became the
kind of place you could show off to Southern slave-owning aristocrats that
you don't hold with, while their freed slaves would sit in the kitchen.

To protect this ideal/materialistic space, the ideal kitchen had to be kept
far to the back. As Clark describes it: "It was important, said the advocates
of housing reform, that the kitchen and other service aspects of the house
be hidden from the eyes of any visitors. . . . If servants were hired, a back
staircase was put in to give them access to the kitchen and keep them out
of sight."[22] Despite Stowe's ideal of the value and worth of women's work
(cf. Ophelia's New England home where the work is unobtrusively "done
up" without servants by the mother and her girls), even in *The American
Woman's Home* kitchens are relegated to the back of the house in the suggested floor plans. As Wright sees it, such designs suggest that in the model
home, "the kitchen area was planned as the hired woman's territory," despite the fact that fewer and fewer homeowners could afford hired help.
Thus, "'Queen Anne in the front, and Mary Anne in the back,' was a quip
of the time, referring to a typical house plan. By this account, the lady of
the house gave all her time and attention to the front parlor, where she
reigned amidst her fashionable English splendor, while her servant . . .
was hidden away in the back kitchen."[23] The ideal became, then, to separate the woman who worked from the True Woman who reigned on the
pedestal of her front parlor, without a hair out of place.

Baby Suggs confronts this alignment of kitchen placement with servanthood and remodels her house to avoid it. Thus the Bodwins' servants'
quarters become a bedroom for the family, and no one ever has to make

the servant's "journey" into the house again. Moreover, Denver's statement that whoever wanted to come into 124 had to get by Baby Suggs's
scrutiny suggests that, although Baby Suggs had a clear understanding
that her house could be invaded, she trusted in her strength as ruler over
her domain, as a working "queen" of her kitchen. And, as further testimony to the strength of her will, she accomplishes this remodeling despite
apparent criticism from the outside: "Said she didn't care what folks said
about her fixing a two-story house like a cabin where you cook inside. She
said they told her visitors with nice dresses don't want to sit in the same
room with the cook stove and the peelings and the grease and the smoke.
She wouldn't pay them no mind, she said" (207). Baby Suggs does not want
to create a separate domain for community and spirituality; it is located in
her kitchen where there is no pretense of servants, lavish displays, or of life
lived without the real work of living. Even kitchen life is holy.

So holy, in fact, that under this philosophy 124 was able to become
known as "a way station." Not a temporary one, as the Quaker settlement,
Garner's Sweet Home, and Stowe's America itself were for the black community, but a communal center:

> . . . 124 had been a cheerful, buzzing house where Baby Suggs, holy, loved,
> cautioned, fed, chastised and soothed. Where not one but two pots sim-
> mered on the stove; where the lamp burned all night long. Strangers rested
> there while children tried on their shoes. Messages were left there, for who-
> ever needed them was sure to stop in one day soon. Talk was low and to the
> point—for Baby Suggs, holy, didn't approve of extra. "Everything depends
> on knowing how much," she said, and "Good is knowing when to stop."
> (86–87)

Rather than trying to shut itself off in the privacy of suburbia, consistent
with the ideal, this remodeled, lively house with a life-giving kitchen at its
heart creates a communal domain. Simultaneously, this center gives Baby
Suggs the kind of power that allows her to lay down the rules in her ax-
iomatic expressions of Quakerly simplicity and balance. Like the Halliday
home, her home functions as both *domus* and *hus* for herself and the community—a place of shelter from the larger society as well as an expression
of their communal power, such as it is, in the face of that society.

Moreover, the religion that binds this community upholds the philosophy that "human life is holy." It centers not on a benevolent patriarchal
God but on an ex-slave female who does not tell the others that they are
"the blessed of the earth, its inheriting meek or its glorybound pure" (88).
That would be to preach that they are best out of power and that they

need to be patient so they can go to the big plantation in the sky, keeping themselves in the self-sacrificing mentality that even haunts the Quaker settlement—the true mentality fit for women and "negroes." Baby Suggs knows that this part of Stowe's religion is not what they need to hear. Rather, they need to be commanded to a bit of selfishness: to love their "flesh that weeps, laughs; flesh that dances on bare feet in grass," because "Yonder they do not love your flesh. They despise it" (88). In Baby Suggs's philosophy, it is this hatred of black flesh that allows white people to claim it. They are able to take the self it encloses for their domain, as Sethe realizes: "[A]nybody white could take your whole self for anything that came to mind. Not just work, kill, or maim you, but dirty you. Dirty you so bad you couldn't like yourself anymore. Dirty you so bad you forgot who you were and couldn't think it up" (251). Even Stowe's use was in some ways a "taking" of their bodies, then, a recreating of black selves in an ideal that also would not threaten "the white status quo," despite her own strong examples to the contrary in George and Cassy. Baby Suggs knows that before being fit for any more self-sacrifice, an ex-slave community living in alien territory needs this love of their own flesh. For that alone will allow her people to claim ownership of themselves, as Sethe does in her twenty-eight days of freedom: "Bit by bit, at 124 and in the Clearing, along with the others, she had claimed herself. Freeing yourself was one thing; claiming ownership of that freed self was another" (95).

When Paul D leaves Sethe, he sees her claim as the community did: "[M]ore important than what Sethe had done was what she claimed" (164). Sethe's claim of love for herself and for her children makes her love "too thick" according to Paul D. Like Cassy's, her motherlove goes beyond what the community can bear: "This here Sethe talked about love like any other woman . . . but what she meant could cleave the bone. This here Sethe talked about safety with a handsaw. This here new Sethe didn't know where the world stopped and she began" (164). Paul D, like the community, wants to be able to draw a clear line between self and the world, but Sethe's love of her children makes that difficult. Ella, for instance, "understood Sethe's rage in the shed twenty years ago, but not her reaction to it, which Ella thought was prideful, misdirected, and Sethe herself too complicated" (256). Everything about Sethe's situation is complicated. Not even Paul D can tell her what "better" options she may have had, but he and the community do not want to see these lengths of the love that Baby Suggs preached. They want Sethe just to talk love; like Baby Suggs's feast, her love is too overwhelming in the flesh. Like Stowe, they want her to be simply crazy and then tamed—not a proud woman who resents their lack of understanding and who can hold a job and get on without them. This communal resentment is voiced again by Ella: "When she got out of jail and made no gesture toward anybody, and lived as though she were alone, Ella junked her" (256).

Hence, although Paul D "knew exactly what she meant: to get to a place where you could love anything you chose—not to need permission for desire—well now, that was freedom," in the same conversation he condemns her for not remembering that she has two feet (162). Sethe refuses the only seeming alternatives to her love: Paul D's suggestion to "love small" and Ella's advice "don't love nothing" (92). She had reclaimed her freedom to love; she could no longer allow schoolteacher to invade, contaminate, and claim the selves of her children, "her best thing," seemingly the only thing she had left that was pure. As she sees it, she was doing her first duty as a mother, "to know what is [as opposed to 'what's worse'] and to keep them away from what I know is terrible" (165).

When faced with schoolteacher's hat, Sethe felt the invasion of Baby Suggs's domain, her own *hus.* He, by sanction of the Fugitive Slave Act, was trying to take away the freedom she had tried to claim as a result of Ohio's domain as a free state. So her reaction to the Fugitive Law was to stop the man by putting her children "on the other side," beyond the domain claimed by whitemen: "I took and put them where they'd be safe" (164). Her pride comes from a triumph over the whiteman's domain. This is not, however, to forget that Sethe's was "a rough choice" that even Baby Suggs "cannot approve or condemn" (180). The nature of her claim is still problematic: did she have the right to the bodies of her children? She sees her action as claiming a domain over herself, but where does "the world stop and she begin"? Good, after all, is knowing when to stop. By killing her children, even out of love, was she staking a claim that was too wide, or just as wide as the Baby Suggs ideal allowed it to be? Most frighteningly, was that act of love crossing the boundary into the acts of hate that were committed by the owners of the slaves' bodies? Her loving action also may be haunted by the presence of Simon Legree and schoolteacher, and for most of the book we do not have the "comforting" knowledge that she is simply another crazy Cassy—and neither does she. In the clearing Sethe observes: "Other people went crazy, why couldn't she?" (70).

Yet if Sethe's action has scarred her, then it also makes us see Ella, again representative of the whole community, as scarred another way. Ella also killed a child, one she was forced to have by "the lowest yet," by refusing to feed it. She killed it out of hatred; it was a "hairy, white thing" that bespoke her violation. Yet her equally understandable decision not to love at all anymore is symptomatic of the community's unwillingness to accept Baby Suggs's love freely. Hence, when "they"—the whitemen—come into the yard of 124, Baby Suggs's belief in the amazing grace that seemed to make her home overflow in a feast for five thousand (that turns out to be a "last supper") disappears. As she stands in the field, sensing the town's disapproval, she feels she has broken her own rule of "knowing when to stop": "And then she knew. Her friends and neighbors were angry at her because she had overstepped, given too much, offended by excess" (138). This refusal of her love marks Ella and the community as being unable to claim the freedom to love, just as Sethe's marks her as one who has overstepped. Everything depends on knowing how much.

But what Baby Suggs sees and what Stamp Paid is beginning to see is that "the heart that pumped out love, the mouth that spoke the Word," all those things that Baby Suggs had been working to get the community to love in themselves seemingly "didn't count. They came in her yard anyway. . . . The whitefolks had tired her out at last" (180). The whitemen seem to have claimed every living domain on the land and every soul in it. Thus, when Sethe argues against her on the side of the whitemen, saying, "They gave you this house," Baby Suggs answers, "Nobody gave me anything" (244). The whitemen's invasion has made Baby Suggs aware that her communal domain never mattered, never was a given. More disturbingly, not even a claim to one's self is a given in a society that justifies slavery. Like Simon Legree's mansion, 124 has always been haunted by the ownership of whitemen—both by Edward Bodwin's literal ownership and the broader political ownership that allowed the men to invade her home in the name of the law, "at the very hour when everyone stopped dropping by" (163).

As with Rachel Halliday's Quaker settlement, the spiritual unity of the town seems to have rested on Baby Suggs's shoulders, and the community refused to go where she was leading them. Particularly after Baby Suggs's death, the family within 124 struggles to create a self-sufficient unity devoid of outside community and entrapped by the memory and haunting of slavery in the form of Beloved. Even Paul D's banishment of the ghost lasts only long enough for Sethe to go out and reestablish a nodding acquaintance with the community. She just becomes able to imagine the solidity of the three hand-holding shadows that she sees as she, Paul D, and Denver walk home from the carnival, when Beloved appears.[24] After that, Beloved demands unity with Sethe alone, Denver with Beloved, and Paul D with Sethe, who, however, still seems to want to mother and love everyone; she wants the three hand-holding shadows as a model family for 124 because that kind of unity represents the binding claim of her motherlove.

Deborah Horvitz does well to remind us that Beloved does "give by taking," by demanding that "Sethe reveal memory and story about her life before Sweet Home, memory about her African-speaking, branded mother and her life right after Sweet Home when she cut Beloved's throat."[25] She does, thereby, help forge links between Sethe, her lost mother, grandmother, and Beloved herself, as Horvitz argues, as well as being the memory tyrant who refuses to share Sethe. This tyrannical aspect of Beloved's haunting is clarified by a connection to the Gothic tradition of ghosts on which both of the novels draw. Karen Halttunen notes that Cassy's "haunting" of Simon Legree in the form of his mother played off and satirized the tradition of ghosts in nineteenth-century Gothic novels; Legree "haunts himself" as the ghost becomes to him the outward realization of his fears and guilt regarding his lost mother and his own lost innocence.[26] So Beloved seems to embody the insecurities of each of the residents of 124: the pervasive, tyrannical memory of the "patriarchal institution" that continues to sap their ability to claim freedom. Because of this memory, her "tyranny" has strong overtones of slavery's patriarchal force. She moves Paul D out of the house and further weakens his manhood by compelling him to have sex with her against his will—like the slave owner Baby Suggs describes as "studding his boys." Importantly, this "violation" takes place in the coldhouse, the house away from the communal flame of the kitchen. In her quasi-patriarchal possession of the house, Beloved even convinces the fiercely independent Sethe that her womanly place, in fact the only domain, is in the house: "Whatever is going on outside my door ain't for me. The world is in this room. This here's all there is and all there needs to be" (183).

Ultimately, Denver realizes that this "possession" has gone too far, but she too has been virtually convinced by her years of seclusion that "the world beyond the edge of the porch" will swallow her up (243). And, as a representative of the community, Stamp Paid recognizes the unintelligible voices that form a noose around 124 as the voices of enslavement—voices that we know ring with "She mine." Beloved has become, at least in part, the embodiment of slavery's patrimony to Sethe and her daughter: a conscience who refuses to understand and forgive the ambiguity of Sethe's simultaneously loving and cruel response to the mock freedom granted by the Fugitive laws. Beloved's presence calls forth from Sethe a boundless retribution that fills up the house and drives all three women to the edge of sanity: "If the whitepeople of Cincinnati had allowed Negroes into their lunatic asylum, they would have found candidates in 124" (250). Although Sethe has seemingly been broken down into a "safe" madwoman like

Cassy, she has become so only after having her claim to herself taken away by this ghost that demands to be her only "best thing." Such a theft of claim represents the epitome of patriarchal possession.

Denver, Stamp Paid, and Ella ultimately lead the rest of the community in a movement of reconciliation that continues to the end of the novel. Denver recognizes the danger of Beloved's possession and determines to seek outside help, even though the world outside of 124 might eat her up. The community, in turn, finds in Denver's expression of need the ties forged by Baby Suggs. Beloved has fulfilled and surpassed the community's vengeful anger at both Sethe's and Baby Suggs's dangerous, boundless loves. In the end the women led by Ella do what they refused to do at Sethe's arrest; they form a "cape of sound" to wrap around her "like arms to hold and steady her on her way" (152). Upon making this effort they see the ghosts of their young selves on the lawn, with Baby Suggs "laugh[ing] and skipp[ing] among them, urging more" (258). They see themselves happy in her bountiful last supper, "not feeling the envy that surfaced the next day" (258). Baby Suggs's ghost once again teaches the wideness of love, and they are now ready to carry her love on.

Yet, at the very moment when everyone starts dropping by again, we are reminded that these women are still the madwomen in Mr. Bodwin's attic as his presence returns to haunt 124 and the community with his power and to haunt Sethe with the memory of schoolteacher's return twenty years earlier. Her passion cannot be broken down like Cassy's; motherlove for her is still a killer. But this time she does not strike her own child. She strikes Bodwin, the good-intentioned whiteman who still carries in him the ghosts of the patriarchal institution—the ghost of "the man without skin" in Beloved's vision who has a whip in his hand and those of the ghostly men who run the slave ship of her narratives, pushing the dead into the sea (215). When Beloved sees this whiteman looking at Sethe and Sethe running toward him, she disappears; the more permanent possessor/ghost has returned to his domain, and her possession simply does not match up. She does not own the walls of 124. When Sethe directly attacks him—the "real" ghost of patriarchal ownership—the ghostly embodiment of her enslavement can disappear.

Yet Morrison provides us with hints of Bodwin's vulnerability, too. Unaware of Sethe with her deadly ice pick, Mr. Bodwin is a seventy-year-old man having "thoughts of mortality" that are "not new" but "still ha[ve] the power to annoy" (260). He is a fragile being who must, after all, be saved by a girl, Denver. His two houses—the one a secluded nest in town, the other a possessed two-story house in the black community—announce his vulnerable, human need for shelter as well as his need for a material domain. Of course, in the end the community members still recognize their dependence on his benevolent power. As with Mr. Garner, "everything rests on him": "He somebody never turned us down. Steady as a rock. I tell you something, if she had got to him, it'd be the worst thing for us" (265). But they also have a new kind of communal strength established by the reciprocal movements out of and toward 124.

Because of this strength, at the very end of the novel we are given a slightly precarious hope that Paul D, Denver, and Sethe will make it there anyway. They will remodel this house and Baby Suggs's ideal in keeping with their love for and mutual dependence on one another—despite Miss Bodwin's desire to get rid of 124 and Mr. Bodwin's feeble resistance. Denver may be growing up and out of the house, but she has been reconciled to Paul D; she no longer sneers at him. She and Paul D have, in fact, worked out a reciprocal, loving relationship to the ill Sethe: "Denver be here in the day. I [Paul D] be here in the night. I'm a take care of you, you hear?" (272). Their model home is being built in a remodeled patriarchal space that only needs painting. Paul D no longer jealously wishes to be the "head" of the family, or for Sethe to be only "the woman he wanted to protect" (132, 127). That is the domestic ideal, the patriarchal ideal that has always haunted the house. This nonpatriarchy does not mean that Paul D is emasculated in the way that readers have complained of or have praised Stowe's Uncle Tom for being.[27] Rather, manhood, too, is redefined; he can still be empowered as a male in this culture. He does not need to be sent to Africa or any such safe, faraway corner of the world. He will, of course, protect Sethe in her current weakness and nurture her back to health. But he will also lay his story next to hers, in an equal reciprocity, so that together they can try to create "some kind of tomorrow" out of their pasts. They are not looking forward to a big plantation in the sky. Rather their story wants to preach Baby Suggs's holy, self-love story, which will allow Sethe to reclaim herself: "You your best thing, Sethe. You are" (273). And the "present" of this is, indeed, a story to pass on and create a future with.

Stowe and Morrison share an acute awareness of the power of the patriarchal culture ostensibly to offer the home as woman's *domus* and *hus* while remaining always threatening and able to invade that domain and shatter its security. Both authors, however, optimistically offer alternative visions to this patriarchal control. Stowe began the remodeling by using the domestic ideal as a new form of global female empowerment. But her matriarchal ideal does not finally alter the basic structure of the patriarchy—as a true remodeling must. It shifts power into the hands of a female head of the household who continues operating under the ultimate control of a patriarchal, slave-owning God. By setting up her text as a conscious parallel to *Uncle Tom's Cabin,* Morrison reentered this structure to continue the remodeling and demonstrated how to alter irreversibly the power structure of the patriarchal home. She suggests a space where a warm, communal center could be made out of the working place of the home: a space where women and men can share themselves in the form of their stories without fear of their stories being claimed by someone else's labels of them as being wrong—animalistic, bad, unwomanly, or unchristian; where painful stories can be made bearable because they are shared by more than one person and accepted by the community; where that community can learn to love anything they choose and claim themselves in the domain of that love. If they indeed accomplish this loving claim, as we are given to hope at the end of *Beloved,* then the ghosts of the patriarchy may finally cease to have power over, if not to cease haunting, the houses of women's fiction.

Notes

1. Amos Rapoport, "Vernacular Architecture and the Cultural Determinants of Form," in *Buildings and Society: Essays on the Social Development of the Built Environment,* ed. Anthony D. King (London: Routledge, 1980), 284.

2. Harriet Beecher Stowe and Catharine Beecher, *The American Woman's Home* (1869; rpt., Watkins Glen, N.Y.: Library of Victorian Culture, 1979), 13. In his introduction to this edition, Joseph Van Why notes that this book was essentially a revision of Catharine Beecher's *Treatise on the Domestic Economy for the Use of Young Ladies at Home and at School* to which Stowe's famous name was attached, although she may have contributed some thoughts from her own series of essays *House and Home Papers,* first published in the *Atlantic Monthly* in 1864. On the differences between the Beecher sisters regarding the domestic ideal, see Jeanne Boydston, Mary Kelley, and Anne Margolis, *The Limits of Sisterhood: The Beecher Sisters on Women's Rights and Woman's Sphere* (Chapel Hill: Univ. of North Carolina Press, 1988), and Gillian Brown, who finds that Stowe seeks a "utopian rehabilitation" of the traditional ideals of domesticity more closely allied with her sister Catharine, in "Getting in the Kitchen with Dinah: Domestic Politics in *Uncle Tom's Cabin,*" *American Quarterly* 36 (1984): 503–23.

3. Arthur C. Danto, "Abide/Abode," in *Housing: Symbol, Structure, Site,* ed. Lisa Taylor (New York: Cooper-Hewitt Museum, 1990), 9.

4. Elizabeth Ammons, "Heroines in *Uncle Tom's Cabin,*" *American Literature* 49 (1977): 161–79; rpt. in *Critical Essays on Harriet Beecher Stowe,* ed. Ammons (Boston: G. K. Hall, 1980), 153. Among others, see also Ammons's "Stowe's Dream of a Mother-Savior:

Uncle Tom's Cabin and American Women Writers before the 1920s," in *New Essays on "Uncle Tom's Cabin,"* ed. Eric J. Sundquist (New York: Cambridge Univ. Press, 1986), 155–95; Gillian Brown, "Getting in the Kitchen with Dinah"; and Jane Tompkins, "Sentimental Power: *Uncle Tom's Cabin* and the Politics of Literary History," in *Sensational Designs: The Cultural Work of American Fiction, 1790–1860* (New York: Oxford Univ. Press, 1985), 122–47.

5. Gwendolyn Wright, *Moralism and the Model Home: Domestic Architecture and Cultural Conflict in Chicago, 1873–1913* (Chicago: Univ. of Chicago Press, 1980), 2.

6. See especially Gillian Brown, "Getting in the Kitchen with Dinah," and Theodore Hovet, *The Master Narrative: Harriet Beecher Stowe's Subversive Story of Master and Slave in "Uncle Tom's Cabin" and "Dred"* (Boston: Univ. Press of America, 1989).

7. Wright, 37.

8. Harriet Beecher Stowe, *Uncle Tom's Cabin, or Life Among the Lowly,* ed. Kenneth S. Lynn (Cambridge: Harvard Univ. Press, 1962), 350. Subsequent references to this edition will be incorporated parenthetically into the text.

9. Hovet, 23.

10. Karen Halttunen, "Gothic Imagination and Social Reform: The Haunted Houses of Lyman Beecher, Henry Ward Beecher and Harriet Beecher Stowe," in *New Essays on "Uncle Tom's Cabin,"* 107–34.

11. Brown concludes her article by noting that, although "men as we know them" cannot exist in Stowe's matriarchal utopia, Stowe's retention of "the name of the male God throughout her matriarchal design suggests that her imagination of a feminized world still requires the sanction of male authority" (523).

12. William L. Andrews, *To Tell a Free Story* (Urbana: Univ. of Illinois Press, 1986), 180.

13. On the use of the term "romantic racialism," see George M. Fredrickson, "Uncle Tom and the Anglo-Saxons: Romantic Racialism in the North," in *The Black Image in the White Mind: The Debate on Afro-American Destiny, 1817–1914* (New York: Harper, 1971), 97–130.

14. In the *Key to "Uncle Tom's Cabin"* (London: Clarke, Beeton, 1853), Stowe does not offer a specific parallel for Cassy's narrative, but she does include a clipping from a newspaper article that describes a slave mother's murdering of her own children and subsequent suicide and the owner's befuddled reaction (273). Later, Stowe also includes a letter from a freed slave whose mother's desire to "fix [him] so they'd never get [him]" reminded him of Cassy (304).

15. Toni Morrison, *Beloved* (New York: Knopf, 1987), 140. Subsequent references to this edition will be incorporated into the text parenthetically.

16. See Karen E. Fields on Morrison's exploration of this possibility of love even between slave and master in "To Embrace Dead Strangers: Toni Morrison's *Beloved,"* in *Mother Puzzles: Daughters and Mothers in Contemporary American Literature,* ed. Mickey Pearlman (New York: Greenwood, 1989), 159–70, esp. 166.

17. On the complex nature of Beloved's ghostly character, see Deborah Horvitz, "Nameless Ghosts: Possession and Dispossession in *Beloved,*" *Studies in American Fiction* 17 (1989): 157–67.

18. Marilyn Chandler does an especially fine job of discussing Denver's relation to 124 Bluestone in her recent comparison of *"Housekeeping* and *Beloved:* When Women Come Home," in *Dwelling in the Text: Houses in American Fiction* (Berkeley: Univ. of California Press, 1991), 291–319.

19. Clifford E. Clark, Jr., "Domestic Architecture as an Index to Social History: The Romantic Revival and the Cult of Domesticity in America, 1840–1870," *Journal of Interdisciplinary History* 7 (1976): 33–56; quotation from 50 (emphasis his).

20. Clark, 41.

21. Wright, *Moralism and the Model Home,* 35.

22. Clark, 50.

23. Wright, 35–36.

24. On the importance of the number three in Morrison's earlier fiction, see Susan Willis, "Eruptions of Funk: Historicizing Toni Morrison," in *Black Literature and Literary Theory,* ed. Henry Louis Gates, Jr. (New York: Routledge, 1990), 263–84.

25. Horvitz, "Nameless Ghosts," 160.

26. Halttunen, "Gothic Imagination and Social Reform," 123–24. I would also like to thank Elizabeth Schultz for her insights on this point.

27. Ammons is one of the foremost admirers of the feminization of Tom, finding that Tom's equation with mothers and Eva/Christ "indicts masculine ethics" and calls for a redefinition of masculinity along more feminine lines, toward a reformation of society as a whole. See especially "Stowe's Dream of a Mother-Savior." She argues, of course, against the anger of such critics as James Baldwin, who asserts that Tom "has been robbed of his humanity and divested of his sex" in "Everybody's Protest Novel," *Partisan Review* 16 (1949): 578–85, rpt. in *Critical Essays on Harriet Beecher Stowe,* ed. Elizabeth Ammons (Boston: G. K. Hall, 1980), 92–97. The quotation appears on 94.

Between Presence and Absence

Beloved, *Postmodernism, and Blackness*

RAFAEL PÉREZ-TORRES

❖　❖　❖

> I am not experimental,
> I am simply trying to recreate something of an old
> art form in my books—
> the something that defines what makes a book
> "black."
>
> —Toni Morrison

HENRY LOUIS GATES, JR., has famously discussed a central dilemma of black literature: its presence marks as well an absence because "black" has in Western European discourse long signified "blank." The problem a black author finds in articulating black identity, Gates argues, "can perhaps be usefully stated in the irony implicit in the attempt to posit a 'black self' in the very Western languages in which blackness itself is a figure of absence, a negation. Ethnocentrism and 'logocentrism' are profoundly interrelated in Western discourse as old as the *Phaedrus* of Plato, in which one finds one of the earliest figures of blackness, a figure of negation" (7). Given sociohistorical conditions compelling it toward silence, African-American literary production questions not what distinguishes itself from other forms but rather how it manages to speak at all. Language at once masks and reveals the social and political structures from which it arises and which it creates. The link between language and ideology presents black writers with a quandary: how to speak when compelled to silence? Consequently, black writers have had to digest both Western and non-Western forms of cultural production in order to create a voice that can affirm and affix identity. Out of this process they have forged a literary discourse that transforms notions of blackness.

One area of transformation presents itself in the attempt to situate Toni

Morrison's *Beloved* within a postmodern context. In *Beloved,* interpretation forms an integral strategy in creating black cultural and social identities. The fictional characters and communities—as objects of exploitation in both slave and free-market societies—transform absence into a powerful presence. A sense of self emerges from experiences of exploitation, marginalization, and denial. Analogously, Morrison's narrative, confronting a facelessness dominant American culture threatens to impose on black expression, forges out of cultural and social absences a voice and identity. *Beloved* creates an aesthetic identity by playing against and through the cultural field of postmodernism. In so doing, it challenges received notions of postmodernism and, more important, engages with the very complex critical issues out of which contemporary American cultural identity is forged.[1]

At a very basic level, *Beloved* makes evident its engagement with postmodernism through the aesthetic play of the novel. Throughout the narrative, *Beloved* reveals a concern with linguistic expression: the evocation of both oral and written discourses, the shifting from third person narration to omniscient narration to interior monologue, the iteration and reiteration of words and phrases and passages. This linguistic and narrative variation demonstrates a concern with the production and meaning of language. The text thus spins a story woven of myth that creates a pattern of elaborate linguistic play. By crossing genres and styles and narrative perspectives, *Beloved* filters the absent or marginalized oral discourse of a precapitalist black community through the self-conscious discourse of the contemporary novel. The novel emerges, then, at an intersection where premodern and postmodern forms of literary expression cross.

The narrative in *Beloved* highlights processes of reinscription and reinterpretation. It intertwines the mythic, folkloric, and poetic threads of an oral literature with the rhetorical and discursive trajectories of a postmodern literary field. The novel stands amid a cultural context in which play, allusion, quotation serve as privileged aesthetic techniques. It is not enough, however, to claim for *Beloved* the mantle of postmodernism. It and other novels that emerge from multicultural histories serve to foreground the relation between cultural text and sociohistorical context. The "blackness" of black literary texts, historically read to signify a lack in Western discourse, becomes in Morrison's hands an important thread tying together the complicated realms of politics and aesthetics. The "not" signified by blackness becomes for Morrison a means by which to weave her tale. A process of interpretation and reinterpretation in *Beloved* serves to form an "is" out of the "nots," helps untie the tangled threads by which Morrison knits together her novel.² *Beloved* challenges us to rethink the relationship between the postmodern and the marginal, to reinterpret and redeploy the decentering impulses associated with postmodernism. The novel forces us to retrace the distinct threads of the historically marginal as they inform the patterns and politics of postmodern culture. Thematizing the suspension between absence and presence, *Beloved* and other multicultural texts hang between being and not being a part of (rather than apart from) contemporary American culture. These texts force a reassessment of what is evoked by the term "American."

Absence is made tangible in *Beloved* from the first page of the novel. We are presented with several historical and geographical facts: the action is set near Cincinnati, Ohio; the year is 1873; the address of the house is 124 Bluestone Road. These concrete details do nothing to obviate the sense of loss that pervades the opening. We are informed that the grandmother, Baby Suggs, is dead and the sons, Howard and Buglar, have run away. Only the escaped slave Sethe, married to Baby Suggs's son Halle, and her daughter Denver remain. Though free, they are scorned by their community and made victim to a ghostly presence, a "spite" that fills the house at 124 Bluestone Road. The historic and geographic specificity that opens the narrative stands opposed to the equally concrete absences evident in the story: the missing ancestor and the missing descendants. Readers are placed generationally in a space that floats somewhere between an absent past and an absent future. Into this static fictional present a ghostly past perpetually attempts to insert itself.³

Absence is present through to the last page of the novel. The reader is told numerous times by the end of the narrative that Beloved's story "is not a story to pass on" (275). "Pass on" signifies both rejection and acceptance. Beloved's story cannot be repeated, the narrative warns, cannot be allowed to occur again in the world. The repeated warning also means that this is a story that cannot be forgotten, that cannot be rejected or "passed" on. Thus the close of the novel evokes again the motif of absence and presence by ambiguously suggesting Beloved's story should neither be forgotten nor remembered.

The interplay between presence and absence, accepting and rejecting, appearing and disappearing, repeats and resurfaces throughout the course of *Beloved*. The demarcation in the text between life and death (the ultimate distinction in the modern West between existence and extinction) blurs and is erased.⁴ These distinctions dissolve as Beloved, Sethe's murdered child, returns incarnate. The erasure of boundaries between self and other, life and death is a motif evident from the very first scene of the book. Though dead, Baby Suggs is from beginning to end a felt and seen presence in the narrative. We are given her image: an old crippled woman, lying in bed, hovering between the memories of an uneasy life and the certainty of a restless death. Too demoralized to care that her grandsons have run off, she is concerned only with the small satisfaction of meditating upon scraps of colored cloth: "Suspended between the emptiness of life and the meanness of the dead, she couldn't get interested in leaving life or living it, let alone the fright of two creeping-off boys. Her past had been like her present—intolerable—and since she knew death was anything but forgetfulness, she used the little energy left her for pondering color" (6). We come to learn of Baby Suggs's slave past that had "busted her legs, back, head, eyes, hands, kidneys, womb and tongue" (87). Her son Halle, who had at the old plantation Sweet Home hired himself out every Sunday for five years in order to buy her freedom, has not managed to make it north to be with his mother, wife, and daughter. Baby Suggs has had to become accustomed to absences. And in this she is not alone.

The story of slavery invoked by *Beloved* and endured by Baby Suggs is premised on the absence of power, the absence of self-determination, the absence of a homeland, the absence of a language. The action of the novel incorporates these historical conditions and draws attention to their many results. The absence of Mr. Garner, who had been a temperate force of oppression at Sweet Home, leads to the slaves' flight. The absence of her children who had escaped earlier and gone ahead of their parents drives Sethe to continue her arduous journey north to Ohio. The absence of Halle leads her to wait for his return and is one of the causes for Baby Suggs's withdrawal into her small world of colored cloth. Sethe learns the lessons of absence and refuses to turn her children over to the slave catchers who have come to take her family back to Sweet Home, only eluding capture by murdering her child. The presence of her baby's ghost as well as its eventual reincarnation serve as a constant reminder of the absence and longing that have led Sethe and Denver to take refuge in their isolated home at 124 Bluestone.

Absence thus comprises the past and the present of the characters' lives in *Beloved*. These absences are due to the presence of and obsession with skin color. While "black" signifies "blank," it also signifies property. It is the insulting and violating practice of commodification that serves as the source for the many absences Baby Suggs and her people have had to learn to survive:

[I]n all of Baby's life, as well as Sethe's own, men and women were moved around like checkers. Anybody Baby Suggs knew, let alone loved, who hadn't run off or been hanged, got rented out, loaned out, bought up, brought back, stored up, mortgaged, won, stolen or seized. So Baby's eight children had six fathers. What she called the nastiness of life was the shock she received upon learning that nobody stopped playing checkers just because the pieces included her children. (23)

Commodity and exchange serve as the only forms of interaction between blacks and whites in *Beloved.* This exchange on its most basic level involves the marketing of human beings, but exchange also occurs in a more subtle though no less invidious manner. The white abolitionists who use Sethe's plight to further their cause turn her story into currency. Their concern is not with her as a person, but with her as a case. Her story disappears in their rush to turn her actions into abolitionist propaganda. This causes Sethe to shy away from repeating her narrative and leads her to put her story away so that it can be neither misused nor misunderstood. Only later, with Beloved's reemergence, does the story of a mother driven to desperation and murder too reemerge. Sethe's story opens between her, Beloved, and Denver channels of exchange (aesthetic, social, personal) similar to the channels of charitable exchange evident among the black community in the novel. The novel thus posits forms of exchange that provide alternatives to modern forms of market exchange.

Morrison's narrative sketches a relation between the black community and material goods that is governed by the use value of those commodities. Her esthetic creation evokes a historical period in which the industrial has not yet infused the lives of the characters. This aspect in some measure explains why many of Morrison's works explicitly or implicitly focus on elements of rural, preindustrial life. By presenting monetary exchange only through the buying or selling of slaves, the narrative suggests a nostalgia for the premodern that implicitly focuses criticism on contemporary social organization.

Rather than view postmodernism as a historically decontextualized field of endless play, as critics such as Fredric Jameson and Hal Foster have suggested, *Beloved* presents us with a different vision of historical reconstruction. The movement in the text among the modern and premodern, the reexamination of historical signification, suggests a critical engagement with history as a narrative, a construction implicated in ideology. Morrison's text suggests a complex relationship to tradition and history, one that is neither a simple reclamation of historical "fact" nor a fanciful reconstruction of some originary "tradition." Instead, it re-members history, revises perceptions of the past and its significance in an implicit critique of contemporary social formations.

This critique based in material history does not center solely around economic exploitation. After all, the reason Baby Suggs's children are used as pieces in the slave traders' game is because of their color. Thus one begins to grasp a vague pun woven into the text: Baby Suggs's fascination with color comes as a result of her suffering a life of deprivation, a life, like her room, that is absent of color ("except for two orange squares in a quilt that made the absence shout" [38]). Color becomes a metonym for the richness of life. Yet Baby Suggs's suffering is due precisely to the color of her skin. The punning on Baby Suggs's fixation with "color" is an appropriate verbal device for a narrative concerning and arising from a black culture. The word "color" in this context is a sign for the literal concept of hue and visual perception. The concept undergoes a literary transformation whereby color serves as a metonym for luxuriousness, comfort, pleasure. Simultaneously it serves to signal not just a racial group called "black" but also the recent sociolinguistic transformations that have replaced the terms "color" and "colored" with "black" and "African-American." The pun helps trace literal as well as historical, political, and social patterns within the weave of the narrative. The language of the text, the effect of pun and play, constructs and dissolves structures that are at once linguistic and ideological.

So while Morrison's narrative shares affinities with other postmodern texts, it also suggests a connection between its narrative strategies and the sociohistorical conditions of Africans in the Americas. Gates argues that the signifying of black narratives—the linguistic playing, punning, coding, decoding, and recoding found in African-American texts—emerges from the pressing necessity for political, social, and economic survival:

> Black people have always been masters of the figurative: saying one thing to mean something quite other has been basic to black survival in oppressive Western cultures. Misreading signs could be, and indeed often was, fatal. "Reading," in this sense, was not play; it was an essential aspect of the "literacy" training of a child. This sort of metaphorical literacy, the learning to decipher codes, is just about the blackest aspect of the black tradition. (6)

Where the term "play" might suggest freedom, innocence, rebellion, the linguistic "play" evident in *Beloved* results from deciphering codes with deadly serious implications. There is in *Beloved* no innocence, no aesthetic word play that does not simultaneously trace political, social, and cultural

meanings. In this respect *Beloved* and other multicultural novels distin-
guish themselves from the full-blown fancy found in texts often termed
postmodern.

The allusions and processes of symbolic exchange evident in *Beloved*
work over and over to reentrench the narrative in a painful social and historical reality.[5] Late in the novel, for example, Denver goes among the
community in search of food and work in order to support her mother,
who has been incapacitated by the demands engendered by Beloved's return. Denver seeks to enter the service of the Bodwins, the abolitionist
family who helped settle Baby Suggs and Sethe on their arrival in Ohio. In
their home she notices on the shelf the small figure of a black boy:

> His head was thrown back farther than a head could go, his hands were
> shoved in his pockets. Bulging like moons, two eyes were all the face he had
> above the gaping red mouth. His hair was a cluster of raised, widely spaced
> dots made of nail heads. And he was on his knees. His mouth wide as a cup,
> held the coins needed to pay for a delivery or some other small service, but
> could just as well have held buttons, pins, crab-apple jelly. Painted across
> the pedestal he knelt on were the words "At Yo Service." (255)

The caricature here is cruel. The image of the black boy at once suggests
commercial exchange (the coins held for delivery or small service), servitude (the kneeling figure), and the grotesquely twisted neck of a lynching
victim. With this brief image the text exhibits a comprehensive critique of
the commercial, racist, and potentially violent nature of the dominant social order. The passage also evokes a series of puns: the "service" of blacks
equated with the "service" of the small cup full of change, the taking of
money from out the black boy's mouth suggestive of the drawing upon
the services performed by blacks, the presence of the grotesque boy "At Yo
Service" evident just as Denver is going to enter the service of the Bodwins.
One meaning slides into the next.

The image of the black figurine exemplifies the unstable processes of
symbolic exchange at work in the novel. The significance of such words as
"color" and "exchange" and "service" configured by the image of the sub-
servient change cup moves toward a critique of social realities. The slipperi-
ness of language is foregrounded in the novel as words glide from one
frame of reference to another, just as characters glide from one defining
identity to another, and the form of the narrative from one genre to another. This shifting is not due to the liberating practice of free linguistic
play and indeterminacy. Rather, it arises from the absences left by previous
literary, discursive, and social forms. As multiplicity and transformation

come to form the privileged components of *Beloved,* the inadequacies of other avant-garde forms of literary expression are made present. In large part, the reason classically postmodern texts move away from connection with sociohistorical reality is their commitment to the hermetic isolation of the aesthetic object.[6] Because of the contested histories from which they emerge, multicultural texts place in the foreground the relationship between language and power. In order to understand alterity and decentralization as historically grounded phenomena rather than reified fetish, a critical understanding of postmodernism takes into account the lessons proffered by multicultural texts. There exists a profoundly complex and critical relationship between the use of language and the exercise of power.

Morrison's narrative "plays" not just with language but also with the traces of ideology that leave their mark in language. At this level, the significance of linguistic play that is not simply play makes itself manifest. Language, never innocent of power, becomes in Morrison's text a central means by which power disperses itself. The language of slavery within *Beloved* comprises signs written with whips, fires, and ropes. It is this discourse that is literally inscribed on Sethe's back by the dispassionate and evil figure of schoolteacher.

Schoolteacher appears after the death of Mr. Garner in order to help Mrs. Garner run Sweet Home. Faceless, nameless, he becomes the speaking subject of slavery's discourse. Taking advantage of his position as the possessor of language, he notes with scientific detachment the animal-like characteristics of Sweet Home's slaves. He has his nephews—studying under his tutelage—do the same: "No, no. That's not the way. I told you to put her human characteristics on the left; her animal ones on the right. And don't forget to line them up" (193). Sethe's identity, circumscribed by these "scientific" practices, is subject to the effects of schoolteacher's discourse. As often happens, the treatment she receives as an object of discourse transforms her into an object of violence. She tells Paul D, the one Sweet Home man to escape slavery alive and whole: "[T]hose boys came in there and took my milk. That's what they came in there for. Held me down and took it. I told Mrs. Garner on em. . . . Them boys found out I told on em. Schoolteacher made one open up my back, and when it closed it made a tree. It grows there still" (16-17). Sethe's body is doubly violated: once when its nutriment is stolen, then again when torn open by a whip. Just like the page of schoolteacher's notebook, Sethe is divided and marked, inscribed with the discourse of slavery and violation.

Throughout the narrative, the hard language of slavery is heard:

Sethe's mother is hanged; Sixo is burned alive then shot; Paul A, mutilated beyond recognition, swings from the trees of the Sweet Home farm. The bodies of these characters become the texts on which their identities are written. In a lesson brought home again and again, the power of the word is made manifest in the world. Power belongs, as schoolteacher tries to show, not to those whom words define but to those who define words.

Yet the defined do not entirely lack power. Those who live with the absence of power reserve to themselves the persistent practice of decoding and recoding signs. The result is that the texts on which the master has inscribed one meaning reinscribe those self-same signs and make them signify something new. The master's texts become the subjects rather than the objects of language, masters of rather than slaves to discourse.

Both Sethe as a black slave and Amy Denver as a white indentured servant know the bonds of slavery and sexual violation. The two women meet as they each seek to escape their position as objects of oppressive discursive practices. For Amy—stumbling on the battered and pregnant Sethe while running away to Boston—the woman's scarred back is not a mark of her slavery. Rather she exclaims, "It's a tree. . . . A chokecherry tree. See, here's the trunk—it's red and split wide open, full of sap, and this here's the parting for the branches. You got a mighty lot of branches. Leaves, too, look like, and dern if there ain't blossoms" (79). Both women have been marked by their position as owned property. As the signs of slavery inscribed on the one are transformed by the other into an image of fruition instead of oppression, Amy gives back to Sethe her identity as a nurturing source.

The power to rename represents a reclamation of agency when other venues that would help the characters establish a sense of subjectivity are closed. At the center of this need to name stands again the sense of absence found throughout *Beloved*. In this instance, the absence of names returns to haunt African-American life. As Toni Morrison explains,

> [A]mong blacks, we have always suffered being nameless. We didn't have names because ours are those of the master which were given to us with indifference and don't represent anything for us. It's become a common practice, among the community, to give a name to someone according to their characteristics: it's life that gives you a name, in a way. (Pasquier 12; my translation)

Blacks are "nameless" because given names cannot recover a preslave past. The community bestows names upon people, constructing through a communal act of rechristening a self meant to counteract the disempow-

erment of a slave past. Kimberly Benston explains that this practice of re-
naming represents a way of creating a historical self-identity. For the
African-American, he notes, "self-creating and reformation of a fragmented familial past are endlessly interwoven: naming is inevitably genealogical revisionism. All of African American literature may be seen as
one vast genealogical poem that attempts to restore continuity to the rup-
tures or discontinuities imposed by the history of black presence in
America" (152). Naming becomes, in other words, a means of bridging the
violent gaps left by history. As Adam McKible notes, naming becomes a
tool of struggle, a way to disrupt, delegitimize, and displace master narratives.

McKible draws upon Walter Benjamin's notions of the monad as a crys-
tallization of historical memory, an opposition to oppression as described
in Benjamin's essay "Theses on the Philosophy of History." The problem
here lies in Benjamin's notions of history. Paul De Man, for example, critiques Benjamin's understanding of history in *The Resistance to Theory*. History, writes De Man, "is not human, because it pertains strictly to the
order of language; it is not natural, for the same reason; it is not phenomenal, in the sense that no cognition, no knowledge about man, can be derived from a history which as such is a purely linguistic complication" (92).
Morrison's novel suggests that history does indeed pertain to the order of
language as the novel demonstrates how history is constructed and reproduced like other narratives. Understanding history as a linguistic complication does not prevent a reclamation and restitution of human identity
from history. *Beloved* suggests that this process of reclamation occurs at
those points of aporia where the human and the historical do not meet. In
"The House a Ghost Built," for example, William Handley argues that
Beloved lies between two cultures with differing literary values. From an
American perspective, the novel invokes a lost culture and so serves an ele-
giac function. From an African context, the novel brings a sense of loss into
existence by the power of the word. The novel then represents both a loss
and a regeneration simultaneously, both an absence and a presence that
point toward the absent and present cultural connections to Africa.

The moment in the novel where Sethe is mostly clearly faced with the
dilemma of absence and presence occurs soon after her escape to Ohio and
her reunion with her children. Sought out by slave catchers and schoolteacher, Sethe refuses to allow her children to be taken back to the inhumanity of slavery. In the face of this threat, Sethe marks her baby with a
most profound form of inscription. She draws a handsaw across her throat.

Sethe stakes her position against the injustice and violence of history by using the only language she has at hand. The power to name is the power to mark, the power to locate and identify. This is the power Sethe assumes for herself in deciding the fate of her children. Yet this power does not emerge from nowhere: the language Sethe uses to mark her child is a language she had learned early in life and had nearly forgotten. Only in a moment of desperation does it reemerge.

Sethe recalls being raised, along with the rest of the slave children, by the one-armed wet nurse Nan. She was the one who took care of the children, nursed the babies, did the cooking:

> And who used different words. Words Sethe understood then but could neither recall nor repeat now. . . . The same language her ma'am spoke, and which would never come back. But the message—that was and had been there all along. . . . She told Sethe that her mother and Nan were together from the sea. Both were taken up many times by the crew. "She threw them all away but you. The one from the crew she threw away on the island. The others from more whites she also threw away. Without names, she threw them. You she gave the name of the black man. She put her arms around him. The others she did not put her arms around. Never. Never. Telling you. I am telling you, small girl Sethe." (62)

The only baby Sethe's mother accepted bears the name of the only man she took in her arms. The other babies she rejected. Sethe learns from Nan not the linguistic code of her African past but another code: one of absence, of silence. This language contests history by denying to it another victim of oppression. Sethe's language, like her mother's language, is one of denial and rejection. Hers is a discourse—a language of desperation— that says No to that which is not acceptable. Sethe practices this discourse in a woodshed. Her instrument is a handsaw; her text is her beloved baby; her sign is the mark of a great refusal: "If she thought anything, it was No. No. Nono. Nonono. Simple" (163).

The meaning of Sethe's refusal—and the assertion of her own agency—is, however, lost. Others appropriate her story of desperation in order to serve their own ends. Her actions and the significance of her discourse are misconstrued in the rush to turn her story into other stories that have, ultimately, nothing to do with Sethe and her family. As the telling is altered, the story told is no longer Sethe's. First the events are circumscribed by the sensationalist newspapers of the day: "A whip of fear broke through her heart chambers as soon as you saw a Negro's face in a paper, since the face was not there because the person had a healthy baby, or outran a street mob" (155–56). After the newspapers, the abolitionists take up Sethe's cause, adding fuel to the fire of antislavery passion. Like Owen Bodwin, the man who helped Sethe and her family escape slavery, the abolitionists find in Sethe a cause and not a human being: "The Society managed to turn infanticide and the cry of savagery around, and build a further case of abolishing slavery. Good years, they were, full of spit and conviction" (260). Caught between the sensationalism of the newspapers and the inflammatory rhetoric of the abolitionists, Sethe's story disappears.

To tell her story again, to make clear the meaning of what she had done, Sethe would like every word delivered by the preacher at her baby's funeral engraved on the headstone: "Dearly Beloved. But what she got, settled for, was the one word that mattered. She thought it would be enough, rutting among the headstones with the engraver. . . . That should certainly be enough. Enough to answer one more preacher, one more abolitionist and a town full of disgust" (5). Beloved is thus twice marked: once with a handsaw and once with a chisel. The first sign brings an absence, creates a lack; the second is Sethe's attempt to fill that lack with an explanation of the emotion that prompted the first. Both, we understand, are legitimate expressions of a difficult discourse, the desperate language of the oppressed. Each rushes to fill the absences left by other discourses pressed physically and psychically upon Sethe and her progeny—slavery, patriarchy, commodity exchange. Together in the novel, these discourses form constellations of meaning that prove insufficient in the face of Sethe's own sense of identity.

However, asserting a self by appropriating discourse, as Sethe learns, is not a simple matter. She thought the inscription of Beloved's tomb would be enough to quiet the past. While that single word may have been enough to answer the preacher, the abolitionist, the town full of disgust, it was not enough to answer Beloved. The future of Sethe has been solely a matter of keeping the past at bay. The past, incarnate in the form of Beloved, finally overwhelms her. Beloved becomes for Sethe a manifestation of history—a living and usurping power, one that controls and subsumes her, one for which she does not have a contesting language:

> Beloved bending over Sethe looked the mother, Sethe the teething child, for other than those times when Beloved need her, Sethe confined herself to a corner chair. The bigger Beloved got, the smaller Sethe became; the brighter Beloved's eyes, the more those eyes that used never to look away became slits of sleeplessness. Sethe no longer combed her hair or splashed her face with water. She sat in the chair licking her lips like a chastised child

while Beloved ate up her life, took it, swelled up with it, grew taller on it.
And the older woman yielded it up without a murmur. (250)

The past mercilessly consumes Sethe. She has not found a language to counteract effectively the intolerance and violation traced by other discourses. Despite her best efforts to respond to a hopeless situation, despite her attempts to assert agency by becoming a speaking subject, Sethe finds herself subject to the tyranny of history.

Over and over, Sethe finds this tyranny associated with signs and language. She becomes a text upon which her white masters inscribe a discourse of slavery. She serves as a symbol of exchange, a commodity as either a piece of property or a social cause. And she becomes a text upon which patriarchy seeks to inscribe her identity, as the actions of Paul D reveal. Not long after Paul D's arrival in Ohio, Sethe ponders why he would want her, suddenly, to bear him a child. She suspects he wants to use her body as a marker, a way of establishing a legacy for himself. By using her body to bear him a child he leaves behind a sign affirming both his manhood and his existence.

The reason Paul D wants a child, finally, is because he does not have the nerve to tell Sethe he has been having sex with Beloved as well as her. The excuse of a child might be, he reasons, what it takes to cause a rift between Sethe and Beloved and finally drive the strange girl out. Sethe herself comes to suspect the truth as she thinks about some of the things Paul D cannot endure: "Sharing her with the girls. Hearing the three of them laughing at something he wasn't in on. The code they used among themselves that he could not break. Maybe even the time spent on their needs and not his. They were a family somehow and he was not the head of it" (132). Paul D's sense of self and power is challenged when he confronts a situation unfamiliar to—indeed exclusive of—him. This sense of unfamiliarity and lack of control makes itself manifest in numerous ways. The most striking and disruptive moment occurs when Sethe finally tells him about the murder of her baby.

When Paul D arrives at 124 and runs the spirit of Beloved out of the house, he thinks he has made the house safe for Sethe and Denver. He assumes he can confront and control powers that others cannot. He realizes when Sethe tells him about her baby's death that he has it all wrong:

And because she had not [run the spirit off] before he got there her own self, he thought it was because she could not do it. That she lived with 124 in helpless, apologetic resignation because she had no choice; that minus husband, sons, mother-in-law, she and her slow-witted daughter had to live there all alone making do. The prickly, mean-eyed Sweet Home girl he knew as Halle's girl was obedient (like Halle), shy (like Halle), and work-crazy (like Halle). He was wrong. This here Sethe was new. (164)

Paul D can only judge Sethe by bringing prescribed models of order into play. She needs the direction of a husband/son/mother-in-law in order to do better than "make do." Sethe is measured in Paul D's eyes by how much she is like her husband, Halle, rather than like herself. Under his gaze, her identity is bounded. When he learns that her words and her actions can transgress those bounds, Paul D is both surprised and scared that this Sweet Home girl can so effectively tear down the walls of social and famil-ial structures and draw a handsaw across her child's throat.

The tension between Sethe and Paul D—and the intractable relation-shp between Sethe and history—moves toward resolution as Paul D re-turns to visit Sethe near the close of the narrative. Beloved has been run off. Sethe feels deserted, dissociated from that which was her best part, which she strove so hard to protect, and which has been lost to her once again. The loss of the past, her daughter, and her ability to name and so claim these threatens to destroy Sethe. Beneath Paul D's hands washing her, her body feels as if it will crumble away. She does not know whether she can withstand the touch of contact: "Nothing left to bathe, assuming he even knows how. Will he do it in sections? First her face, then her hands, her thighs, her feet, her back? Ending with her exhausted breasts? And if he bathes her in sections, will the parts hold? She opens her eyes, knowing the danger of looking at him. She looks at him" (272). The narrative marks a moment of commitment on Sethe's part. She realizes the need to connect with and to rely upon another.

For his part, Paul D does not know what to think of Sethe lying on Baby Suggs's bed seemingly—like the old woman before her—waiting only for death: "There are too many things to feel about this woman. His head hurts. Suddenly he remembers Sixo trying to describe what he felt about the Thirty-Mile Woman. 'She is a friend of mine. She gather me man. The pieces I am, she gather them and give them back to me in all the right order. It's good, you know, when you got a woman who is a friend of your mind'" (272). Like the Thirty-Mile Woman of Sixo's affections, Sethe helps form the syntax of Paul D's life. Because of this, "he wants to put his story next to hers" (273). Together they might form a story different from the suffering of Beloved's story and from the tyranny of history that her story represents.

It is this tyranny to which Paul D refers when he tells Sethe, "[M]e and you, we got more yesterday than anybody. We need some kind of tomorrow" (273). Paul D tries to move Sethe away from the destructive past toward a new beginning. Suggesting a movement beyond the structures of patriarchy and the violence of slavery, Paul D realizes the need to rename and reidentify what their past was. As a result of this new syntax, as a consequence of putting together previously disparate stories and histories, they can begin to articulate what a future may be. Paul D wants to put his story next to hers, to rewrite and so reroute the course of their narrative.

After all, Beloved's story "is not a story to pass on" (275). The ambiguity of this phrase reveals the ambiguity of the relation between history and the dispossessed. On the one hand, history is eternally reinvoked and reinforced: Beloved's is a story that cannot be ignored. On the other hand, history must be contested and refused: Beloved's is a story that cannot be passed down. A possible means out of this impasse may be the reconfiguration of history, the putting together of disparate narratives in the formation of a new syntax.[7]

The drawing together of stories signals a primary strategy in Morrison's text. Here at the level of narrative performance lies the resistant and critical postmodern qualities of the novel. The play of the novel is not simply a pastiche of various narrative forms. Rather, it is a conjoining of different discourses, a tracing of their different social significances. The construction of the text serves to voice mixed forms, to articulate the mestizaje of contemporary multicultural literary production. This is the presentation of a new and heretofore absent expression in an attempt to speak a missing aspect of history. The novel works to weave together into one narrative stories seemingly as dissimilar as those by Sethe and Paul D. Throughout, the text highlights the various processes by which stories, both traditional and contemporary, oral and written, historical and fictional, are told. The tale of Sethe's escape and Denver's birth, the infanticide and the aftermath, all are told by or remembered through the consciousness of various characters—Denver, Sethe, Beloved—as well as through the contemporary narrator whose voice frames the entire narrative. From the first page of the novel, this voice creates a tension between the fictional past and the present moment of narration. The narrator explains that the site of the novel, 124 Bluestone Road, "didn't have a number then, because Cincinnati didn't stretch that far. In fact, Ohio had been calling itself a state only seventy years" (36). The narrative brings to the fore the temporal disjuncture between the narrative present and the fictional past characteristic of the novel form. *Beloved* also focuses on how stories are told by one person to another as a means of articulating the accumulated wisdom of communal thought and of hearing the dead through the voices of the living. The novel thus evokes numerous forms of narrative—and numerous forms of telling history—as it forms a critical postmodern pastiche.

Pastiche is of course quite a loaded term within discussions of postmodernism. One position, as articulated by Fredric Jameson, asserts that pastiche is a neutral practice of parody, "without any of parody's ulterior motives, amputated of the satiric impulse, devoid of laughter. . . . Pastiche is thus blank parody" (65). Hal Foster similarly views artists employing pastiche as being "foot-loose in time, culture, and metaphor" (16). On the other hand, David Antin, discussing postmodern poetry, argues that the "weaker" logical relations between the assembled objects of pastiche allow "a greater degree of uncertainty of interpretation or, more specifically, more degrees of freedom in the reading of the sign-objects and their ensemble relations" (21). Contra Jameson, in *Beloved* the use of pastiche is not a "blank" parody but rather a liberating technique that frees the signifier from a fixed frame of reference. In *Beloved,* the pastiche suggests that each narrative form evoked by the novel—novelistic, modernistic, oral, preliterate, journalistic, and, most significantly, historical—becomes a metanarrative at play in the field of the narrative. The novel evokes a narrative that has been decentered by history, the communal voice articulating African-American experiences. It places this voice within the same discursive space as a central narrative form, an aesthetically decentered but culturally privileged modernism. By juxtaposing these against the historical configuration of slavery and its aftermath, *Beloved* takes quite literally the decentering impulse that informs postmodern culture. The novel places into play an aesthetically decentered novel with a historically dispossessed constituency to reenvision the relationship between storytelling and power. The novel deploys a narrative pastiche in order to contest history as a master narrative.[8]

The importance of historically decentered narratives in all of Morrison's works cannot be overestimated. In an interview with Nellie McKay, Morrison talks about the evocation of a community voice in her novels:

> The fact is that the stories look as though they come from people who are not even authors. No author tells these stories, they are just told—meanderingly—as though they are going in several directions at the same time. . . . I am not experimental, I am simply trying to recreate something of an old art form in my books—the something that defines what makes a book

"black." And that has nothing to do with whether the people in the book are black or not. The open-ended quality that is sometimes a problematic in the novel form reminds me of the uses to which stories are put in the black community. The stories are constantly being retold, constantly being imagined within a framework. (427)

Morrison's explanation suggests a reliance upon collective thinking and impersonal memory, the telling and interpretation of stories through multiple voices. Her work does not engage with the infinite progress of aesthetic experimentation. If nothing else, postmodernism has at the very least allowed us to see the links between a drive for aesthetic avant-gardism and the mind-set of technological modernization. The need for endless aesthetic invention can no longer effectively drive contemporary culture.[9] It is worth emphasizing here: evident in Morrison's text is a break with the ideology of progress overtly and covertly evident in modernist texts. Morrison's novel and the work of other multicultural writers represent a strategic break. Her novel revisits history neither for sheer aesthetic play nor as a neoconservative call upon staid forms of tradition. Rather, Morrison's text offers a radical revisioning and recounting of history. This recounting seeks to highlight the erasure enacted on those who have often paid the dearest price in the race for economic and technological "progress." Rather than make her art new—a view linked to a belief in the infinite progress of modern civilization—Morrison discusses her works in terms of rewriting and reinterpreting established forms. Her work, in other words, assumes a postmodernist position.

This position resonates with the analysis of storytelling posited by modernist visionary Walter Benjamin. "Experience which is passed on from mouth to mouth," Benjamin writes, "is the source from which all storytellers have drawn. And among those who have written down the tales, it is the great ones whose written version differs least from the speech of the many nameless storytellers" (84). The storyteller draws on the voice of community. Most significantly, the storyteller creates community, uniting, through narrative, the lives of the teller, the listener, and the greater world of experience from which the story is drawn. In this respect, storytelling distinguishes itself from the simple conveyance of information. Storytelling "sinks the thing into the life of the storyteller, in order to bring it out of him again. Thus traces of the storyteller cling to the story the way the handprints of the potter cling to the clay vessel" (91–92). There evolves an interconnectivity between experience, the teller, the auditor.

What separates Morrison's use of storytelling in *Beloved* from Benjamin's romantic vision in "The Storyteller" is its ability to dehierarchize narrative forms. Rather than confirm storytelling as a singularly "authentic" form of communication, Morrison's text engages with the numerous ways narratives—official and unofficial, central and decentralized, privileged and marginal, historical and aesthetic–function in multicultural spaces. While the novel questions the master's discourse, it does not suggest a simple call back to the village as the sole source of "authentic" knowledge and learning. There is no turning away from the numerous voices that contribute to the narrative. Often these voices evoke an oral quality; often—as with the framing narrative voices—they do not. Each in its own way recounts the same event, each from a different perspective, none taking precedence over the others.

The retelling of Denver's birth provides an illustrative example. The story emerges at different points in the narrative, and, with each telling, a different facet of the story emerges. While each teller evokes an orality in the telling of the story, the overall problematic of Morrison's novel does not disappear: each of these "oral" stories merges with a highly complex and narratively elaborate postmodern novel.[10]

The first telling of the birth story comes just after Denver sees an apparition of Beloved hugging Sethe. Denver turns from the window and follows the well-worn path around the house: "Easily she stepped into the told story that lay before her eyes on the path she followed away from the window. . . . And to get back to the part of the story she liked best, she had to start way back: hear the birds in the thick woods, the crunch of leaves underfoot" (29). Though we know that "the magic of her birth, its miracle in fact, testified to . . . friendliness as did her own name," it is not until fifty pages later that we learn the source of Denver's appellation—the white girl in search of velvet, Amy Denver. Sethe too tells a version, though abbreviated, of Denver's birth to Paul D: "Nothing bad can happen to her. Look at it. Everybody I knew dead or gone or dead and gone. Not her. Not my Denver. Even when I was carrying her, when it got clear that I wasn't going to make it—which meant she wasn't going to make it either—she pulled a whitegirl out of the hill. The last thing you'd expect to help" (42). Later still, Denver prepares to tell the same story to Beloved: "She swallowed twice to prepare for the telling, to construct out of the strings she had heard all her life a net to hold Beloved" (76). And then the story: "She had good hands, she said. The whitegirl, she said, had thin little arms but good hands. She saw that right away, she said. Hair enough for five heads and good hands, she said" (76–77). Presently, the narrative gives way to another voice, the omniscient narration told by the contemporary speaker.

Each telling, each version of Denver's birth, shares similar phrases and images: the wild onions into which Sethe falls, the bloody back of the runaway slave, the good hands of the white girl, the river birth. The repetition and variation create a sense that the story has always been present, that an already familiar story is being told once more. In this respect the strategy suggests orality. The repetition and variation also suggest that there is no authoritative view by which to judge Denver's birth. Despite a potential desire to locate in the oral elements of *Beloved* a privileged discourse, their presence serves incessantly to disrupt authority.

Authority in *Beloved* becomes subject to a double impulse. One is a move toward an original source, a "true" and powerful form of discourse—the slave narrative, the rural narrative, the folk narrative—as an integral part of Morrison's technique. Simultaneously, there is the implicit and explicit argument made that *Beloved*'s is a story that has yet to be told, that cannot be told, cannot be understood. Consequently, numerous forms of narration are called upon to convey the partial information of an inevitably fragmented story. The first move may be characterized as an evocation of the premodern, the second of the postmodern. The decentered and residual storytelling tradition in *Beloved* is mediated through the complex and decentered form of the postmodern novel. As a result, *Beloved* makes overt the often covert connections between language and power, narrative and politics. It draws upon the idea of tradition without yielding to the exigencies of political, social, and cultural conservatism. It resists notions of a centralized authority while not denying that forms of authority—both central and marginal—exist in the world. The novel composes a pastiche of discourses intimately tied to forms of power. Simultaneously, it sets those discourses in tension by examining their contested claims to authority. Nowhere is this tension more evident, finally, than in the contested form of the novel itself.

Beloved creates this tension by relying upon the authority of the community in order to speak while employing that most alienated and isolated form of contemporary literary creation—the novel. The tension between the modern and the premodern forms the point at which the strategies of Morrison's narrative converge. The work refers to various discourses as it assumes and transforms them. It both points toward the alienated world of modern aesthetic production and evokes the oral tradition of the black community. This tradition forms a critique of the master's authority, a critique of authority altogether. *Beloved* is born of a dissatisfaction with the present through an invocation of the already present past. The novel can be read, then, as a "rememory" of the discursive powers of community. It becomes a metanarrative that critiques the oppressive practices of authority. From this perspective the novel stands as a postmodern text that challenges a postmodernism comprising endless aesthetic play and reified alterity. *Beloved* knits together various discursive threads in order to counter this reification with historical and cultural specificity, with a presence premised upon absence. The novel seeks to forge out of this absence a new and more inclusive story. The story of absence and exclusion that Beloved's story represents becomes, indeed, not a story to pass on. The novel interweaves its narrative as a commentary on the difficult history of America that has brought people of all races together in hatred and love. The only resolution to this interweaving is to insist that Beloved's story be closed off in order for new stories to be told. The last word of the text merges with the title of the novel. Together they form an inscription and create a sense of finality and hope for renewal even a tombstone could not provide: Beloved.

Notes

An earlier version of this essay appeared as "Knitting and Knotting the Narrative Thread—*Beloved* as Postmodern Novel," *Modern Fiction Studies* 39, nos. 3–4 (Fall–Winter 1993): 689–707.

1. Here I find myself disagreeing with Marjorie Perloff's assessment of *Beloved* as a comfortable historical novel. Perloff argues that the book—with its virtuous characters, sequential story line, causality, collective memory, and melodrama—most resembles nineteenth-century realism.

2. The notion of being between "is" and "not" indeed proves central to the novel, dedicated as it is to the sixty million Africans who died during the Middle Passage between freedom and slavery. In an interview with Angel Carabi, Morrison notes that with the novel she was "trying to insert this memory [of the Middle Passage] that was unbearable and unspeakable into the literature. . . . It was a silence within the race. So it's a kind of healing experience. There are certain things that are repressed because they are unthinkable, and the only way to come free of that is to go back and deal with them" (38). Morrison highlights the interplay between absence and presence, between silence and voicing, evocative of Gates's discussion of blackness.

3. For a discussion of the use of ghosts as a link between the visible and invisible

in novels by Morrison, Philip Roth, and Leslie Marmon Silko, see Naomi Rand, "Surviving What Haunts You."

4. Robert Broad suggests that the distinction between individual and community is likewise blurred in *Beloved*. In this he argues that the novel contests the veneration of individuality by Western culture.

5. For a discussion of pain and its role in self-development, see Kristin Boudreau, "Pain and the Unmaking of Self in Toni Morrison's *Beloved*."

6. In this regard, we might think of the influence poststructural thought has had on a formalized notion of postmodernism. R. Radhakrishnan argues that poststructuralism can lead to a process of endless regression: "Post-structuralist thought perpetuates itself on the guarantee that no 'break' (Althusser) is possible with the past even though its initial intentional trajectory was precisely to make visible this very 'break,' valorize it qua 'break,' and then proceed towards a different and differential creation. Post-structuralist intentionality thus dessicates itself, allegorizes this dessication, and offers this allegorically perennial revolution as the most appropriate defense against the reproduction of such categories and structures as, Self, Subject, Identity, etc." (190). As Andreas Huyssen points out, poststructuralism actually is better understood as the end game of modernism, what Huyssen calls the "archeology of modernity," a theory of modernism at the stage of its exhaustion (39). Thus the conflation of the "indeterminacy" of poststructuralism with postmodernism leads to the often confusing conflation of high modernism with postmodernism. For a critical work premised on this conflation, see Marjorie Perloff, *The Poetics of Indeterminacy*.

7. Iyunolu Osagie argues that the novel shows "recorded history (which often presents certain information to the exclusion of some other) is a social construction reflecting a particular consciousness, a particular agenda. Indeed, with the lingering shadow of dark memories and the appearance and disappearance of ghosts in *Beloved*, Morrison states simply: There is more than meets the eye in the construction of history" (423). While Osagie highlights Morrison's application of psychoanalytic material as a rhetorical strategy, I find it useful to foreground the dehierarchizing quality of *Beloved*. The novel displaces a privileged position of history by putting it in proximity to other narratives. History is, as De Man suggests, a purely linguistic complication that, as *Beloved* strains to show, has real consequences in the suffering and devaluation of dispossessed populations.

8. M. M. Bakhtin's concern with the dialogic nature of hybrid languages is illustrative here. In *The Dialogic Imagination*, Bakhtin asks: "What is a hybridization? It is a mixture of two social languages within the limits of a single utterance, an encounter, within the arena of an utterance, between two different linguistic consciousnesses, separated from one another by an epoch, by social differentiation or

by some other factor" (358). The genius of the novel, as Bakhtin's familiar argument goes, is its ability to put these social languages into dialogue against each other in a strategy meant to subvert authoritative discourse. As this modernist intervention by the narrative represents a cornerstone of the critical function of the novel, *Beloved* helps illustrate that postmodernism does not supercede modernism but both contains it and contests it.

9. As Andreas Huyssen observes, many aspects of modernism are not obsolete: "What has become obsolete, however, are those codifications of modernism in critical discourse which, however subliminally, are based on a teleological view of progress and modernization" (49).

10. Of this complexity, Robert Broad observes: "Let's face it: Toni Morrison's *Beloved* can only be re-read" (189).

Works Cited

Antin, David. "Modernism and Postmodernism: Approaching the Present in American Poetry." *Boundary 2* 1, no. 1 (Fall 1972): 98–133.

Benjamin, Walter. "The Storyteller: Reflections on the Works of Nikolai Leskov." *Illuminations.* Ed. Hannah Arendt. Trans. Harry Zohn. New York: Shocken Books, 1969. 83–109.

——. "Theses on the Philosophy of History." *Illuminations.* Ed. Hannah Arendt. Trans. Harry Zohn. New York: Shocken Books, 1969, 253–65.

Benston, Kimberly. "I Yam What I Am: The Topos of Un(naming) in Afro-American Literature." *Black Literature and Literary Theory.* Ed. Henry Louis Gates, Jr. New York: Methuen, 1984. 151–72.

Boudreau, Kristen. "Pain and the Unmaking of Self in Toni Morrison's *Beloved.*" *Contemporary Literature* 36, no. 3 (Fall 1995): 445–64.

Broad, Robert L. "Giving Blood to the Scraps: Haints, History, and Hosea in *Beloved.*" *African American Review* 28, no. 2 (Summer 1994): 189–97.

Carabi, Angel. "Toni Morrison." *Belles Lettres: A Review of Books by Women* 9, no. 3 (1994): 38–45.

De Man, Paul. *The Resistance to Theory.* Minneapolis: University of Minnesota Press, 1986.

Foster, Hal. "Against Pluralism." *Recodings: Art, Spectacle, Cultural Politics.* Ed. Hal Foster. Port Townsend, Wash.: Bay Press, 1985. 13–32.

Gates, Henry Louis, Jr. "Criticism in the Jungle." *Black Literature and Literary Theory.* Ed. Henry Louis Gates, Jr. New York: Methuen, 1984. 1–24.

Handley, William R. "The House a Ghost Built: Nommo, Allegory and the Ethics of Reading in Toni Morrison's *Beloved.*" *Contemporary Literature* 36, no. 4 (Winter 1995): 676–702.

Huyssen, Andreas. "Mapping the Postmodern." *New German Critique* 33 (Fall 1984): 5–52.

Jameson, Fredric. "Postmodernism, or the Cultural Logic of Late Capitalism." *New Left Review* 146 (1984): 53–92.

McKay, Nellie Y. "An Interview with Toni Morrison." *Contemporary Literature* 14, no. 4 (1983): 413–29.

McKible, Adam. "'These Are the Facts of the Darky's History': Thinking History and Reading Names in Four African American Texts." *African American Review* 28, no. 2 (Summer 1994): 223–36.

Morrison, Toni. *Beloved.* New York: Knopf, 1987.

Osagie, Iyunolu. "Is Morrison Also among the Prophets?: 'Psychoanalytic' Strategies in *Beloved.*" *African American Review* 28, no. 3 (Fall 1994): 423–41.

Pasquier, Marie-Claire. "Toni Morrison: 'Dans ma famille, on racontait tout le temps des histoires.'" *La Quinzaine Littéraire,* Mar. 1–15, 1985, 12–13.

Perloff, Marjorie. *The Poetics of Indeterminacy: Rimbaud to Cage.* Princeton: Princeton University Press, 1981.

———. "Great American Novel?" *ANQ* 5, no. 4 (Oct. 1992): 229–231.

Radhakrishnan, R. "Feminist Historiography and Post-Structuralist Thought: Intersections and Departures." *The Difference Within: Feminism and Critical Theory.* Ed. Elizabeth Meese and Alice Parker. Philadelphia: John Benjamins, 1989. 189–205.

Rand, Naomi R. "Surviving What Haunts You: The Art of Invisibility in *Ceremony, The Ghost Writer,* and *Beloved.*" *MELUS* 20, no. 3 (Fall 1995): 21–33.

A Conversation on
Toni Morrison's *Beloved*

BARBARA CHRISTIAN

DEBORAH MCDOWELL

NELLIE Y. MCKAY

◆   ◆   ◆

NM: I would like to thank both of you for taking the time to talk with me about Toni Morrison's *Beloved*. I have always felt that this book embodies many oral qualities, perhaps because we learn a great deal about the narrative through the dialogues that the characters have with each other as well as with themselves as they struggle with their memories. Consequently, I believe that an oral component in this book makes an appropriate contribution to the collection. I have no prepared questions to lead us into the discussion since I envisioned a more spontaneous and less structured dialogue: something that captures some of the flavor of the oral tradition. So, I now invite you to relax and jump in with your questions and ideas as they come to you. We'll bounce our ideas off of each other for the next hour or so.

Let me begin by saying that I am presently teaching a course on Morrison's novels to fifty-four undergraduates in one of our four-week Summer School sessions. I've arranged my syllabus to end the class with *Beloved* in two weeks, so we have not gotten to it yet. But as we talk today, even as I project myself into the next ten days or so when I will be teaching *Beloved*, I will be downloading the lecture on *Song of Solomon* that I gave this morning and which I am carrying around in my head. A good place for us to start may be to tap into something Barbara mentioned to me the other night on the phone about the diasporic qualities in the novel. Barbara, would you mind explaining to Deborah and me what constitutes these diasporic elements and how they function in this novel?

BC: Well, interestingly, *Song of Solomon* gives me a way to enter *Beloved*. What I see in *Song of Solomon* is Morrison pushing further and further into the black past from her previous novels. I mean, *Song of Solomon* moves us back from Lorain, Ohio (*The Bluest Eye*), and Medallion (*Sula*) in a reverse migration from Michigan to Pennsylvania and then Virginia, to consider the long ago: the dead ones. In *Tar Baby*, which follows *Song of Solomon*, we see her making a move forward again. One of the things that I thought about when I read *Beloved* and *Jazz* was that the historical process in *Beloved* stopped her from moving directly back to Africa; and it seemed to me that what stopped here was the Middle Passage. There has been so little information about the Middle Passage that in order to move further back or across the ocean, there was a whole section [of history] that had to be filled in. So because a lot of people have written about *Beloved* as evoking the Middle Passage, that brings out a lot of information on it. The Middle Passage has become a lot more interesting to me since Morrison published that book. In other words, now historians are talking more about the Middle Passage and what it means.

But that wasn't exactly what I meant by diasporic, although we can talk about the Middle Passage in relation to that concept. It seems to me that throughout the book there are echoes of different kinds of African retentions. One that is really striking, which one of my students worked on, was the dance of the antelope. Sethe recalls the antelope dances in relation to her mother. And the language! She can no longer speak the language of her mother. There is also the information that she gets on how her mother threw away all of the children she conceived or gave birth to while coming across the ocean except her (Sethe), because she was the child of the black man around whom her mother put her arms. One keeps hearing this echo, this echo in the lives of the slaves of a life that happened previous to their enslavement, that is, a life in Africa. And so one gets that kind of diasporic resonance in relationship to Africa, and also I would say, in relation to the Caribbean. That, for me, especially, the way in which Morrison uses memory in the novel, in terms of the return of Beloved, is very much rooted in Caribbean storytelling, in the folklore of the Caribbean. The dead come back, they come back when people die in a way that is not understandable to them, or in a terrible or brutal manner, they come back as babies. They literally return. Stories from Haiti as well as from the English-speaking Caribbean are similar. So these beliefs are very much embedded in Caribbean culture. When I read *Beloved,* I read it very much through a Caribbean lens. Am I making sense to you? You see, some people character-ize this return as part of the psychoanalytic, but in the Caribbean it's not characterized that way; it is literally part of the spiritual folklore: it is possi-ble for the dead to return, especially in the form of children.

NM: But that's not only Caribbean, it is also African, and in the Caribbean the stories are African retentions.

BC: Yes, that's why I'm saying the idea of the dead returned is diasporic. It's got diasporic resonances. It's not only African in the sense of being left be-hind in Africa, it's also Caribbean, and I would say it's probably African-American up to a certain point, maybe not through the present, I'm not sure. But I'm sure it's rooted in nineteenth-century black life in the New World, so that life in the out-of-Africa homeland has that diasporic quality that comes from Africa to the Caribbean, to blacks in North America who influence the Caribbean a second time, you know. Moving back and forth. So that was part of what I was thinking about. And there are also actual in-cidents in the novel such as the antelope dance and the way in which music is used, these seem to me to be very diasporic.

NM: I'm sure that you are correct on these assumptions. Morrison's work is so multifaceted that there are many ways from which one can approach everything she's written, and *Beloved* is an especially rich text. I would be very interested in more work on this aspect of the book. Any comments, Debbie?

DM: No, I don't have any comments on that. I find it very, very intriguing, but I've done no cross-cultural research and so must take Barbara's read-ings on faith.

BC: What I did in a piece already was this: I went back to Africa to find, ac-tually I mean I went to the works of John Mbiti and to some of the research that's been done in African religions and philosophies. It was really difficult to do, because in all of the material about the ancestors, many different points of view surface on such issues as ancestor worship. But the point is that there's a lot of discussion about it in much of West African religions where this idea of the ancestral return is central. If an individual has a trau-matic—a really traumatic—death, the dead do return. Someone else also told me, and I haven't been able to follow this up yet, but a professor from SUNY-Albany, where Morrison used to teach, told me that she (Morrison) did a lot of research in Brazil particularly looking at the work of the scholar who wrote *Flash of the Spirit.*

DM: Robert Farris Thompson.

BC: Right, and in his book there are discussions of the phenomenon.

NM: You mean, that Morrison did a lot of this research prior to writing *Beloved* to gather information to write about the return of Beloved?

BC: Yes, that's what he told me, that she actually read a lot of this material.

NM: I have no doubt of that because she has such a broad, wide net: a knowledge base through which she seems to filter everything that shows up in her novels. Her broad knowledge makes everything she writes extraordinarily rich and complex because she's pulling from various strands of ways of knowing. And because she is as knowledgeable and so well grounded in diverse myths and cultures, readers seldom resist suspending belief and follow her excursions that blend Western epistemology with other cultured views of reality.

BC: And for me that was really an important part of it, you see, because when *Beloved* came out I felt that there were so many psychoanalytical readings of the book that showed little awareness, I would say, or willingness to admit that there were other systems which also explained the book and the character Beloved herself; that it didn't have to be exclusively the return of the repressed, right, which is the way psychoanalytic critics read it. There is an African, a diasporic, way of thinking about a trauma that a people go through or a trauma that a person goes through, a black family goes through, that explains it. You know, there are many narratives in this narrative.

DM: And the various systems within which Morrison works are not counterposed to each other, nor mutually exclusive.

BC: Not at all; in fact, in many ways they intersect.

DM: And because there is always this really thick and dense layering of knowledge systems and intellectual currents in Morrison's writings, that there is a psychoanalytic dimension to *Beloved* as there is to *Jazz* and to much else that Morrison writes is indisputable, but that dimension is not incompatible with the solid grounding of these books in specific cultural and folkloric traditions as well.

BC: Right, I don't think these systems are incompatible, but I was concerned about the feminist emphasis among critics in the academy who tend to note only the psychoanalytic and not the other narratives. These critics who give the novel a kind of one-dimensional status. So I think it was important to include other ways of looking at it. When I was in Paris, it was fascinating to me that most of the African students I met there read it in terms of an African narrative rather than a psychoanalytic one. So it's not that different approaches are incompatible; I am just concerned about the way in which academic critics can take hold of one narrative and make that one the only narrative.

NM: I also think, Barbara, that what I meant by the wide net that Morrison casts is exactly what Deborah said a few minutes ago: the layering in the novels. One can keep digging deeper and deeper into Morrison's work and find the same issues dealt with in so many ways and from so many different cultural references that she destablizes our tendencies toward safe one-dimensional meanings. She brings elements from diverse cultures into the African-American narrative. But, far from creating destructive opposition within her texts, in as far as such opposition exists in the layering, it enriches each story, each novel, and each text she produces seems richer than the one that went before because of her experiments with this sort of multilayered narrative. I think, for instance, that many of the initial responses to *Song of Solomon* that came from very well known and influential critics who liked that book because they could read it through European symbols and myths, fell short because they were totally unaware of the myths and elements in it that belonged to African and African-American culture and various other sources that Morrison used. We've now been able to, I think, convince many people, or convince many critics at least, that there is a cultured layering that's taking place in the novels, and while there is one set of textures that come from one mode of thought or from one culture, there are many others that come from other sources.

BC: Well, I think that's Morrison's distinctive gift.

DM: I would agree with that.

BC: Yes, when I use the word layers, and many of us use that term, even in titles of our works on Morrison, I mean her adeptness at weaving language. You know, I actually think of it as rhythms on top of rhythms, like you get in chords in jazz. That she's able to do that like no other writer I know of is partly why I think so many different audiences connect with her. The layers, the rhythms, also involve certain kinds of silences for the reader to fill in from her culture and tradition. And one of the things I'm trying to figure out is how Morrison does this. I mean, really in a very formal way, I'm talking about the formal quality. I mean, we know she does it, but to actually look at incidents where she does it, it's fascinating. The different kinds of techniques she uses produce work with many layers. And one element that gives her that ability is, as you said, because she reads so much. She knows so much about different cultures and also cultures that are gone. I mean, there's a lot of Greek mythology, for example, in *Beloved*.

NM: And that's because she's fascinated with those cultures. I mean, it's clear that her own fascination with various cultures and modes of thinking are things that she brings directly to the fiction. I tell students that reading Morrison's novels is or can be an exercise in discovery if one wants to trace the many sources from which she draws to achieve both the depth and richness that make reading her as rewarding as it is.

BC: And she does this in a real syncretic way; I mean, the kind of synthesis that she's able to do is remarkable. There are some people who know a lot but they somehow are not able to pull their knowledge together in a way that the reader does not see the piecing together. As she says, "the seams don't show," you know. So, Deborah, I was wondering, have you been doing any kind of work specifically on *Beloved*?

DM: No, I have not been doing any work on *Beloved* recently.

BC: I was interested in whether you are or not because of the piece you did on *Sula*, how you related some of the ways in which you talk about that very complicated character Sula, to what you can say about *Beloved*. Because Sula is a character in which one can see her both as oppositional and nonoppositional, how would you look at Sethe in this light or from that perspective?

DM: Well, what I was trying to do in the *Sula* essay was to respond to something in the same way as you are looking at the diasporic elements in *Beloved*: as the kind of corrective to a body of criticism that was leaning too intently in one direction. I was doing that on a different critical matter in the essay on *Sula*, and that was to really try to challenge the fixation that so many black critics had in the '80s on positive imaging, criticism that stemmed from the popular success of books like *The Color Purple* and plays like *For Colored Girls*. I was impatient with such rigid notions about what makes a positive black character and particularly what makes a positive black male character. So I was trying to challenge those notions through a reading of *Sula*, which is a text I think that, perhaps more than any other of Morrison's, really does resist conventional notions of character, understood to mean coherent and whole. And I think that resistance has some implications for ideas about race and culture. Typically we bring spatial logic to discussions of culture, as if cultures exist within specific physical boundaries and do not migrate beyond those boundaries. And I think that what we're calling this interweaving and layering in Morrison gets at that very issue. There is a way in which African myths of flying and Western myths of flying intermingle in *Song of Solomon,* and I think you can see that. That's just an example of one metaphor, but you can take any kind of structuring motif in practically any Morrison work and you see that there is an intermingling that resists notions of sealing off or cordoning off one metaphoric or symbolic system from another. Issues of culture are migratory, and one thing about *Beloved,* going back to your point about the Middle Passage, is that from the moment of contact, those cultures began a process of syncresis in which the artifacts, the belief systems, the assumptions of each became inextricably entwined with the other, and it is sometimes hard to know where the one stops and the other starts.

BC: I find your points really fascinating in terms of the characters themselves in *Beloved.* You have one like, let's say Denver, who is born while her mother is escaping slavery and is on the way to freedom. From my point of view, Denver is a free African-American in the sense that she's never been a slave. But, what happens to her around her birth?

NM: Sethe would probably have died in the woods had not Amy Denver come along, and against all the cultural expectations of the racial issues involved, the white girl helped the escaping black slave mother and baby in such a way as to give both the chance to escape and survive. Their survival depended on the actions, the human, benevolent actions we might say, of Amy Denver.

BC: And Sethe names her daughter Denver. That's an American name. But I'd like to ask a question about Paul D because I recalled that Deborah's essay had something to do with the response to the way men were being viewed in men's and black women's books in the '80s, and I've often wondered if perhaps Morrison is responding partly to those kinds of concerns in her characterization of Paul D?

DM: Hmm, I don't know. The one thing that I would say about Morrison's characters in general, because I don't think I can answer your question, is, I don't know if she's responding to that kind of general controversy in the late '70s or early '80s, but I think what is clear about how she creates characters in general is that there is a tendency for us to sympathize with practically everybody she creates, even those whom conventional assumptions would lead us to conclude are evil, dastardly, or craven people. Like Sula for instance.

NM: I want to make two points. First, to Barbara's question, I don't know either if Morrison is responding directly to the controversy you mention. But one thing we all know is that Morrison is perhaps one of the most culturally aware of our contemporary critics and that the acuity of her critical intelligence misses nothing that has any significant meaning to the community. Black imaging is one of those things of which she is very both conscious and critical, as in her problem with the 1960s "Black Is Beautiful" slogan. My second point fills out Deborah's observations. One important part of Morrison's project is to avoid demonizing the characters she creates. She spends a lot of time, even on the most terrible among them, working out how they become what they've become and how they've been affected by the forces beyond themselves that they have to contend with. So, yes, there is a way in which it is very difficult not to be sympathetic to even those who seem to embody some of the traits that we least admire in people.

DM: Yes, this strategy speaks to the historical temper of her work, that there is an effort to, when you say to explain, you have to place them in a historical context. Halle sees the men taking Sethe's milk, but it is Paul D who provides the historical dimension to the aftermath of the occurrence. Before Paul D's arrival, Sethe could only say that Halle wasn't there (where they were supposed to meet), that he abandoned her and their children. Paul D provides the information that lets her know her husband was up above in the loft, that he saw them take her milk, and he couldn't do a damned thing about it. He conveys to Sethe and the reader that somehow that scene devastated Halle emotionally; I mean, it cracked him; it broke him; in a manner of speaking, it paralyzed him.

BC: Yes, and you just brought up something else that I really love about *Beloved* because one of the things I think the novel really conveys to us is the way in which it is not enough to have one person's memory or two persons' memories, but we need to have a community of memory. And the whole novel, it seems to me, is infused in terms of this chorus of memories playing with, singing with, against, creating new kinds of memories, some against and for and so forth.

DM: And also the understanding of memory as a creative process.

NM: Exactly.

DM: Again, we typically think of memory according to a documentary logic or as facts, memory as fact: this happened, I remember that. But what Sethe understands, and I think conveys through that really interesting locution called "re-memory," is that every revisitation of an actual event recreates or re-members, puts back together that which was, but that putting back together doesn't bear a uniform relation to what was there before: memory is a creative process.

NM: That triggers something for me. I mean I like that a lot, because it takes me back to power and art in the story of Denver's birth, which is told at least three separate times in the text. Denver's telling of the story of her birth and Sethe's telling the same story on different occasions are quite interesting and emphasize the creativity of memory. The power and the art are even more phenomenal in the part of the story in which the voices of Sethe, Beloved, and Denver constitute a chorus of need and remembering. But the story of Denver's birth is pretty powerful too.

DM: What would Denver know about her birth other than what she had been told?

NM: Exactly. But she has a story that's her own and not Sethe's.

BC: A story, yes, and Morrison says this herself very well in her Nobel Prize speech when she says narrative creates us at the very moment that we are creating it.

DM: Absolutely. And you see, it goes back to the issue with which we began. I mean, the whole idea of the myth of the eternal return, especially the return of that from which one was traumatically sundered—the community, the family, etc.—the return of that. And that is an active imagination; that is fantasy. You know, that represents the interior workings of a people, fantasy, longing, desire, wish fulfillment, that is the psychoanalytic, that's the interior matter of us.

BC: Right, and that's what this novel is so much about: it's so much about a people who are not a people. That's the way it begins, and it's not only through laws, it's through what you just talked about, that desire, that creation, that narrative. Every people has a narrative.

DM: Exactly. And throughout human history we see how these narratives have intersected with various discrete traditions; they might have a different name, but you know every culture, for example, has a creation story.

BC: And so how do we become a people? For African-Americans it takes on a relatively unique quality because of the traumatic sundering that took place during the Middle Passage, and so the very idea of using that quote from the Bible at the beginning of the novel, "I will call them my people,/ which were not my people;/ and her beloved,/ which was not beloved," reminds us that African-Americans themselves are syncretic, from Africa that is, that they're all different peoples who had to figure out a way to become a people. And that was not long ago. It was a very short time ago.

DM: Precisely. To become a people. One of my favorite scenes in *Beloved* is the scene of the picnic that results in the split in the community, a split caused by jealousy and envy. The community that feasted on Baby Suggs's bounty really turns on them, turns them in. And that's nothing but the result of plain, unmitigated envy.

NM: It was their refusal to warn Baby Suggs and her family of the danger coming their way, that deliberate nonaction that caused the tragedy for everyone.

DM: But how does one forge a common identity in the face of such realities of the human history of conflicts and power asymmetries: those who have not, resenting those who have? I think what I find most engaging and continual about Morrison's work is her refusal of sentimentality, a refusal of pietism and I think in this book any pietism about motherhood. I mean this is one of the most complicated dramatizations of the complexities of the maternal that I know. You know, again the resonance is to Medea from the classical tradition, but I mean, here are issues of infanticide, I mean the very reality of infanticide, I mean seeing it, breaking it apart, even in the context of slavery and even with the understanding of why it was committed. That is still a powerful taboo. All of her texts are about taboos of one kind or another, it seems to me.

NM: Who is this woman? That's a central question. Who is this woman with the audacity to take it into her own hands to decide whether someone should live or die?

DM: And you know, in mothering, there are so many different shadings and reversals of the maternal impulse in this novel. At one point Denver must become Sethe's mother.

BC: That's right, but that is not incompatible with the whole concept of African cosmology in relation to the mother. "Because mother is gold," for example, is a standard idea in West Africa. Go to the African-American spirituals. "Sometimes I feel like a motherless child"—there's nothing worse than that, and if you look at all of the major characters in the book except Denver, they do not know their mothers. They operate in a space in which the women don't know, they have not had the benefit of a mother to make them knowing of how to mother.

NM: Exactly right.

BC: And they don't have a motherland. So there's all that to cope with. I mean, what if the concepts of mother that we know, the "universal," I hate to use that word, but the ideal of mother existing in many traditions is the double figure, the mother who loves and the mother who can destroy. Morrison plays with that a lot in all of her work, not only in *Beloved* but in *Bluest Eye,* in *Sula, Song of Solomon,* in *Jazz,* in *Tar Baby,* and it's very important to me because of the way in which black women have so often been seen primarily and only completely as mother.

NM: And they're always only a certain kind of mother: the ideal or the destroyer.

DM: Yes, the black woman is always already a mother. That is the prototypical position of the black woman.

NM: That's right.

BC: And so Morrison's both on the cutting edge and at the same time she's also extending it, you know, it's so interesting. Because I remember in one interview she said she disagreed with feminists at the time because her motherhood was a very liberating thing. And Bill Moyers asked her why. This is on a tape with Bill Moyers, and she said because children will make you become the best thing you can possibly be, or the worst thing you can be. In other words, they put you to the test of being human, they look at you completely in terms of what's real, not whether your fingernail polish, and I remember that she used that example, is correct. But she's looking at a mother as a powerful kind of construct, at the same time as one whose definition restricts African-American women because of the narrow definitions applied to it. And so, *Beloved* is as powerful as I think it is partly because of Sethe's act, the one act that no woman, definitely no black woman, right, would ever do: kill her child.

NM: Because although it is known that there were slave mothers who killed their children, the fact is that's a story that has been covered up, that's a story that nobody really wants to talk about because it's the taboo, the black mother, certainly of all mothers, would not act in that way toward her child. "We are a people who love life," Mama Younger tells her driven-to-the-wall pregnant daughter-in-law in Hansberry's *Raisin in the Sun.*

BC: Yes, and in fact, mothers would also die for their children.

NM: Exactly.

BC: What's also interesting to me is the way in which Morrison changes Margaret Garner's story because it tells us something about the terms of motherhood. In the actual Garner story, the case itself, which one of my students read, the child that Garner kills is a mulatto, actually a child that probably was sired by her owner.

NM: That would put a whole other spin on things too, wouldn't it?

BC: Yes, from my point of view, Morrison changes that because she doesn't want the rationale of Garner having been raped and so killing the child is her way of getting back at the master. These children come from a family that is as close to a legal marriage as you can have in the slave structure. So Morrison's not bringing that in because a lot of people would like to read it as saying okay, she hated the man so she killed the child.

DM: I'm so glad you inserted that, she makes the story more complicated and more interesting because we already have that other narrative.

BC: That's right, and she says that she wants to invent something, there's an invention going on in the novel, it is not about what we already know. So she changes some elements of the case, the Garner case. The historical Margaret Garner was tried for theft rather than for murder. There was a certain way in which Margaret Garner, who couldn't speak in court because she was a slave, but was spoken for, laid claim to her child by killing her child. In other words, her child was no longer a possession of hers or of the system. It became her child. According to the law, the slave master owned her child. By killing her child, "I own this child, not you. This is my child." And that's such a complicated notion: the mother's ownership of the child. We see it in all kinds of myths all over the world too. It's not only in this context, the context of slavery, that the whole question of laying claim to children and asking who possesses them, who owns them, comes up, but it is intensified by the system of slavery. And whether children should be owned by their parents to the extent of determining whether they live or die is of course partly the question that Beloved comes back to ask.

NM: Exactly.

BC: Did Sethe have a right to do this? So the maternal is really complicated. Something that comes back to me also is how everybody expects her/his mother to love her/him, and I just taught *Sula* in the spring, and I had at least four students who wrote about the scene in *Sula* when Sula hears her mother say she loves her but does not like her. Sula was truly upset by this. But, in fact, we all know that as mothers, and among people we know who are mothers, there are some children whom their mothers don't like.

NM: There are some people whom we are in a sense forced to love, but we don't like. We can even understand that in some of our other personal relationships, but we refuse to admit that mothers are humans who have the same range of reactions to the children they bring into the world as they do to everyone else with whom they interact. I don't think that motherhood alters that part of the human dimension, no matter what the institution prescribes.

DM: No, and it's only the sentimentalization of motherhood that leads us to believe that motherhood equals love, or to mother is to love. It doesn't follow. Motherhood is a social institution complete with ideologies, and Morrison keeps puncturing these idealogies. In a way that really does grate. For instance, you can't take it neutrally when Hannah confronts her mother in *Sula* and asks Eva: "Did you love us?" and Eva replies: "What do you mean did I love you? I kept you alive didn't I?"

BC: That's an African-American response.

DM: And Eva goes on to repeat the narrative, the "three beet" story that Hannah does not want to hear for the umpteenth time, because what Hannah wants is to be affirmed in the knowledge of her mother's love, and Eva is not able to give her what she needs. The equation of motherhood with keeping the child fed and shod is what Eva's working with, but Hannah's working with something else because these are generational differences between them—they come at motherhood from different historical moments.

BC: Hannah wants to know, "Did you play with us?" That's a different definition of motherhood.

DM: Precisely, but you see what Morrison is doing is really giving us a subtle history of this institution, in the same way that she is implicitly giving us a subtle history of childhood. The institution of childhood as a stage in human development is a very recent phenomenon in the entire sweep of human history; it's relatively new. I think of the lengths to which we've taken that whole concept these days—in this the era of the hothouse babies, who require more and more "precious" forms of mothering, of attention. I think Eva's little conversation with Hannah in that scene is saying that, because she says, "In eighteen and ninety-five, I had three beets to my name." In *that* time. In *that* place, to paraphrase the opening paragraph of *Sula*.

NM: Emphasizing time and economic context.

BC: And that year, 1895, was at the very height of lynching, which adds the sociopolitical context.

DM: Right, as Eva puts it to Hannah, who had time to "ring around the rosie" when starvation stands at the door?

BC: And we see that in *Beloved,* but also in *Jazz*—that's one of the books we're not getting into, but in *Jazz* you see that question coming up again with Violet's mother—the mother who kills herself.

DM: Right, and in fact that entire book. I think to talk about *Beloved* we really cannot avoid talking about Morrison's corpus because there is a way in which *Beloved* is so epic in its scale that it not only invites the references to things outside itself that we've been talking about, the larger cultural and cross-cultural metaphors and myths and resonances, but it also really compels us to read it in relation to the rest of Morrison's corpus. Because there you see this continuation very clearly.

NM: The definition of the project that engages her.

DM: Yes, exactly. And in it we see the continuation of the signal scenes in *Beloved* that are in *Jazz,* everything, every trauma, every devastating act including the one at the center of that book, Joe Trace's murder of Dorcas. Everything in the realm of this novel is traceable to mother stuff. It's so interesting that when Joe traces Dorcas he tracks her to a house party in a borough of New York City. Tracing her comes on the heels of his fantasizing once again about tracking the woman who was alleged to be his mother to a burrow in the Virginia countryside. The murder of Dorcas, the love object, somehow links to Joe's absent mother, the missing mother.

BC: Yes, but you see, with Violet, there is a kind of reversal to what happens in *Beloved* because in *Beloved,* Sethe kills her child to save her (the child). In *Jazz,* Rosedear kills herself.

And that also has a kind of historical resonance, to get back to what you were saying, Deborah, because there's a different historical moment here when we consider that she waited until her kids are all together and Bell has come back, and so on, and then she jumps in the well.

DM: And jumping in the well suggests psychoanalytic theory.

BC: That is the return to the womb.

DM: To the womb, that's what the well becomes, it's a kind of external symbol: a physical symbol of the womb.

BC: As her mother has returned. So there's all that emphasis on the maternal. But getting back to *Beloved*. One of the other things that I find very striking about the novel is the way in which, and I just wrote a long piece on it called "Beloved, She's Ours," and it's about the question of ownership and possessiveness. Because throughout the novel Morrison constantly uses images of currency. Denver has a nickel face, Paul D knows his worth, and so on. Now in one sense that's the whole issue of the way in which Morrison makes us really feel slavery the way it was, as a system of ownership, that is, the ownership of people. But the question that I think she asks is not so simple. It has to do with motherhood as well. The whole question of when love becomes possession. That is, where the love seeks to own. And the question in *Song of Solomon* is one that comes up all the time in Morrison, this whole question of the thin line between love and the desire to possess. When does love stop being love and become possessiveness? Or, is it possible to love and not possess? So it is not only the question of being owned in terms of the legal system of slavery, it's also one that I call the interior imperial landscape. Slavery itself made slaves as persons very aware of what their monetary worth was, and that affected how the characters dealt with one another. Beloved is always insisting to Sethe that she owes her something. The novel is full of these images of currency and ownership and possession.

DM: That's absolutely right.

BC: . . . and that is part of what it means for a group that is still going through becoming a people.

NM: There's another area also of significance here: slaves did not own anything, not even themselves. And what was even worse was that on the scale of human worth, they were worth nothing. They were only valuable in as much as they could work and their work improved their owners' financial status. Women slaves were most valuable for their ability to be reproductive; to create more slaves, men for being studs and for their stamina for hard work.

BC: Yes, and that's what you have in the cent and the nickel and the dime, but then they used those terms with one another. There's a way in which, for example, Sethe sees herself completely as her milk, that is, she pares herself down to one thing, which is the way in which slaves were considered—the penises were worth a certain amount, they're itemized, commodified—and one of the things that Sethe works through in this novel, has to work through, is the way in which she is not her milk.

NM: While the milk is also the main source of life for her child.

BC: That's right. So it's this continuous process of how to stop being, seeing oneself as a commodity because that was the way one had been viewed and the way in which the characters related to one another. That's why that party picnic, when Baby Suggs is like Jesus Christ getting enough food for a crowd out of two loaves, and so on, is so important, because the rest of the community sees it in terms of what she has, right.

NM: But it's also interesting in that scene, and I meant to say this earlier, that, in fact, the neighbors who come to Baby Suggs's party partake of her bounty and do so quite heartily. The next morning when they woke up the first thing they realized was how much they had overeaten, and that makes them feel badly for themselves. But instead of looking at themselves and their gluttony, they project their anger onto Baby Suggs, who, in her joy at having at least part of her family with her, shares her happiness with everyone else by having the party. That's when the community becomes envious of what she is able to do, and I think that's one of the interesting things here in terms of what Morrison is doing relative to her overall project. Here we see her ability and willingness to explore, in depth, what is hardly praiseworthy in the black community. This is one of those time when, as Deborah mentioned earlier, we see her backing away from sentimentalizing the community and instead taking a hard look at what is actually going on within the "village."

DM: Because I think that's one of the things that most hamstrings us as a people. We really always let these larger idealisms dominate our conceptions of ourselves as a people and leave ourselves no space for entertaining the range of human emotions. We always want to be at one end or the other of any continuum, typically the most idealistic end.

NM: But that's also reaction.

DM: Yes, it is.

NM: Reaction to the negativity that racism projects onto us all the time. So we know why people behave the way they do, and that makes everything very complicated. There are always external forces driving many people to block out some of the humanness we should allow ourselves. So that it seems to me that it has taken us until these last years of the twentieth century for some of us, now at a distance from 1865, and it's certainly not a large number of us, to feel sufficiently secure in ourselves to have the luxury to examine ourselves and to try to set the record straight, to face ourselves in our weaknesses without denial, and not just worry about what other people or how other people see us, and what those other people think of us. A writer like Toni Morrison has, in fact, led this charge in which we are taking control of all of our history and saying we want to face up to who we are, and we engage in serious self-exploration, looking at ourselves in all our many complexities.

BC: Yes, and of course we have, as you say, a certain kind of freedom, and that may well be why an author like Morrison does go back, because she points out that *Beloved* comes from the slave narrative tradition. Slave narrators could not say certain things because they were involved in . . .

NM: They had another project, a different project.

BC: Their project was the abolition of slavery, so they spoke more about the institution rather than of the internal landscape, because they couldn't. And also what's interesting to me is that they couldn't afford to remember. It's not only that other people wanted to forget how awful slavery was, but they themselves couldn't afford to remember because they were so close to it, and it was so terrible, that it would not have been possible to continue their lives in any reasonable way if they remembered. I recall that when I started teaching some years ago many of my students said they did not want to hear about slavery. I think that was because they were overwhelmed by it because it was still pretty close in historical time. But as we move further away from it in time, from the actual events of the nineteenth century, although there are other things that we must deal with now, we have a certain kind of freedom and distance that permits us to see it in another way. And yes, Morrison, and I think a large group of our writers, not only Morrison.

NM: Sure, she's not the only one, but she's one of the leaders in this area.

BC: Yes, that's true. And they are insisting that the only way for us to heal ourselves is to face the meaning of slavery. "Healing" is another word that I want to use about this novel, not in a sentimental way, but as the outcome of the process of confronting the trauma of what slavery meant to the group. It's the psychoanalytic method in a way, isn't it?

DM: It is, working through, memory, repeating and working through, to borrow the title of one of Freud's essays.

BC: Talking it through until we get to the other side. This is what I call ritual; it's the ritual that we have to go through, a certain kind of ritual to get to the other side, the healing. And we are now in a position to do that. I think that this is one of the projects of the contemporary novel; because unless we get this done, that is, achieve a healing, and unless the country takes part in it, we're going to be repeating the trauma again.

NM: And that issue makes of the novel a cautionary tale, which is a good place to end this conversation because it leaves it as wide open as Morrison's end of the novel. Obviously, we could say a great deal more about *Beloved*, but we will have to leave that for another time. In the meantime, like the three of us, many scholars and teachers in our country and elsewhere will continue to feast on the inexhaustible wealth of both pleasure and challenge that this extraordinary book offers the reader's imagination.

This is not a story to pass on!

Suggested Reading

Atlas, Marilyn Judith. "Toni Morrison's *Beloved* and the Reviewers." *Midwestern Miscellany* 18 (1990): 45–57.

Berger, James. "Ghosts of Liberalism: Morrison's *Beloved* and the Moynihan Report." *PMLA* 111, no. 3 (May 1996): 408–20.

Boudreau, Kristin. "Pain and the Unmaking of Self in Toni Morrison's *Beloved*." *Contemporary Literature* 36, no. 3 (Fall 1995): 447–65.

Davies, Carole Boyce. "Mother Right/Write Revisited: *Beloved* and *Dessa Rose* and the Construction of Motherhood in Black Women's Fiction." *Narrating Mothers: Theorizing Maternal Subjectivites.* Ed. Brenda O. Daly and Maureen T. Reddy. Knoxville: University of Tennessee Press, 1991. 44–57.

Finney, Brian. "Temporal Defamiliarization in Toni Morrison's *Beloved.*" *Obsidian II* 5, no. 1 (Spring 1990): 20–36.

Gates, Henry Louis, Jr., and K. A. Appiah, eds. *Toni Morrison: Critical Perspectives Past and Present.* New York: Amistad, 1993.

Goldman, Ann E. "'I Made the Ink': (Literary) Production and Reproduction in *Dessa Rose* and *Beloved.*" *Feminist Studies* 16 (Summer 1990): 313–330.

Grewel, Gurleen. "Memory and the Matrix of History: The Poetics of Loss and Recovery in Joy Kogawa's *Obasan* and Toni Morrison's *Beloved.*" *Memory and Cultural Politics: New Approaches to American Ethnic Literatures.* Ed. Amritjit Singh, Joseph T.

Skerrett, Jr., and Robert E. Hogan. Boston: Northeastern Univ. Press, 1996. 140–74.

Hartman, Geoffrey. "Public Memory and Its Discontents." *Raritan* 13, no. 4 (Spring 1994): 24–40.

Handley, William R. "The House a Ghost Built: Nommo, Allegory, and the Ethics of Reading in Toni Morrison's *Beloved.*" *Contemporary Literature* 36, no. 4 (Winter 1995): 676–701.

Hirsch, Marianne. "Maternity and Rememory: Toni Morrison's *Beloved.*" *Representations of Motherhood.* Ed. Donna Bassin, Margaret Honey, Meryle Mahrer Kaplan. New Haven: Yale Univ. Press, 1994. 92–110.

Holloway, Karla F. C., and Stephanie Demetrakopoulos. *New Dimensions of Spirituality: A Biracial and Bicultural Reading of the Novels of Toni Morrison.* New York: Greenwood Press, 1987.

Keenan, Sally. "'Four Hundred Years of Silence': Myth, History, and Motherhood in Toni Morrison's *Beloved.*" *Recasting the World: Writing after Colonialism.* Ed. Jonathan White. Baltimore: Johns Hopkins Univ. Press, 1993. 45–81.

Kolmerten, Carol A., Stephen M. Ross, and Judith Bryant Wittenberg, eds. *Unflinching Gaze : Morrison and Faulkner Re-envisioned.* Jackson: Univ. Press of Mississippi, 1997.

Koolish, Lynda. "Fictive Strategies and Cinematic Representations in Toni Morrison's *Beloved*: Postcolonial Theory/Postcolonial Text." *African American Review* 29, no. 3 (Fall 1995): 421–38.

Levy, Andrew. "Telling *Beloved.*" *Texas Studies in Literature and Language* 33, no. 1 (Spring 1991): 114–23.

Mayer, Sulvia. "'You Like Huckleberries?' Toni Morrison's *Beloved* and Mark Twain's *Adventures of Huckleberry Finn.*" *The Black Columbiad: Defining Moments in African American Literature and Culture.* Ed. Werner Sollors and Maria Diedrich. Cambridge: Harvard Univ. Press, 1994. 337–46.

McKay, Nellie Y., ed. *Critical Essays on Toni Morrison.* Boston: G. K. Hall, 1988.

Middleton, David L., ed. *Toni Morrison's Fiction: Contemporary Criticism.* New York: Garland, 1997.

Morrison, Toni. "Memory, Creation, and Writing." *Thought: A Review of Culture and Idea* 59 (Dec. 1984): 385–390.

————. "Unspeakable Things Unspoken: The Afro-American Presence in American Literature." *Michigan Quarterly Review 28, no. 1* (Winter 1989): 1–34.

————. *Playing in the Dark : Whiteness and the Literary Imagination.* Cambridge: Harvard Univ. Press, 1992.

Rockwood, Bruce L. "Retakings: Perspectives on the Nature of Property and Politics from the Law and Literature of Slavery." *Law and the Conflict of Ideologies: Ninth*

Round Table on Law and Semiotics. Ed. Roberta Kevelson. New York: Peter Lang, 1996. 211–36.

Rody, Caroline. "Toni Morrison's *Beloved*: History, 'Rememory,' and a 'Clamor for a Kiss.' " *American Literary History* 7, no. 1 (Spring 1995): 92–119.

Sale, Maggie. "Call and Response as Critical Method: African American Oral Traditions and *Beloved." African American Review* 26 (Spring 1992): 41–50.

Samuels, Wilfred D., and Clenora Hudson-Weems. *Toni Morrison.* Boston: Twayne Publishers, 1980.

Schapiro, Barbara. "The Bonds of Love and the Boundaries of Self in Toni Morrison's *Beloved." Contemporary Literature* 32, no. 2 (Summer 1991): 194–210.

Scruggs, Charles. "The Invisible City in Toni Morrison's *Beloved." Arizona Quarterly* 48, no. 3 (Autumn 1992): 95–132.

Taylor-Guthrie, Danille, ed. *Conversations with Toni Morrison.* Jackson: Univ. Press of Mississippi, 1994.

———. "Who Are the Beloved? Old and New Testaments, Old and New Communities of Faith." *Religion and Learning* 27, no. 1 (Spring 1995): 119–29.

"Toni Morrison: A Special Section." *Callaloo* 13. no. 3 (Summer 1990): 471–525.

"Toni Morrison." *In Black and White: Conversations with Afro-American Writers, Part 3.* Prod. and Dir. Matteo Bellino. Written by Barbara Christian. SSR-RTSI Swiss Television production. Princeton, N.J.: Films for the Humanities & Sciences, 1994.

Wolff, Cynthia Griffin. "'Margaret Garner': A Cincinnati Story." *Discovering Difference: Contemporary Essays in American Culture.* Ed. Christoph K. Lohmann. Bloomington: Indiana Univ. Press, 1993. 105–22.

Wyatt, Jean. "Giving Body to the Word: The Maternal Symbolic in Toni Morrison's *Beloved." PMLA* 108, no. 3 (May 1993): 474–88.

Yanuck, Julius. "The Garner Fugitive Slave Case." *Mississippi Valley Historical Review* 40 (June 1953): 47–66.